Getting Started With Paradox 5.0 For Windows

Henry Gaylord

Pace Computer Learning Center
School of Computer Science and Information Systems
Pace University

Babette Kronstadt
David Sachs

Series Editors
Pace Computer Learning Center
School of Computer Science and Information Systems
Pace University

JOHN WILEY & SONS, INC.
New York / Chichester / Brisbane / Toronto / Singapore

ISBN 0-471-12069-3

Printed in the United States of America

10 9 8 7 6 5 4 3 2 1

Getting Started

With

Paradox 5.0

For Windows

Preface

Getting Started with Paradox 5.0 for Windows provides a step-by-step, hands-on introduction to *Paradox*. It is designed for students with basic PC and Windows skills who have little or no experience with *Paradox*. Basic skills are taught in short, focused activities which build to create actual applications.

Key Elements

Each lesson in *Getting Started with Paradox 5.0 for Windows* uses eight key elements to help students master specific database concepts and skills and develop the ability to apply them in the future.

- **Learning objectives**, located at the beginning of each lesson, focus students on the skills to be learned.

- **Project orientation** allows the students to meet the objectives while creating a real-world application. Skills are developed as they are needed to complete projects, not to follow menus or other artificial organization.

- **Motivation** for each activity is supplied so that students learn *why* and *when* to perform an activity, rather than how to follow a series of instructions by rote.

- **Bulleted lists of step-by-step general procedures** introduce the tasks and provide a handy, quick reference.

- **Activities with step-by-step instructions** guide students as they apply the general procedures to solve the problems presented by the projects.

- **Screen displays** provide visual aids for learning and illustrate major steps.

- **Independent projects** provide opportunities to practice newly acquired skills with decreasing level of support.

- **Feature reference** at the end of the book allows students to have a single place to look for commands to carry out the activities learned in the book.

Stop and Go

The steps for completing each *Paradox* feature introduced in this book are covered in two ways. First they are described clearly in a bulleted list, which can also be used for reference. Then the steps are used in a hands-on Activity. Be sure to wait until the Activity to practice each feature on the computer.

Taking Advantage of Windows

Getting Started with Paradox 5.0 for Windows provides a balanced approach to using a Windows application. The use of the mouse and buttons for carrying out commands is emphasized. However, familiarity with the menus is developed so that students can take advantage of the wider range of options available in menu commands. Shortcut keys are introduced when appropriate. The convenient **Feature Reference** at the end of the book summarizes menu commands and mouse and keyboard shortcuts for each of the features covered in the lessons. Students can use this both to review procedures or learn alternate ways of carrying out commands.

Flexible Use

Getting Started with Paradox 5.0 for Windows is designed for use in an introductory computer course. As a "getting started" book, it does not attempt to cover all of the features of the software. However, the topics included in later lessons allow instructors to provide opportunities for individualized or extra credit assignments or use the book in short courses focused specifically on *Paradox*. While designed to be used in conjunction with lectures or other instructor supervision, basic concepts are explained so that students can use the book in independent learning settings. Students should be able to follow specific instructions with minimal instructor assistance.

Data Disk

Data disks are provided to the instructors for distribution to the students. A few of the projects use files from the data disk so that the focus of the lesson is on the new skills being learned in each project. Initial projects require that students develop applications from the beginning, and later projects build on those applications. Enough explanation is always included so that students understand the full application that they are building.

Acknowledgments

While the author has written the words, this book represents the work and effort of many individuals and organizations. Babette Kronstadt provided energetic leadership and orchestrated the production of not only this book but all of Pace's books in the *Getting Started* series. Nancy Treuer and Matthew Poli worked miracles with the layout and text formatting. Janet Smith patiently and exhaustingly examined the text and activities, locating many of my errors and offering innumerable suggestions.

I received enormous institutional support from Pace University and the School of Computer Science and Information Systems (CSIS). In particular, much personal support and personal leadership for the work has come from the Dean, Dr. Susan Merritt.

From another perspective, this book is also a product of the Pace Computer Learning Center which is a loose affiliation of approximately 15 faculty and staff who have provided more than 7,000 days of instruction to over 60,000 individuals in corporate settings throughout the United States and around the world during the past nine years. My shared experiences in the development and teaching of these non-credit workshops, as well as credit bearing courses through the Pace University School of Computer Science and Information Systems, was an ideal preparation for writing this book. In addition, none of the books for Wiley would have been possible without the continuing support of Dr. David Sachs, the director of the Computer Learning Center.

The *Getting Started* series has received many invaluable comments and suggestions from instructors at other schools who were kind enough to review our earlier books and offer their suggestions for the current books. My thanks go to Jack D. Cundiff, Horry-Georgetown Technical College; Pat Fenton, West Valley College; Sharon Ann Hill, University of Maryland; E. Gladys Norman, Linn-Benton Community College; and Barbara Jean Silvia, University of Rhode Island.

My thanks also go to the many people at Wiley who provided needed support and assistance. The editor, Beth Lang Golub, and editorial program assistant, David Kear, have been very responsive to concerns, and supportive of all of the Pace Computer Learning Center's writing projects. Andrea Bryant was invaluable in her management of all aspects of the production of this book.

Henry Gaylord

April, 1995
White Plains, New York

Contents

2 WORKING WITH A TABLE'S DATA 49

3 ALTERNATIVE VIEWS OF ONE OR MORE TABLES 69

4 QUERIES 105

5 MULTIPLE CRITERIA AND MULTI-TABLE QUERIES   127

6 REPORTS   149

Students and Instructors
Before Getting Started Please Note:

WINDOWS INTRODUCTION

Getting Started with Paradox 5.0 for Windows assumes that students are familiar with basic Windows concepts and can use a mouse. If not, instructors may consider using the companion book, *Getting Started with Windows 3.1*, also published by Wiley. Windows has a tutorial which can also help students learn or review basic mouse and Windows skills. To use the Windows Tutorial: 1) turn on the computer; 2) type: **win** or select Windows from the menu or ask your instructor how to start Windows on your system; 3) press the **ALT** key; 4) press the **H** key; 5) when the **Help** menu opens, type a **W**; and 6) follow the tutorial instructions, beginning with the mouse lesson if you do not already know how to use the mouse, or going directly to the Windows Basic lesson if you are a skilled mouse user.

STUDENT DATA DISKS

Most of the projects in this book require the use of a Data Disk. Instructors who have adopted this text are granted the right to distribute the files on the Data Disk to any student who has purchased a copy of the text. Instructors are free to post the files to standalone workstations or a network or provide individual copies of the disk to students. This book assumes that students who use their own disk know the name of the disk drive that they will be using it from. When using a network, students must know the name(s) of the drives and directories which will be used to open and save files.

SETUP OF WINDOWS AND PARADOX 5.0 FOR WINDOWS

One of the strengths of Windows and *Paradox* is the ease with which the screens and even some of the program's responses to commands can be customized. This, however, can cause problems for students trying to learn how to use the programs. This book assumes that Windows and *Paradox for Windows* have been installed using the default settings and that they have not been changed by those using the programs. Some hints are given about where to look if the computer responds differently from the way it would under standard settings. If your screen looks different from those in the book, ask your instructor or laboratory assistant to check that the defaults have not been changed.

VERSION OF THE SOFTWARE

All of the screenshots in this book have been taken using Version 5.0 of *Paradox for Windows*. If you are using a different version, the appearance of your screen and the effect of some commands may vary slightly from those used in this book.

Paradox for
Windows

Introduction

Objectives

In this lesson you will learn:

- What a database is
- How to start *Paradox for Windows*
- The parts of the screen
- How to use the menus and dialog boxes in *Paradox for Windows*
- How to use the toolbar in *Paradox for Windows*

- Database terminology
- How to use the Help System
- How to exit from *Paradox for Windows*
- The typographical conventions used in this book

PURPOSE OF THE INTRODUCTION

Unlike the other lessons in this book, which contain specific steps to complete database projects, this introduction will discuss databases and *Paradox for Windows* in general. It will start with how to get *Paradox for Windows* running, review the Windows aspects of *Paradox*, point out the features that are different from other Windows programs you may have used, and examine the Help system. It will also explain several terms that are used in database work. The final section describes the typographical conventions used by this book.

WHAT IS *PARADOX FOR WINDOWS*?

Every business and institution needs to keep lists of facts. A customer list, an inventory list, a sales invoice list, and a list of course enrollments would be but four examples. Such lists are called *databases*, and the facts and figures they contain are called *data*. To work with these databases on the computer, businesses and institutions, as well as individuals, use database programs. One such program is *Paradox for Windows*.

Paradox for Windows is a powerful, yet remarkably straightforward, database tool. It is a *RDBMS*, or Relational Database Management System, which means it handles multiple lists of data simultaneously. It allows you to organize, edit, search for, report on, and calculate with your data. Since most people despise keeping and working on long lists of data on paper, using *Paradox* on a computer makes an otherwise tedious job quick and painless; many would say fun.

GETTING STARTED

Paradox for Windows is a Windows program. That is good news, because if you know how to start and work with any other Windows program, you already know a portion of how to work with *Paradox for Windows*. This book assumes you have previously used a mouse, and that you know how to run Windows on the computer you are using, as well as the fundamentals of operating Windows. Any basic procedures that are unique to *Paradox for Windows* will be discussed in this introduction.

Because *Paradox for Windows* is a Windows program, and both *Paradox for Windows* and Windows can be customized in various ways, there might be small differences between the appearance of your screen and the illustrations in this book. For example, the thickness of the frames around the windows can be changed in Windows from the normal 3 dots wide to a larger or smaller value. If someone made the frames 20 dots thick, the frame lines would look peculiar in every Windows program, including *Paradox for Windows*. They would still work the same way, however. By simply setting the frame width back to 3, all would appear normal again.

Like any Windows program, there are ways to perform operations with the mouse and with the keyboard. While *Paradox for Windows* was designed for a mouse, often a key combination is easier. This book will favor whichever method is easier, although both ways will be described.

> The steps for completing each *Paradox* feature introduced in this book are covered in two ways. First, they are described in a **bulleted** list, that can also be used for reference. The steps are used in a hands-on *Activity*. Be sure to wait until the **numbered** instructions in the *Activity* to practice each feature on the computer.

To start *Paradox for Windows*:

- Turn on the computer and start Windows.

- Locate the *Paradox for Windows* icon that represents the program.

- Double-click on the *Paradox for Windows* icon or name. Alternatively, click once to highlight the icon's name, then press the **ENTER** key.

Activity I.1: Starting **Paradox for Windows**

1. Turn on the computer and start Windows.

2. Locate the *Paradox for Windows* icon. To find the icon you may need to open the program group that contains the icon by double-clicking on the group icon, or clicking once on the group icon and choosing **Restore** from the control menu that appears.

   The Paradox for Windows icon could be in almost any program group, but the likely candidates would be groups named **Paradox for Windows** *or* **Windows Apps**. *If neither of those groups contains Paradox for Windows, consult your instructor or lab assistant.*

3. Run *Paradox for Windows* by double-clicking on the *Paradox for Windows* icon or clicking once to highlight the name and pressing the **ENTER** key.

   As it takes a few moments to load all of Paradox for Windows, the progress will be monitored in a box in the middle of the screen.

THE *PARADOX* WELCOME SCREEN

When *Paradox for Windows 5.0* first begins, you **may** see a "Welcome to Paradox" screen like Figure I - 1. While you might want to explore on your own the use of the "Coaches" as an introduction to several beginning topics (and see Independent Project I.1), once you have worked with *Paradox for Windows* for a while you will already know most of the information that the Coaches offer.

At the bottom middle of that screen (see Figure I - 1) is a box that can be checked so it will not be displayed the next time *Paradox for Windows* is run. If anyone who previously used the computer you are now using checked that box when they used *Paradox for Windows*, this screen will not appear. (Also, if you are using an earlier version than 5.0 of *Paradox for Windows*, this screen will not appear.) Do not worry if it didn't appear as you do not need the Welcome screen; we do not do anything with it. In fact, the next thing we will do is close it if it is showing.

Closing the Welcome screen:

- If the "Welcome to Paradox" screen is displayed, click the mouse near the lower left corner of the screen on the gray button that says **Paradox**.

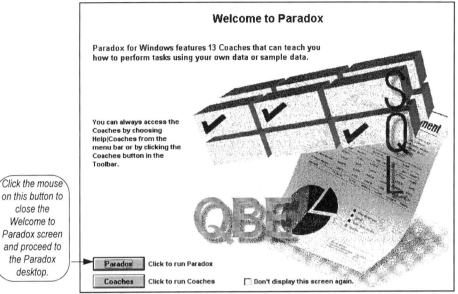

Figure I - 1

Activity I.2: Closing the Welcome screen

1. If the "Welcome to Paradox" screen is not displayed, skip directly to step 3.

2. Click the left mouse button once on the **Paradox** button near the lower left corner of the screen.

3. If the window that contains *Paradox for Windows* is not covering the entire screen, click the **Maximize** ▲ button (see Figure I - 2) to make the *Paradox* workspace as large as possible.

   *The **Maximize Button** is the button with the upward pointing triangle at the extreme right end of the line that says Paradox for Windows. If the window is already maximized (covering the entire screen), however, the **Maximize** button is replaced by the **Restore** button, a button showing a pair of triangles, one pointing up, the other pointing down. The **Restore** button puts the program back into a less-than-full-screen window.*

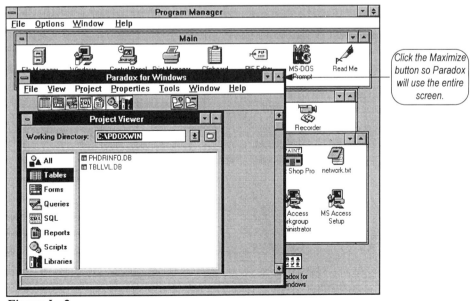

Figure I - 2

THE *PARADOX FOR WINDOWS* SCREEN

Once the Welcome screen is out of the way, you will see the *Paradox for Windows desktop* (see Figure I - 3). The Project Viewer will probably be open. While we will use the Project Viewer later in these lessons, we would like to concentrate on the remainder of the screen at this moment. Thus, we will close the Project Viewer window.

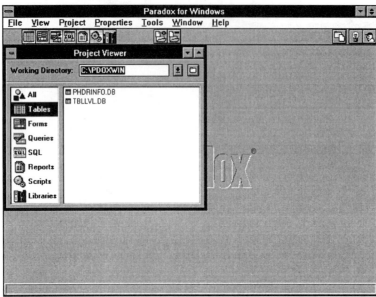

Figure I - 3

To close the Project Viewer:

- Choose **Close All** in the **WINDOW** menu or **Close** in the **FILE** menu.

Activity I.3: Closing the Project Viewer

1. If the Project Viewer window is not open on your screen, skip to the paragraph that follows step 3.

2. Move the mouse pointer so it points at the **WINDOW** menu and click the left mouse button once to open that menu.

3. Click the left mouse button on **Close All** within that menu.

THE *PARADOX FOR WINDOWS* DESKTOP

The *desktop* should resemble a typical Windows screen (see Figure I - 4) with a *title bar* at the top, the *menu bar* on the second line, the *toolbar* on the third line, and the *status bar* at the bottom. (If your screen resembles but doesn't look exactly like Figure I - 4, we will adjust it in the next section so it matches.)

The Title Bar

The *title bar* is the colored bar at the very top of *Paradox*'s window. It contains the name of the program in the center, the *Application Control Menu* at the left end, and the ***Minimize*** *button* and ***Restore*** *button* at the right end (see Figure I - 4). These are all common to every Windows program.

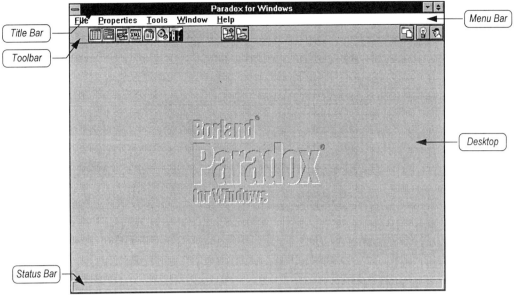

Figure I - 4

The Menu Bar

The second line contains the *menu bar* (see Figure I - 4). There are different menu bars for working on different items. *Paradox for Windows* automatically displays the appropriate menu bar. Since no data has been opened on the desktop, there is nothing to work on, and *Paradox* is currently displaying a minimal menu bar. The menu bar is common to all major Windows programs.

The Status Bar

The bottom line of the window is the *status bar* (see Figure I - 4). Its left section displays various messages about the current operation. Two of the more useful messages are the name of the toolbar button that the mouse pointer is on top of and the current position within a data table. On the right end of the status bar in indented boxes, *Paradox* will display the current modes. It is important to read the status bar during operations in *Paradox* to obtain such information.

The Scroll Bars

When the length of the listings in any *Paradox for Windows* list extends beyond the size of the window that displays those listings, *scroll bars* will automatically appear at the right side of the list, the bottom of the list, or both (see Figure I - 10 for an example). To operate the scroll bars, click the mouse on the arrow that points in the desired direction of movement at one end or the other of the scroll bar. The listings in the window will scroll. Continue clicking until the desired listings or columns scroll into view. The box within the scroll bar will travel along it to indicate the position of the listings that currently show relative to the entire set of listings.

The Toolbar

The third line at the top of the window is the *toolbar* (see Figure I - 4). It contains buttons that provide shortcuts to the most frequently used activities in *Paradox for Windows*. The toolbar will automatically switch among the different built-in toolbars to supply the appropriate tools for the item you are currently working on.

The last person to use this copy of *Paradox for Windows* might have hidden the toolbar or changed it to a floating toolbar. If so, you will see in the following Activity how to adjust it or make it reappear. It is normally displayed on the third line at the top of the window.

To display the toolbar on the third line of the window:

- Click the left mouse button once on the **PROPERTIES** menu.

- Pick **Desktop** by clicking the left mouse button once on that choice within the open menu.

- In the **Toolbar:** section (see Figure I - 5), neither **Floating** nor **Hidden** should have an X in the box to its left. If either one does, click the left mouse button once on top of the box to remove the X.

- Click on the **OK** button to close the **Desktop Properties** box.

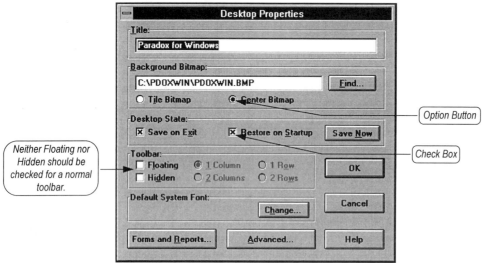

Figure I - 5

Activity I.4: Displaying the toolbar

We will verify that the toolbar is displayed on the third line at the top of the desktop.

1. Move the mouse pointer on top of the **PROPERTIES** menu and click the left mouse button once to open that menu.

2. Within the open menu, move the mouse pointer on top of **Desktop** and click the left mouse button once to open the Desktop Properties options.

3. If either of the choices **Floating** or **Hidden** has an X in the box to its left, click the left mouse button once on top of the box to remove the X.

4. When neither box contains an X, click on the **OK** button to close the **Desktop Properties** box.

   Your screen should now match Figure I - 5.

THE MOUSE POINTER

There are several different shapes for the mouse pointer, depending on what tool or item the mouse pointer is on top of. First, you must not confuse the mouse pointer with the text cursor. The text cursor is a blinking vertical bar that will be seen within text only while you are typing or ready to type. Clicking the mouse button while the mouse pointer is on top of some text will cause the text cursor to move to that spot. Otherwise, there is no relationship between the two.

The various mouse pointer shapes include the regular diagonal arrow ( ) for choosing items on the screen like a menu, the I beam ( ) to position the text cursor, various hollow double-headed arrows (for example ⟺) for sizing items, and the hourglass ( ) for those occurrences when an operation will take a little time. These mouse pointers will be described at each place in the book when they are encountered. For the moment, simply be ready to see many different shapes.

USING THE MENU

The menu in *Paradox for Windows* works exactly the same way any other Windows program's menu operates. That is, you push the mouse until the mouse pointer is on top of the desired choice on the menu bar and click the left mouse button once to open that menu. You then click on the particular choice within the menu to initiate an action. The choices within the menus are commands.

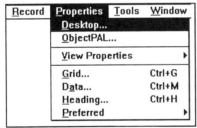

Figure I - 6

Three things can happen when you click on a command. If the choice within the menu has a triangle to the right of its name (see Figure I - 6), a submenu will open (see Figure I - 7) and you may pick from its choices. If the command name ends with an elipsis (...) like most of the commands in the **PROPERTIES** menu that is shown in Figure I - 6, a *dialog box* will appear for the selection of options pertaining to that command. Dialog boxes will be fully described in the next section. If just the command name appears on the line within the menu, the command will be carried out directly. If the command is displayed in pale letters it is currently unavailable; it will become available when the proper items are open on the desktop. Clicking on a pale command will accomplish nothing.

Occasionally you will see a check mark to the left of a menu choice. The check means that command option has been activated. It will remain active as long as the check remains. Clicking a command that is checked deactivates that action and removes the check mark. Of course, you can click that command yet again to reactivate it.

Also, there are some key combinations that will initiate certain menu commands. Those keys are named at the right of any command that has a keyboard equivalent, like the three shown in the **PROPERTIES** menu in Figure I - 4.

Figure I - 7

To initiate any menu command:

- Push the mouse until the mouse pointer is on top of the desired menu.

- Click the left mouse button once to open that menu.

- In the open menu, move the mouse on top of the desired choice.

- Click the left mouse button once to initiate that command.

- If a submenu opens, choose from it by clicking on the desired command.

- If a dialog box opens, fill out the various items as described in the next section.

KEYBOARD ALTERNATIVE: Press the **ALT** key to activate the menu bar, then tap the underlined letter in the desired menu name to open that menu. Within the menu, tap the underlined letter or digit in the desired command name. Note that in both cases the underlined letter is not necessarily the first letter of the menu or command name.

To close a menu:

- Click the left mouse button again on the menu name. The quickest keyboard method is to press the **ALT** key.

DIALOG BOXES

A dialog box is the Windows tool you use to select options for a command. For example, if the menu command you pick is to open a database table, which table do you want, on which disk drive is it recorded, and in which directory?

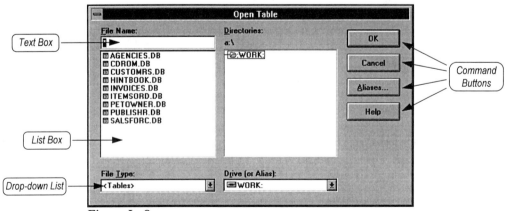

Figure I - 8

Element	How it Works	Figure Showing an Example
Text Box	Click within the box and type the desired entry. You may need to remove the default entry that is already in the text box.	Figure I - 5 and Figure I - 8
List Box	Click on the desired item within the ordered list. Sometimes the list will be longer than the allowed space, in which case there will be a scroll bar. To consume less space within the dialog box, the list is often a drop-down list with an arrow you can click to open the list (see File Type in Figure I - 8).	Figure I - 8
Check Box	A square box that if turned on will have an X in the box. To switch the setting, click on either the box or the name of the option. You may activate any, all, or none of the check box choices.	Figure I - 5
Option Button (or Radio Button)	A round button that always comes in groups. One option within the group must be selected and only one can be selected. The black dot within the circle denotes the chosen option. Click the mouse on the circle or name of the desired option.	Figure I - 5
Command Button	These are the action buttons. Click the mouse on top of the desired action. The two most common command buttons are OK and Cancel. The OK button carries out the options selected in the dialog box. The Cancel button closes the dialog box without making any of the changes you selected.	Figure I - 5 and Figure I - 8

Table I - 1

There are five different active elements that can appear in a dialog box in *Paradox for Windows*. Table I - 1 describes each item, and Figure I - 5 and Figure I - 8 show examples.

Often a text box and a list box will be associated so that clicking on a name in the list substitutes for typing the name into the text box. When this association exists, the list box will be directly underneath the text box and will not have a title of its own, like the **File Name** combination in Figure I - 8.

Activity I.5: Using the menu and dialog boxes

We will work with the menu and a dialog box to see how their components function. Our task is to open the **CUSTOMRS.DB** database that is supplied on the Student Diskette. We will not do anything with the database at this time, except to open and close it.

1. Insert your copy of the Student Exercise Diskette into the A: drive.

    If the disk drive you will be using is some other drive, substitute its name into the instructions in this book each time you see A:.

2. Move the mouse pointer on top of the **FILE** menu and click the left mouse button once to open that menu.

3. Move the mouse pointer on top of **Open** within that menu and click the left mouse button once to choose that command.

4. In the submenu that opens, move the mouse pointer on top of **Table**.

    Notice the elipsis (...) that follows the command name, indicating that a dialog box will open so you can pick the various options that accompany opening a database table.

5. Click the left mouse button once to choose **Table**.

*The **Open Table** dialog box appears on the desktop (see Figure I - 8).*

6. The currently selected drive is probably not A:, so, to switch there, click the left mouse button once on top of the drop-down arrow at the right end of the box titled **Drive (or Alias):** to open the list of the drives that are available to you (see Figure I - 9).

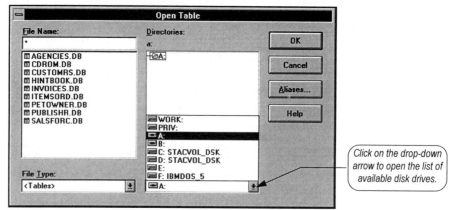

Figure I - 9

The names of some of the drives that will be in your list will probably differ from the names in Figure I - 9. If you use the A: drive, the other names do not matter.

7. Click the mouse button once while the mouse pointer is on top of **A:**.

*If you get a **Could not access drive.** message, make sure you have properly put a diskette into drive A:, then click the mouse pointer on the **OK** button. Then, click on the **Cancel** button in the Open Table dialog box and begin the process again with step 2.*

If you are not going to use drive A:, select the drive that you will be using from the list.

*The name **CUSTOMRS.DB** should be showing in the File Name list box (see Figure I - 8).*

8. Click the left mouse button once on the name **CUSTOMRS.DB** in the list box under File Name.

The name will be highlighted to show it has been selected.

9. Click on the **OK** command button to complete the operation.

*Several things happen when the **CUSTOMRS.DB** table opens onto the desktop (see Figure I - 10). First, the database table appears in a **Table** window. Second, since there is now an object on the desktop, the menu changes to offer the appropriate choices for that object. Third, the toolbar buttons change to match the object.*

10. Move the mouse pointer on top of the **FILE** menu and click the left mouse button once to open that menu.

11. Move the mouse pointer on top of **Close** within that menu.

There is no elipsis following the command name, so no dialog box will appear. This command is carried out immediately with no options.

12. Click the left mouse button once on **Close**.

*The **Table** window disappears and the table is closed. The menu bar reverts to its minimal form. The toolbar changes back to its original set of tools for opening objects. The desktop should again resemble Figure I - 4.*

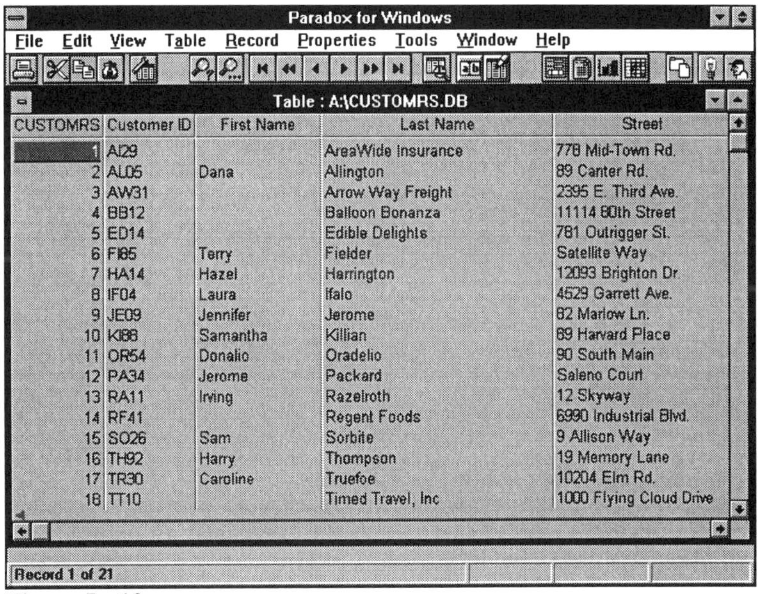

Figure I - 10

USING THE TOOLBAR BUTTONS

As mentioned previously, the *toolbar buttons*, which are sometimes called tools, are shortcuts to the most common operations in *Paradox for Windows*. There is nothing the toolbar buttons can do that cannot be accomplished through the menus or with a key combination; it's just much quicker with the toolbar buttons. For example, the first button on the toolbar is the **Open Table** tool. Therefore, to initiate opening a database table, you could either click on the **FILE** menu, then **Open**, and then click on **Table** in the sub menu, or you could make a single click on the toolbar button. Clearly, one click is quicker than three.

While the picture on each button is designed to remind you of the button's purpose, to see the name of any tool on the toolbar, move the mouse pointer on top of the tool without pressing any mouse buttons, and read the name on the status bar.

To use a toolbar tool:

- Click the left mouse button once while the mouse pointer is on top of the tool.

- If a dialog box opens, fill out the dialog box.

Activity I.6: Using the toolbar tools

To practice with the toolbar tools, we will open the **CUSTOMRS.DB** table again.

1. Move the mouse pointer on top of the first button on the toolbar. Do **not** press the mouse button yet.

   What is the name of this first tool? Read the status bar to find out.

2. Move the mouse pointer on top of the second button on the toolbar. Note its name, **Open Form**. Do **not** press the mouse button.

3. Move the mouse pointer back on top of the first button, **Open Table**  , and press the left mouse button once to activate the tool.

*The **Open Database** dialog box opens, just as it did in the last activity when we chose **FILE/Open/Table**. Paradox was not told that we wanted to permanently switch to the A: drive, so we need to repeat those steps. If the Student Exercise Diskette is not in the disk drive, you will need to put it in again.*

4. To switch to the A: drive, click the left mouse button once on top of the drop-down arrow at the right end of the box titled **Drive (or Alias):** to open the list of the drives that are available to you and click the mouse button once while the mouse pointer is on top of **A:**.

5. Click the mouse button on top of the name **CUSTOMRS.DB** in the list under File Name and click the **OK** button.

*The **Table** window appears on the desktop (see Figure I - 10). The toolbar has changed to reflect that you are now working on a table.*

6. On the toolbar, move the mouse pointer on top of the first button, the **Print** button , and click the mouse button once to activate it.

*The **Print File** dialog box opens (see Figure I - 11). We will leave all of the options in the dialog box as they are. In a later lesson we will explore the printing options.*

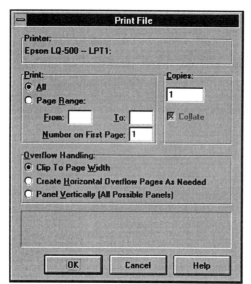

Figure I - 11

7. Click the **OK** button to begin printing.

The printout that you get is not a designed report, it is merely a quick printing with as many fields as would fit laid out across the page. It is the best Paradox could do with no guidance. Our intention here was not to create a beautiful report; designed reports will be covered in a later lesson. The intention was to use a toolbar button and we have done that.

8. Move the mouse pointer on top of each of the remaining toolbar buttons to see what their names are. Do **not** press the mouse button.

9. Click the mouse button on **FILE** to open that menu.

10. Click on **Close** within that menu to close the **CUSTOMRS** table.

11. Click the mouse button on the **Open Project Viewer** button.

12. Click on the **FILE** menu and pick **Close** to close the Project Viewer.

The desktop is again empty.

TERMS

There is a set of terms that you will encounter again and again within this or any book that discusses databases. Since it is important to understand what those terms mean, we will describe them here.

- *Data* are the facts and figures that are stored by *Paradox*. Names, addresses, telephone numbers, and prices are all examples of data.

- A *table* is a single set of data. It might be a list of customers, a list of sales, or an inventory list.

- A *database* is one or more tables of data. Typically, multiple tables are related, like a table of salespersons and the table of sales that they made, or a table of employees and a table of their family members.

- Multiple related tables are called a *relational database system.*

- A *record* is a single listing within the table of data. Thus, a table with 25 listings has 25 records.

- A *field* is a column of similar data. For example, in Figure I - 10 the CUSTOMRS table has four fields showing : Customer ID, First Name, Last Name, and Street.

- The *field name* is the title or heading given to a field.

THE HELP SYSTEM

As with all major Windows programs, there is an extensive help system available any time you get stuck or need more information about any *Paradox for Windows* topic. Either the Help menu or the F1 key will run the *Paradox for Windows* Help program. The Help system is a separate program from *Paradox for Windows*, and, thus, runs in its own window with its own menu bar and buttons. Since the Help system is a part of Windows, if you have used Help in any other Windows program, you already know most of how the Help system works.

Each of the two methods you can use to run the Help program enters Help in a different place. Table I - 2 outlines the two methods, and describes the three top choices in the Help menu.

Additionally, the Help menu contains three other choices for different types of assistance. The Help menu's fourth choice, Experts, opens a dialog box containing buttons for running the Form Expert, the Mailing Labels Expert, and the Report Expert. Experts are a sequence of dialog boxes that ask questions as to the options for a design, and proceed to create the design for you based on your selected options. The Help menu's fifth choice, Coaches, opens a screen containing the four categories of basic information about how to work in *Paradox*. The Help menu's sixth choice, About, opens a dialog box with information about your particular version and copy of *Paradox*.

Method of Starting the Help System	What You Get
HELP/Contents	Runs the Help program and displays the Contents page.
HELP/ObjectPAL Contents	Runs the Help program and displays the ObjectPAL Contents page. ObjectPAL is the programming part of Paradox and beyond the scope of this book.
HELP/Search for help on	Displays the Search dialog box and, when a topic is selected, opens the Help program onto that page.
F1	Runs the Help system and displays the page with the topic closest to whatever you were working on in *Paradox for Windows*. This is called context-sensitive help.

Table I - 2

Once in the Help system, a screen can contain three types of items. The information to be read will be displayed as text. A word or phrase that is underlined with a solid line (and will be green on a color screen) is a *jump term*. A *jump term* is the name of another topic that you might want to jump to in order to see the information on its screen. A dotted underlined phrase (which will also be green on a color screen) will pop open a box of information without changing topics. To activate either kind of underlined item, move the mouse pointer on top of the phrase and click the left mouse button once. When you move the mouse on top of an underlined term, the mouse pointer will change to a hand with a pointing index finger ( ).

In *Paradox for Windows* the pop-up box from clicking on a dotted underlined phrase could contain two different types of information. When the word or phrase is part of a sentence, its definition will appear in the pop-up box. Those terms are called *glossary terms*. When finished reading the definition, click again anywhere on the screen to close the definition box. When the word or phrase stands alone, a list of additional topics that are related to the current term will pop up. Since all of the related topics in the pop-up box will be jump terms (underlined with a solid line), you may click on one to jump to that new topic.

The row of buttons immediately below the menu bar includes buttons to jump to the **Contents** screen, open the **Search** dialog box, move **Back** to any previous topic one screen at a time, see the complete **History** of the topics you have viewed in case you want to jump back to one, move to the next (>>) or previous (<<) topic in the current sequence, open the Search dialog box with both regular Paradox and ObjectPAL topics (**Search All**), and switch to the **ObjectPAL** set of help screens. ObjectPAL is the programming language that comes with *Paradox for Windows*. Additionally, the File menu contains the choice Print Topic to print the current screen's information.

To use the Help system:

- Click on **HELP** in the menu bar.

- Click on **Contents** in the **HELP** menu to open the Help system to the Contents page, or **Search** to open the **Search** dialog box.

- Starting on the Contents page, choose each successive jump term until you arrive at the desired topic.

- In the **Search** dialog box, choose a topic from the list in the upper section and click the **Show Topics** button, and then pick the individual page name in the lower section of the dialog box and click the **Go To** button to jump to that screen of help.

Activity I.7: Using the Help system

To experience the Help system, we will look for information about the Table window and toolbars.

1. Click the mouse on the **HELP** menu to open that menu.

2. In the **HELP** menu, click on **Contents**.

    The Help Contents screen appears in its own window (see Figure I - 12).

3. If the help window is not covering the entire screen, click on the **Maximize** button.

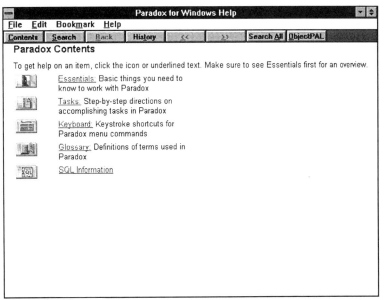

Figure I - 12

4. Move the mouse pointer on top of the **Tasks** jump term.

    The mouse pointer becomes a hand with a pointing index finger.

5. Click the mouse button on **Tasks** to jump to the **Performing Tasks in Paradox** screen.

    *More jump terms appear on the **Performing Tasks in Paradox** screen (see Figure I - 13).*

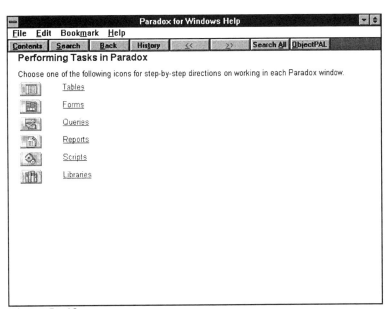

Figure I - 13

6. Click the mouse on **Tables** to jump to that topic (see Figure I - 14).

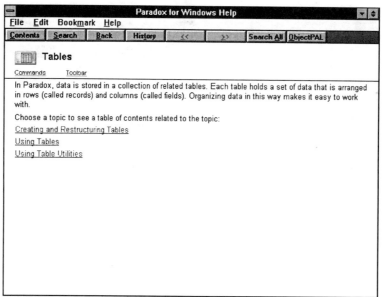

Figure I - 14

7. On the Tables screen, click the mouse on the **Using Tables** jump term to jump to that topic.

   The dotted underlined terms on this screen (see Figure I - 15) will open lists of related topics.

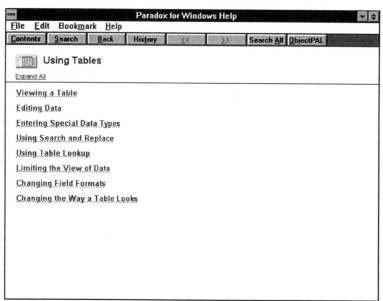

Figure I - 15

8. Click once on **Viewing a Table** to see the list of related topics (see Figure I - 16).

9. Click the mouse once outside of the **Viewing a Table** box to close the box without choosing any of its topics.

10. Click again on **Viewing a Table** to see the list of related topics.

11. In the box, click on the **Viewing a Table** jump term to jump to that screen (see Figure I - 17).

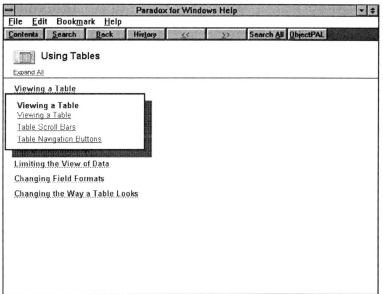

Figure I - 16

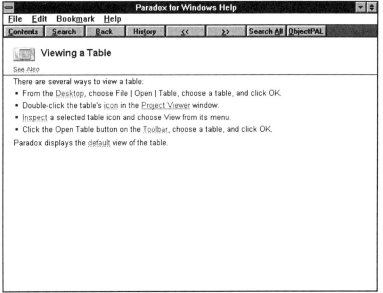

Figure I - 17

12. On the **Viewing a Table** screen, click on the glossary term **Desktop** in the first bulleted point.

    The glossary definition of that term appears (see Figure I - 18).

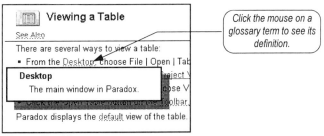

Figure I - 18

13. Once you have examined its definition, click the mouse one more time to close the box.

14. Click on **icon** in the second bulleted point to see its glossary meaning, and then click again to close the box.

15. Click on the **Back** button to return to the previous screen.

16. Click on the **Back** button a second time to return to the **Tables** screen.

17. Click on **Back** again to return to the **Performing Tasks in Paradox** screen.

18. Click on the **Search** button near the top of the window.

*The **Search** dialog box opens (see Figure I - 19). It has an upper section where you type in the text box or pick from the list the category from which you want to choose a particular topic.*

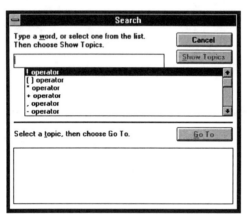

Figure I - 19

19. Type: **toolbar**

20. Click on the **Show Topics** button.

The names of many topics dealing with toolbars appear in the lower section of the dialog box (see Figure I - 20).

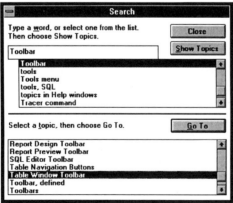

Figure I - 20

21. Scroll down in the list until you see **Table Window Toolbar** and click on that name.

22. Click the **Go To** button.

*The Help system jumps to the **Table Window Toolbar** screen (see Figure I - 21). The button pictures are jump terms.*

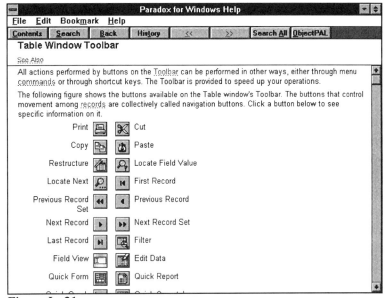

Figure I - 21

23. Click on the **button picture** next to **Print**.

*The **File/Print** screen opens. This screen describes the function of the **Print** button on the toolbar.*

24. Click the mouse on the **FILE** menu to open it and pick **Exit** to close the Help system and return to *Paradox for Windows*.

EXITING FROM *PARADOX FOR WINDOWS*

Although *Paradox for Windows* automatically saves the data you type, there is no guarantee it has saved yet. Thus, you must **never** turn the computer off without properly exiting from *Paradox for Windows*. There is nothing you can do to prevent the electricity from going off occasionally, and that may cause a corruption and force you to retrieve a backup version of a table to repair the problem, but don't do it to yourself by turning the computer off prematurely.

Also, if you are using a floppy diskette for your data, **never** switch floppy diskettes while a database is open in *Paradox for Windows*, even if you switch programs first. *Paradox* is expecting that same diskette to be there at all times, will complain if it cannot locate it, and may even overwrite the second diskette.

It is also a good idea to properly exit from Windows, as it saves the screen arrangement and cleans up temporary files when you exit properly.

To exit from *Paradox for Windows*:

- Click on **Exit** in the **FILE** menu.

- If there are design changes that have not been saved yet, *Paradox for Windows* will ask in an *alert box* (see Figure I - 22 for a typical example) whether to save them or not before exiting.

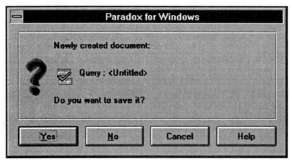

Figure I - 22

- If you get an *alert box*, click **Yes** to save and exit, **No** to exit without saving, **Cancel** to cancel the request to exit and return to where you were in *Paradox*, and **Help** if you do not understand the question in the alert box. An *alert box* is like a dialog box with only command buttons and operates the same way.

To exit from Windows:

- Click on **Exit** in the Program Manager **FILE** menu.
- Click **OK** in the **This will end your Windows session.** alert box.

Activity I.8: Exiting from **Paradox for Windows**

If you will be stopping rather than moving on to Lesson 1, you should exit from *Paradox for Windows*.

1. Click on the **FILE** menu.
2. Click on **Exit**.

SUMMARY

In this introduction you have run *Paradox for Windows*, explored its screen components, used its basic tools (the menu, dialog boxes, and the toolbar, among others), and run the Help program. The major terms were also defined. You opened a supplied table and printed it. You closed the table and exited from *Paradox for Windows*. These are the fundamentals. In later lessons in this book, feel free to come back to review these procedures or terms. Keep in mind that the Help system is an enormous source of information about *Paradox for Windows* and should be used.

KEY TERMS

Alert box	Field	Record
Application Control menu	Field name	Relational Database System
Check box	Glossary term	Restore button
Command button	Jump term	Scroll bar
Control menu	List box	Status bar
Data	Maximize button	Table
Database	Menu bar	Text box
Desktop	Minimize button	Title bar
Dialog box	Option button	Toolbar
Drop-down list	RDBMS	Toolbar button

CONVENTIONS FOLLOWED IN THIS BOOK

Table I - 3 explains the conventions used in this book when giving instructions.

Task	Notation in the Book	What To Do
Highlighting a choice, opening a menu, or activating a button with the mouse	click on, click the mouse button	Move the mouse pointer on top of the menu name, button, or choice in a list and press the left mouse button once
Selecting directly from a list with the mouse	double-click on	Move the mouse pointer on top of the choice in a list and click the left mouse button two times rapidly without moving the mouse.
Moving or sizing an object with the mouse	drag the mouse	Move the mouse on top of the item to be moved or sized, hold down the left mouse button, move the mouse with the button still held down until the position or size of the object is as desired, and release the mouse button.
Open an object's or button's self-contained menu (which is called "inspecting" the object)	click the right mouse button on, inspect	Move the mouse pointer on top of the object or button and press the right mouse button once. The self-contained menu will pop open.
Choosing a menu command	Pick **MENU/Command** Choose **MENU/Command/ Submenu Command**	(1) Move the mouse pointer on top of the **MENU** name and click the left mouse button once. (2) Within the menu that opens, move the mouse pointer on top of the desired **Command** name and click the left mouse button once. (3) If a submenu appears, move the mouse pointer on top of the desired **Submenu Command** name in the submenu and click the left mouse button once.
Pressing a key	Press **ENTER**	Press the **ENTER** key on the keyboard.
Using a key combination	Press **SHIFT+TAB**	Hold down the first key (**SHIFT**) and while it's down tap the second key (**TAB**).

Table I - 3

INDEPENDENT PROJECTS

Independent Project I.1: The Coaches

Coaches are a source of information about the fundamental procedures in *Paradox for Windows*. They list step-by-step instructions for performing simple operations and allow you to actually click on buttons and various choices while examining the steps. They remain on top of the right edge of the desktop while you work in *Paradox for Windows*.

This project will begin exploring the Coaches by examining the information in its **A Quick Look At Paradox** topic under **Paradox Basics**.

1. Run *Paradox for Windows*.

2. Maximize the *Paradox for Windows* window if it does not already cover the entire screen.

3. Click on the **HELP** menu.

4. Click on **Coaches** in that menu to open the Coaches main screen (see Figure I - 23).

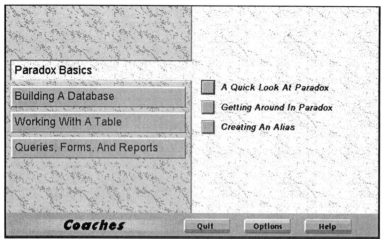

Figure I - 23

5. Click the mouse on the large rectangular button that says **Building A Database** on it.

   A new list of topics appears on the right side of the window.

6. Click on the square button for **Database And Table Basics**.

   A window opens on the right edge of the desktop with introductory messages (see Figure I - 24). The right arrow button will proceed to the next screen and the red X button will return to the main Coaches menu. Future screens will have a left arrow button for returning to the preceding screen.

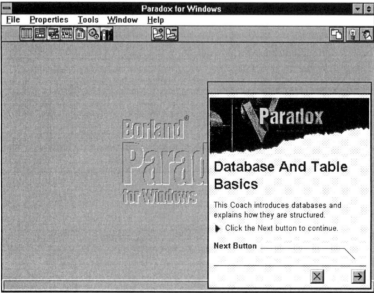

Figure I - 24

7. Click on the **Right Arrow** button for the next screen.

8. Examine this screen's information and click the **Right Arrow** button when finished.

9. Repeat step 8 until the "Congratulations! You have completed this lesson." screen appears.

10. On the "Congratulations!" screen, click the **red X** button to return to the Coaches main menu.

    *A check mark will appear on the button for **Database And Table Basics** if you completed the entire sequence of screens. You could explore other topics on your own, or click the **Quit** button to return Paradox.*

11. If you want to explore other Coaches, feel free to do so.

12. When you are finished, return to the main Coaches menu and click on the **Quit** button.

13. Exit from *Paradox for Windows* with **FILE/Exit**.

14. If you are finished with Windows, exit from Windows with **FILE/Exit Windows** and a click on the **OK** button in the **This will end your Windows session.** alert box.

Creating Tables

Objectives

In this lesson you will learn how to:

- Design and create a database table
- Distinguish between the data types in *Paradox for Windows*
- Save the table design

- Enter data into a table
- Modify the structure of a table
- Create a key field
- Print a table

PROJECT DESCRIPTION

The project that we will pursue through these lessons is that of a small retailer of CDROMs for computers. This lesson will begin by creating the employee file, which will contain the employees' names, identification numbers, date of hire, salary, phone extension, and any important notes. Subsequent lessons will build other components using tables of invoices, products, and customers. All of these tables of data will fit together by the final lesson into a system of related tables, a relational database system.

At the end of this first lesson you will have created the table of data shown in Figure 1 - 1.

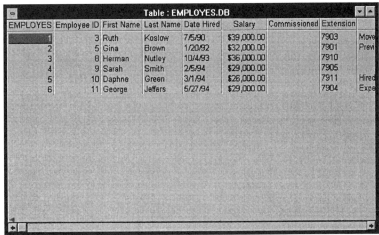

EMPLOYES	Employee ID	First Name	Last Name	Date Hired	Salary	Commissioned	Extension	
1	3	Ruth	Koslow	7/5/90	$39,000.00		7903	Move
2	5	Gina	Brown	1/20/92	$32,000.00		7901	Previ
3	8	Herman	Nutley	10/4/93	$36,000.00		7910	
4	9	Sarah	Smith	2/5/94	$29,000.00		7905	
5	10	Daphne	Green	3/1/94	$26,000.00		7911	Hired
6	11	George	Jeffers	5/27/94	$29,000.00		7904	Expe

Figure 1 - 1

THE WORKING DIRECTORY

As you work with tables of data, *Paradox* reads the data from and writes the data to a particular directory on a disk. A directory is merely a named section of the disk. The directory you are currently working in is called the *Working Directory*. If you decide to work with data in another directory, you change the Working Directory. *Paradox* remembers from one session to the next where that Working Directory is and automatically looks there the next time you run *Paradox*.

If you have not set the Working Directory, or when you wish to change it to another directory, you choose **Working Directory** in the **FILE** menu and pick a different drive/directory. Since we have not set it yet, we will begin by setting the Working Directory so that all created tables, reports, forms, and queries will be recorded in the correct place. You will need to check the Working Directory each time you run *Paradox* if you share the computer with others who might change it.

REMEMBER: Read the bulleted list that follows, but do not actually perform the steps until you reach *Activity 1.1*.

To set the Working Directory:

- Choose **FILE/Working Directory**.

- If the correct drive and directory are not already listed in the **Working Directory:** text box, click the **Browse** button to open the list of directories on the current drive.

- If the drive is not correct in the **Directory Browser:** dialog box, click on the **drop-down arrow** at the right end of the **Drive (or Alias):** list and click on the desired drive.

- Click on the desired directory in the **Directories:** list and click the **OK** button.

- Click the **OK** button in the Set **Working Directory:** dialog box.

Activity 1.1: Setting the Working Directory

Before we can create a data table, we must set the Working Directory to the correct drive and directory so that Paradox will save the design in the proper place.

1. Insert your copy of the Student Data Diskette into the A: drive.

   If you are using a different drive, substitute its name each time this book uses A:.

2. If you are not already in *Paradox*, run the program.

3. If the Welcome to Paradox screen appears, click the **Paradox** button.

4. If the Project Viewer is open, choose either **FILE/Close** or **WINDOW/Close All** to close it.

5. Choose **FILE/Working Directory**.

6. If the correct drive and directory are not already listed in the **Working Directory:** text box (see Figure 1 - 2), click the **Browse** button to open the list of directories on the current drive.

   *If the Working Directory is already correct, click the **Cancel** button and skip the rest of this Activity.*

Figure 1 - 2

7. If the drive is not correct in the **Directory Browser:** dialog box (Figure 1 - 3), click on the **drop-down arrow** at the right end of the **Drive (or Alias):** list and click on the desired drive.

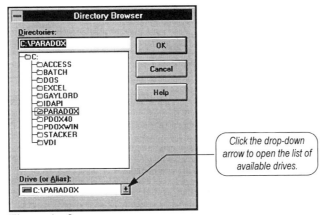

Figure 1 - 3

If you are using the Student Data Diskette in the A:drive, you will select A:(see Figure 1 - 4).

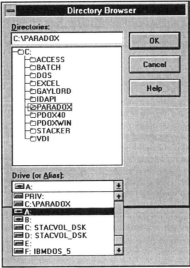

Figure 1 - 4

8. If there is a choice of directories in the **Directories:** list, click on the desired directory.

   The Student Data Diskette probably does not have any directories other than the root. If you are using it, you can skip step 8.

9. Click the **OK** button in the **Directory Browser** dialog box.

10. Click the **OK** button in the **Set Working Directory** dialog box.

    Although nothing shows on the Paradox desktop, the Working Directory is now set.

CREATING A TABLE

To create the table that will hold the employee data, begin by deciding what data the table must contain. Sometimes this is a straightforward task. Other times careful consideration must be given to what the system is to accomplish. For example, if a printed report needs a particular piece of data, either that data must be in the table, or you must be able to derive it from the data in the table by calculation.

Once you know what data needs to be stored, decide on the name, the type of data, and the size in characters for each field.

The field names within a table need to conform to the *Paradox* rules for names. Those rules are:

- The length of a field name may to be up to 25 characters long.

- Any characters except the square brackets [ ], parentheses (), curly braces {}, or combination -> are legal.

- While the pound sign # may be used in combination with other characters (as in ID #), it may not be a field name by itself.

- Spaces are allowed anywhere within a field name, but not on the ends.

The names of the fields should fully describe their function. As there are few restrictions, you should not name a field **FRSTNM** when it could be **First Name**. Similarly, **Equipment ID** is better than **EQPID**, and **Amount Receivable** fully describes a field whereas **AR** or **AMTRECV** is potentially confusing.

To create a table:

- Choose **FILE/New/Table**.

- Pick the type of table. While *Paradox* can create six different types of tables, we will always pick **Paradox 5.0 for Windows**.

- Fill in the grid in the **Create Paradox 5.0 for Windows Table** dialog box with the names for the fields, the data types, and the sizes.

- There is also a column for any **Keys**. We will discuss Keys later in this Lesson.

Filling in the Table Dialog Box

The dialog box for designing tables (see Figure 1 - 6) has four columns in the top left section (Field Roster:) and a group of Table Properties in the right section. To fill in the four columns, type the desired Field Name for a field in your table following the rules listed in the paragraphs above, select a *data type* (see the next section), and for Alpha and Memo fields enter a size (see Table 1 - 1). The fourth column, Key, will be left empty until the end of this lesson.

The field type in the second column is entered as a single character. Consult Table 1 - 1 for the character for each type of data. When in the Type column, you may press the **SPACEBAR** to open a complete list of the data types and pick the desired classification with the mouse, or you may type the representative character (the underlined character) on the keyboard.

The Size column only needs a value for Alpha and the two kinds of Memo fields. While the value entered for Size for an Alpha field is a size limitation, for Memo fields it is not. Both kinds of Memo fields are limited in size only by the amount of disk storage. However, you enter a number in the Size column of each memo field to tell Paradox how many characters from the beginning of the memo should show in the column in the table at all times. The memo field's characters beyond the size specified can be seen only when the user specifically opens the entire memo. Opening a memo field will be discussed in a later section.

Data Types

There are seventeen types of data that can be stored in a *Paradox* table. When designing a table, you must plan carefully and select the proper type for each column of data. The details of each type are listed in Table 1 - 1 below. Pay particular attention to the limitations, as they often dictate what type cannot be used for a specific purpose. (The three complex or rare types named BCD, Binary, and Bytes are not included in this table.)

Data Type	Letter	Size	Special Characteristics
Alpha	A	1-255 characters	most common field type
Number	N		a decimal number with up to 15 digits from -10^{307} to 10^{308}
Money	$		same as a Number field, but show a currency symbol and two decimal places
Short	S		whole numbers only between -32,767 and 32,767
Long Integer	I		whole numbers only between -2,147,483,648 and 2,147,483,647
Date	D		any date up to the year 9999, including BC dates
Time	T		the time of day
Timestamp	@		combination of date and time
Memo	M	1-240 (but read the last paragraph of the previous section)	any characters, to the limit of disk space
Formatted Memo	F	0-240 (but read the last paragraph of the previous section)	similar to Memo, but can contain formatted text (fonts, tabs, justification, etc.)
Graphic	G		a picture in .BMP format
OLE	O		an object from another Windows application such as an Excel spreadsheet
Logical	L		true (T) or false (F) only
Autoincrement	+		automatically numbers each record when the record is entered; the number assigned cannot be changed

Table 1 - 1

Activity 1.2: Creating a Table

In this activity you will create the fields that are needed in the Employees table. The company will need the name, an identification number, the hired date, the salary, the phone extension, and a place for important notes.

1. Choose **FILE/New/Table** to begin creating the table.

2. Select **Paradox 5.0 for Windows** in the **Table Type** list (see Figure 1 - 5), then click the **OK** button.

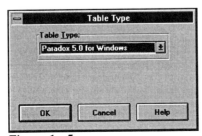

Figure 1 - 5

*The **Create Paradox 5.0 for Windows Table** dialog box that opens is where you define the fields for the new table (see Figure 1 - 6).*

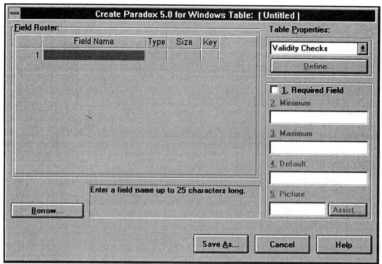

Figure 1 - 6

3. On the first row in the **Field Name** column, type the name of the first field: **Employee ID**

4. Press the **ENTER** key to move to the **Type** column.

5. Press the **SPACEBAR** to open the list of data types and pick **Short** by either typing an **S** or clicking the mouse on **Short** (see Figure 1 - 7).

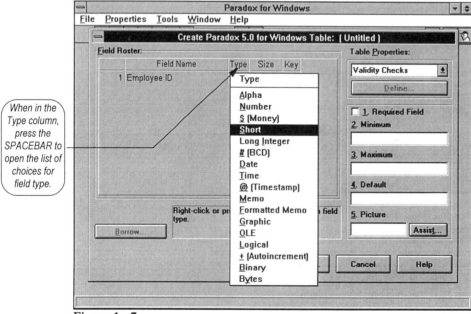

When in the Type column, press the SPACEBAR to open the list of choices for field type.

Figure 1 - 7

*The Employee ID numbers will not need decimal places and are not likely to exceed 32,767, so we can use **Short** as the Field Type. **Short** requires less storage space (on disk and in memory) than the other two numerical types.*

6. Press **ENTER** to move to the next column.

   *Paradox skips the Size column as Short fields do not have an option for size. As we are not ready to assign Key fields yet, be careful not to type anything in the Key column. If an asterisk (*) accidentally shows up there, press the **SPACEBAR** to remove the asterisk.*

7. Press **ENTER** to move to the second line.

8. On the second row in the **Field Name** column, type the field name: **First Name**

9. Press the **ENTER** key to move to the **Type** column.

10. Type an **A** for Alpha.

11. Press **ENTER** to move to the **Size** column.

12. Type **15** for the Size as shown in Figure 1 - 8.

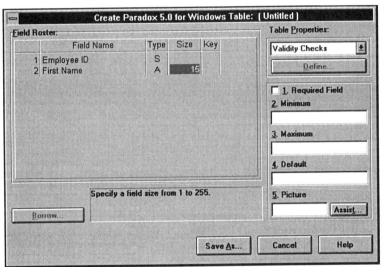

Figure 1 - 8

13. Press **ENTER** to move to the next line.

    Paradox skips the Key field column and will continue to do so from now on since any Keys must be the first fields. As we did not assign the first field to be a Key, the subsequent fields cannot be Keys either.

14. Enter the remaining five fields as shown in Table 1 - 2. When finished, the grid should look like Figure 1 - 9.

Field Name	Type	Size
Employee ID	S (Short)	
First Name	A (Alpha)	15
Last Name	A (Alpha)	20
Date Hired	D (Date)	
Salary	$ (Money)	
Extension	A (Alpha)	4
Notes	M (Memo)	30

Table 1 - 2

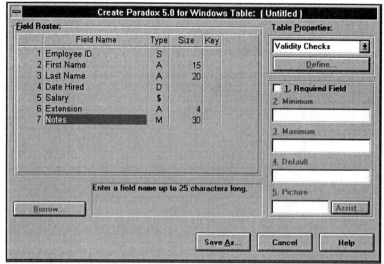

Figure 1 - 9

*Notice that the **Extension** was created as an Alpha field even though a phone extension contains only digits and looks like a number. When a field will contain only digits, but they are never involved in calculations, it is usually more efficient to make them Alpha fields. Zip codes and area codes are two more examples.*

SAVING THE TABLE DESIGN

With the design completed, you need to save the table structure. We will name it **Employes**. The name is misspelled because this is the name by which it is recorded on the disk, and the names of files recorded on disks must follow the DOS naming rules. Those rules only allow names of up to eight characters with no spaces. The word Employees has one character too many, so we will leave out the final e.

Should you try to close the table design without saving, *Paradox* will ask whether you want to cancel without saving changes. You may discard the design by choosing **Yes** or return to the design with **No**.

Activity 1.3: Saving the Table

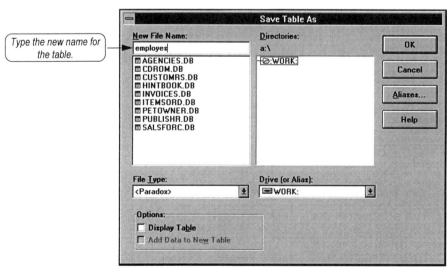

Figure 1 - 10

We will save the table with the name **Employes**.

1. Click the **Save As** button at the bottom of the **Create** dialog box.

2. In the **Save Table As** dialog box, type the name for this table: **Employes** (see Figure 1 - 10).

   You do not need to type the extension .db (for da<u>tab</u>ase) that you see on the other file names. Paradox will automatically add .db to the end of the name you enter. You may not use any other extension than .db.

3. Click the **OK** button.

   The design dialog box closes.

ENTERING DATA IN A TABLE

The next step is to enter the data into the new Employee table. To type new data into a table, open the table, switch into Edit Mode, move to the desired place in the table, and type each item of data. When you are finished editing, switch out of Edit Mode.

To switch into Edit Mode:

- Press the **F9** Edit key, click the **Edit Data** button ▓ on the toolbar, or choose **VIEW/Edit Data** in the menu.

To move to the proper field while entering data into an *Paradox* table:

- The **TAB** key, the **ENTER** key, or the **RIGHT ARROW** key will move to the next field.

- Should you need to back up to a previous field, press either the **SHIFT+TAB** key combination or the **LEFT ARROW**.

- You may click the mouse in any field to move the cursor there.

- If you are in the last field, the rightward movement keys wrap around to the first field on the next line so that you are ready to type another record.

Keep the following points in mind while entering data in a *Paradox* table:

- If you move back to a field that already contains data, the entire set of characters in that field will be selected. Should you begin typing when the whole field is highlighted, the first character you type will replace the entire previous set of characters! While this is handy when replacing outdated data, be very careful that it does not happen accidentally. The **ESC** key will restore the old value if you have not left the field. <u>Do not</u> use Undo in the **EDIT** menu for this, since it operates on the entire record and will undo every change you have made to the record.

- To substitute a cursor for the highlighting, press the **F2** key to switch into *Field View*. Alternatively, click the mouse in the field or click the **Field View** button on the toolbar. Any of these methods places the text cursor within the field so that you can edit characters instead of replacing the entire entry.

To fix typing errors while entering data:

- If you notice a typing error before moving to a new field, press the **BACKSPACE** key to remove the error, then retype.

- Should you notice an error in a previous field, either move to the field and retype the entire entry, or click the mouse cursor next to the mistaken character(s), press the **BACKSPACE** key to remove characters to the left of the cursor or press the **DELETE** key to erase characters to the right of the cursor, and retype the required characters.

To leave Edit Mode:

- Press the **F9** Edit key, click the **Edit Data** button on the toolbar, or choose **VIEW/View Data** in the menu.

Activity 1.4: Entering Data into the Table

In this activity you will enter the data for the six employees of the company.

1. Choose **FILE/Open/Table** or click the **Open Table** button on the toolbar.

2. Click on the name **EMPLOYES.DB** in the **File Name:** list of the **Open Table** dialog box (see Figure 1 - 11).

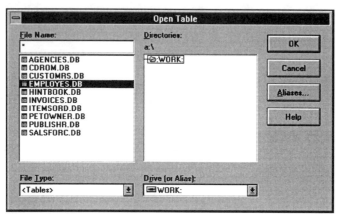

Figure 1 - 11

3. Click the **OK** button.

   The empty table opens in a window on the desktop (see Figure 1 - 12). The menu and toolbar change to present tools for working on the table.

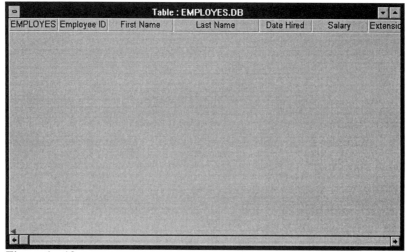

Figure 1 - 12

4. Press the **F9** key to switch into Edit mode. Alternatively, click the **Edit Data** button on the toolbar.

The right side of the status bar will show the notation Edit. The highlight should be in the Employee ID field.

5. Type: **3** for the first employee's ID number and press the **ENTER** key to move to the next field.

    Numbers are not aligned until you leave the field. Thus, the 3 was on the left side of the field when you typed it, but moved over to the right side when you moved to the next field.

6. In the **First Name** field, type: **Ruth** and press **ENTER**.

7. For **Last Name** enter: **Koslow** and move to the next field.

8. In **Date Hired** type: **7/5/90** and move to the next field.

9. Enter: **39,000** for **Salary**.

    Although you may type them, you do not need to type a dollar sign or comma. Nor is it necessary to enter the decimal point or two zeros any time the decimal places are .00. Those will be added automatically when you leave the field.

10. Move to **Extension** and type: **7903**.

    If the table scrolls within the window, that is normal when the fields cannot all fit within the width of the current window frame. As you move within the table, Paradox will automatically scroll the table so that you can see the field on which you are working. To scroll the table yourself, use the scroll bars.

    When only a portion of a number field will fit at the right edge of the window, asterisks may appear rather than part of the number. This is normal, as well.

11. Press **ENTER** to move to the **Notes** field.

    *A memo field is edited differently from other fields. You must press the **Memo View** key, which is **SHIFT+F2** to open a window in which to type or edit the memo. The memo cannot be edited in the column in the table. Of course, you must be in Edit mode as well, or you will only be able to read the memo.*

12. Press **SHIFT+F2** to get into Memo View.

13. Type: **Moved from Hawaii.**

    *Memo View covers the entire table with a full screen window where you may type the memo. Notice the message on the left end of the status bar that **SHIFT+F2** will leave Memo View. Also, note the notation "Memo" on the right end of the status bar*

    *Do **not** press the ENTER key to move to the next field when in Memo View. ENTER would begin a new line in the memo.*

14. Press **SHIFT+F2** to get out of Memo View and back to the table.

15. Press **ENTER** to finish this record and move to the next line.

16. Type the five additional records as shown in Table 1 - 3.

Employee ID	First Name	Last Name	Date Hired	Salary	Extension	Notes
5	Gina	Brown	1/20/92	32,000	7901	Previous job with MTV.
8	Herman	Nutley	10/4/93	36,000	7910	
9	Sarah	Smith	2/5/94	29,000	7905	
10	Daphne	Green	3/1/94	26,000	7911	Hired on a trial basis.
11	George	Jeffers	5/27/94	29,000	7904	Experience in electronics.

Table 1 - 3

The word "electronics" probably does not show, but it is there. We will see in the next lesson how to widen the column to show additional characters.

17. As we are finished with data entry, close the table with **FILE/Close**.

*The records are automatically saved and the **Table** window is closed.*

MODIFYING A TABLE

After working with a table of data for a while, it usually becomes evident that some alterations need to be made. Perhaps new requirements demand changes, or you might see a better way of accomplishing your objectives.

The company decides that placing the sales staff on a base salary plus commissions will spur sales. Non-sales staff will continue with a full salary. Thus, the employee table needs to record who is on commission in a new field that must be added.

To modify a table's structure:

- Open the table that needs to be modified. (It is possible to restructure a table without opening it first by choosing **TOOLS/Utilities/Restructure** and picking the table name. However, since you usually want to see the resulting changes, you will probably open the table eventually. Thus, you may as well open the table first.)

- Pick **TABLE/Restructure Table** in the menu or click the **Restructure** button on the toolbar.

- In the **Restructure** dialog box, move to any field that needs to be altered and type any changes.

- To insert a new field, move to the field that currently occupies the position where you want the new field to be and press the **INSERT** key. On the new blank line, type the new name, data type, and size.

- To add a new field at the end of the current group of fields, click on the last field name and press the **DOWN ARROW** key. Then type the new name, data type, and size.

- To remove a field, click anywhere on the line that contains the field and press the **CTRL+DELETE** key combination. Confirm the deletion in the dialog box that follows.

Activity 1.5: Modifying the Table Structure

You decide to insert the new Commissioned field between Salary and Extension.

1. Begin opening the **EMPLOYES.DB** table by clicking on **FILE/Open/Table** or clicking the **Open Table** button on the toolbar.

2. Click the mouse on the name **EMPLOYES.DB** and click the **OK** button.

3. With **EMPLOYES.DB** open on the desktop, click the **Restructure** button on the toolbar.

4. Click the mouse button on the field name **Extension** to move onto that line.

5. Press the **INSERT** key to insert a new line, which will push Extension and Notes down a row (see Figure 1 - 13).

6. Type the new field name: **Commissioned** and press **ENTER**.

7. Type an **A** for the Type and press **ENTER**.

8. Enter **1** for the Size and press **ENTER**.

We need only enter a Y for Yes or an N for No in the table.

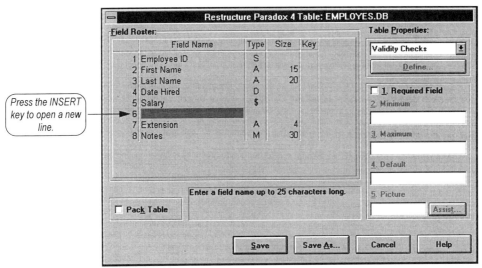

Press the INSERT key to open a new line.

Figure 1 - 13

9. Save this alteration by clicking the **Save** button at the bottom of the dialog box.

KEY FIELDS

If the data in a table is kept in order, finding a particular listing is much quicker. For example, since the telephone book is in alphabetical name order, to locate the name Quinn, one could open the book in the exact middle and look at the first name on the page to see whether Quinn was further along in the book or in the first half of the book. Suppose Quinn is further along than the middle, and so you can ignore the first half of the book, for you know Quinn cannot be there. If you then divided the second half in half again and looked to see which of those quarters Quinn was in, you have narrowed the search down to only one fourth of all listings in just two tries. Continuing in similar fashion, you could search thousands of listings in about a dozen tries.

If, however, the names in the telephone book were not in order, you would need to read every name to locate a particular listing, a process that could take thousands of tries to search thousands of records. *Paradox* reaps the same benefit from having the records in order, and, thus, has what is called a *key* field to keep the records in order.

A *key* can consist of one or more fields in the table design. They must be the first fields in the design. Thus, the key could consist of the first field, the first two fields, the first three, etc. You should select as a key a single field that will have unique values in it like an ID field, or a combination of fields that taken together will be unique. Uniqueness is a requirement for the data in a key field. Once established, *Paradox* will not accept duplicate entries in a key field (or the combination of fields), and only one record may have a blank key field.

To designate a key field:

- Select the field in the table design dialog box.

- Move to the Key column in the design grid.

- Press any key or double-click the mouse. An asterisk (*) will appear in the Key column.

Activity 1.6: Assigning a Key Field

We will select the Employee ID field as the key since it contains a unique value for each employee.

1. With **EMPLOYES.DB** open on the desktop, click the **Restructure** button on the toolbar.

2. Click on the line for the **Employee ID** field if the highlight is not already there.

3. Either click the mouse in the Key column or press the **ENTER** key three times to move to the Key column.

4. Press the **SPACEBAR** to switch the field to a key field.

   An asterisk will appear in the field (see Figure 1 - 14).

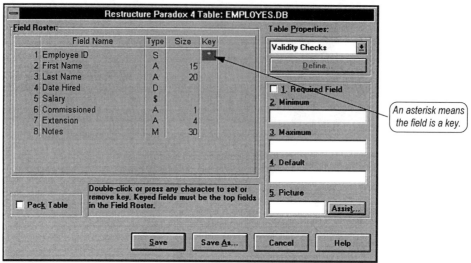

Figure 1 - 14

5. Click the **Save** button to save the design.

   This altered design is saved over the previous version of **EMPLOYES.DB**, *so the table design is updated.*

   We will update the data by filling in whether the employees are on commission or not in the next lesson.

6. Select **FILE/Close** to close the **EMPLOYES.DB** table.

PRINTING A TABLE

When you need a paper copy of the data in a table, the table can be printed. You can either design a report or merely accept Paradox's quick report design. While a later lesson will explore designed reports, this section will use quick reports. All fields are included on a quick report. Also, no calculations, font changes, titles, or other frills are included. It is a dump of the data onto paper.

While all selections for the design of a quick report are automatic, one change usually needs to be made in the **Print File** dialog box. That is to select the "Create Horizontal Overflow Pages As Needed" option. If the default of "Clip To Page Width" is left as the selection, any fields that do not fit across the first sheet of paper are ignored and are not printed. With Overflow Pages, any fields that do not fit are printed on a second sheet, which can be placed side by side with the first sheet. While this side-by-side sheet arrangement would not be desirable on a designed report, for this quick printing of the table data we will accept it.

To print a quick report for a table:

- Open the table.

- Choose **FILE/Print** in the menu, or click the **Print** button 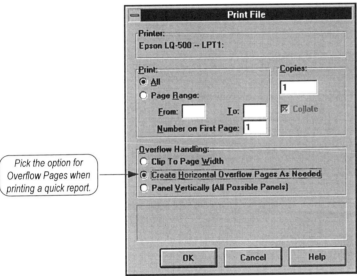 on the toolbar.
- In the **Print File** dialog box, set the **Create Horizontal Overflow Pages As Needed** option.
- Click the **OK** command button.

Activity 1.7: Printing a Table

1. Open the employees table by clicking the **Open Table** button on the toolbar and double-clicking on **EMPLOYES.DB**.

2. Click the mouse on the **FILE** menu to open it, and then pick **Print** within that menu by clicking on that choice.

   *Alternatively, you could click the **Print** toolbar button.*

3. In the **Print File** dialog box (see Figure 1 - 15), click on **Create Horizontal Overflow Pages As Needed**. **All** should be the option in the Print: group and Copies: should have a 1 in the text box.

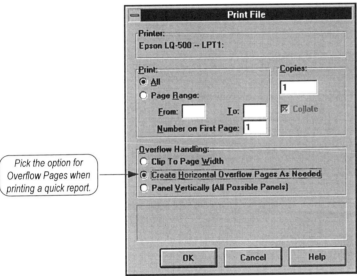

Pick the option for Overflow Pages when printing a quick report.

Figure 1 - 15

Your computer will probably have a different printer listed at the top of the dialog box.

4. Click the **OK** button.

5. When the printing is finished select **FILE/Close** to close the table.

SUMMARY

In this project you set the Working Directory and built the first table for the employees' data. You entered records into the table, modified the structure of the table, and established a key field. Finally, you printed the table. In Lesson 2 you will explore *Paradox's* editing and searching capabilities.

KEY TERMS

Data type	Key	Working directory
Field view	Table	

INDEPENDENT PROJECTS

The following four independent projects give you a chance to work with *Paradox* in creating tables. The first two projects give explicit directions to complete the steps. The third leaves more of the decisions and details to you. The fourth project merely outlines the project and leaves most of the planning to you.

Independent Project 1.1: The School Newspaper

The school newspaper needs your help. They are currently recording the advertisements they solicit in composition books. However, they are going to need summary statistics and the thought of performing them by hand is not appealing.

They ask you to design a table for recording the ads. The paper records they show you have six columns of data: Ad Number, Purchased By, Size, Price, Date Paid, and Salesperson ID. Ad Number is a unique number that is preprinted on each sheet the sales force uses to write up a sale. Since it is unique, Ad Number will be the key field. The field named Size will contain a two letter code where FP=Full page, HP=Half page, QP =Quarter page, and EP=Eighth page. Salesperson ID is the letter plus two digit code for the salesperson. The structure of the table is outlined in Table 1 - 4. Table 1 - 5 shows the data you will need to get started.

Field Name	Character for Data Type	Size
Ad Number	N (Number)	(Size is automatic)
Purchased By	A (Alpha)	30
Size	A (Alpha)	2
Price	$ (Money)	(Size is automatic)
Date Paid	D (Date)	(Size is automatic)
Salesperson ID	A (Alpha)	3

Table 1 - 4

	Ad Number	Purchased By	Size	Price	Date Paid	Salesperson ID
1	2387	College Books	FP	$85.00	5/8/95	K17
2	2388	Diamond Tunes	HP	$45.00	5/8/95	S23
3	2389	Pizza Plus	HP	$45.00	5/9/95	K17
4	2391	Harry Hertz	EP	$15.00	5/9/95	F11
5	2392	College Movies	QP	$25.00		S23
6	2393	Sports Booster Club	QP	$25.00	5/9/95	K17
7	2394	Dean's Office	EP	$15.00		F11
8	2395	Lou's LaundroMat	QP	$25.00		F11
9	2396	Student Grill	HP	$45.00		K17
10	2398	The Sports Palace	FP	$85.00	5/10/95	S23

Table 1 - 5

1. Run *Paradox*.

2. Maximize the *Paradox* window if it does not already cover the entire screen.

3. If the Welcome To Paradox screen opens, click the **Paradox** button.

4. If the Project Viewer is open, choose **FILE/Close**.

5. Check or set the Working Directory by picking **FILE/Working Directory**. If the listed name is not correct, click the **Browse** button, pick the desired drive and directory, and click **OK**. Click **OK** in the Set Working Directory dialog box, as well.

6. Begin a new table with **FILE/New/Table**.

7. Make certain **Paradox 5.0 for Windows** is showing in the **Table Type** box and click **OK**.

8. Type the first Field Name, **Ad Number**, and press **ENTER**.

9. Type an **N** to make Ad Number a Number field and press **ENTER**.

10. Press the **SPACEBAR** to make Ad Number a Key. An asterisk will appear in the Key column. Press **ENTER**.

11. Fill in the five remaining fields as shown in Table 1 - 4 by typing the Field Name and Type for each. Fill in the Size for each Alpha field. Do not make any of the remaining five fields a key; Ad Number is the only key.

12. Save the table by clicking the **Save As** button, entering the name: **Ads**, and clicking the **OK** button.

13. To open the table for data entry, click the **Open Table** button, click on **ADS.DB**, and click the **OK** button.

14. Switch into Edit Mode by clicking the **Edit Data** button on the toolbar or pressing the **F9** key.

15. Enter the ten records shown in Table 1 - 5. Be careful to match the upper or lowercase characters for each entry. You do not need to type the dollar sign or .00 in each price. The Ad Number field will automatically show commas and two decimal places.

16. When finished, close the table with **FILE/Close**.

The newspaper had previously kept the ads for different issues of the paper on separate sheets in the ad book. That won't work in a database table, so you realize after working with the data a while that the table will need an additional column to record the issue of the newspaper. Rather than the issue number, which would not mean much by itself, you decide to add the date of issue to the table structure.

17. Click the **Open Table** button on the toolbar. Either double-click on **ADS.DB** or click once on the name and click the **OK** button.

18. With the table open, pick **TABLE/Restructure Table**.

19. Press the **DOWN ARROW** key six times to move to the next available line, line 7.

20. Type the field name: **Issue Date** and press **ENTER** to move to the Type column.

21. It will be a **Date** field, so type a **D** and press **ENTER**. The size is automatic so you do not need to type anything into the Size column.

22. Save the altered design by clicking the **Save** button.

23. Press the **F9** Edit key.

24. Move to the **Issue Date** column and enter: **5/20/95** for all ten records. (As a shortcut, type 5/20/95 in the first record, move down with the **DOWN ARROW**, and press the **Ditto** key for each of the remaining records. The **Ditto** key is **CTRL+D** , that is hold down **CTRL** and tap the letter **d**. Continue until all ten are done. The **Ditto** key copies whatever is in the field immediately above into the current field.)

25. Print the table by clicking the **Print** button on the toolbar. Remember to pick the **Create Horizontal Overflow Pages As Needed** option. Click the **OK** button.

26. Close the table with **FILE/Close**.

27. If you are finished with *Paradox*, exit from *Paradox for Windows* with **FILE/Exit**.

28. If you are finished with Windows, exit from Windows with **FILE/Exit Windows**.

Independent Project 1.2: The Bookstore

The local bookstore has asked you to create a database to keep track of the books that it stocks and their publishers. The owner has written out the items that need to be recorded. That list names Title, Author, Year of Publication, Publisher Code, Price, and Quantity in Stock.

After reviewing the owner's plans, you spot one problem with the list. You want to include a key field, but nothing in the list is sure to be unique. Therefore, you decide to add to the six suggested fields a Book Code as the first field in the design. The resulting table structure is displayed in Table 1 - 6. The data you are given to get started and test the table is shown in Table 1 - 7.

Field Name	Character for Data Type	Size
Book Code	A (Alpha)	6
Title	A (Alpha)	40
Author	A (Alpha)	40
Year of Publication	A (Alpha)	4
Publisher Code	A (Alpha)	4
Price	$ (Money)	(Size is automatic)
Quantity in Stock	N (Number)	(Size is automatic)

Table 1 - 6

	Book Code	Title	Author	Year of Publication	Publisher Code	Price	Quantity in Stock
1	ATL11	Art Through Life	Jane Rick	1994	AW30	$22.95	86
2	CAL28	Calculus	Henry Slate	1977	TT12	$42.95	152
3	ECC22	Economically Correct	Lester Dane	1974	CE03	$32.95	81
4	EMP19	Even More Poems	Sina Grant	1976	BP07	$21.00	47
5	LOP18	Lots of Poems	Sina Grant	1973	BP07	$18.00	7
6	LUI81	Look Up In The Sky	Bruce Tipple	1989	TT12	$28.95	63
7	MOR47	Modern Russian	Igora Bylov	1990	CE03	$28.50	59
8	MUC17	Music Composition	Eliza Smith	1985	AW30	$32.95	127
9	MUH16	Music Harmony	Eliza Smith	1986	AW30	$32.95	86
10	POG17	The Physics of Glass	Kate Rice	1993	BP07	$7.95	80
11	PWM51	Philosophize With Me	Whyle Jones	1975	TT12	$30.95	115
12	WOH23	World of History	James Dyce	1988	CE03	$34.95	39

Table 1 - 7

1. Run *Paradox*.

2. Maximize the *Paradox* window if it does not already cover the entire screen.

3. If the Welcome To Paradox screen opens, click the **Paradox** button.

4. If the Project Viewer is open, choose **FILE/Close**.

5. Check or set the Working Directory by picking **FILE/Working Directory**. If the listed name is not correct, click the **Browse** button, pick the desired drive and directory, and click **OK**. Click **OK** in the Set Working Directory dialog box, as well.

6. Begin a new table with **FILE/New/Table**.

7. Make certain **Paradox 5.0 for Windows** is showing in the **Table Type** box and click **OK**.

8. Type the first Field Name, **Book Code**, and press **ENTER**.

9. Type an **A** to make Book Code an Alpha field and press **ENTER**.

10. Enter the Size as **6** and press **ENTER**.

11. Press the **SPACEBAR** to make Book Code a Key. An asterisk will appear in the Key column. Press **ENTER**.

12. Fill in the six remaining fields as shown in Table 1 - 6 by typing the Field Name and Type for each. Fill in the Size for each Alpha field. Do not make any of the remaining six fields a key; Book Code is the only key.

13. Save the table by clicking the **Save As** button, entering the name: **Books**, and clicking the **OK** button.

14. To open the table for data entry, click the **Open Table** button, click on **BOOKS.DB**, and click the **OK** button.

15. Switch into Edit mode by clicking the **Edit Data** button on the toolbar or pressing the **F9** key.

16. Enter the twelve records shown in Table 1 - 7. Be careful to match the upper or lowercase characters for each entry. The Quantity in Stock field will automatically get two decimal places.

17. When finished, close the table with **FILE/Close**.

The bookstore owner comes to you with the realization that she forgot to include the cost of a book, which is an important piece of data. You need to modify the table structure to add the Cost.

18. Click the **Open Table** button, click on **BOOKS.DB**, and click the **OK** button.

19. Choose **Restructure Table** in the **TABLE** menu.

20. Since Cost should be placed before Price, press the **DOWN ARROW** five times to move onto the line that currently contains the **Price** field. Alternatively, click the mouse on Price.

21. When on the line with Price, press the **INSERT** key to open a new line, which will push Price down to line 7.

22. Type the field name: **Cost** and press **ENTER** to move to the Type column.

23. Cost will be a **Money** field, so type a **$** and press **ENTER**. The size will be automatic.

24. Save the altered design by clicking the **Save** button.

25. Move to the **Cost** column and enter the values shown in the Cost column in Figure 1 - 16. (Asterisks appear in the Quantity in Stock column because there is not enough room to show the whole number.)

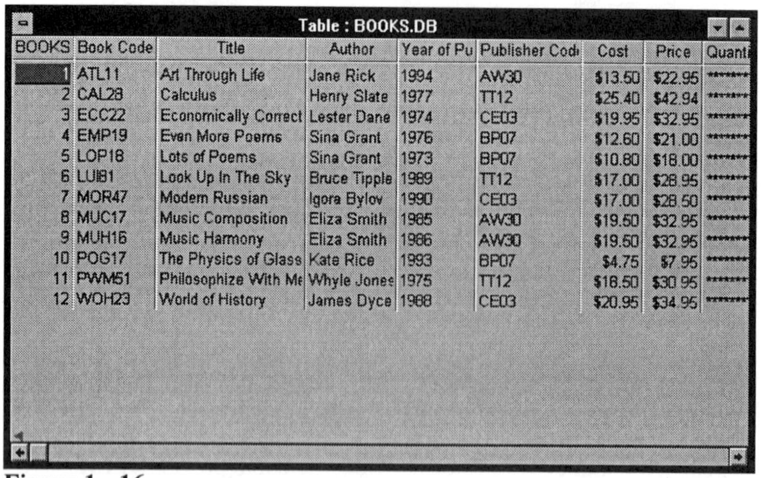

Table : BOOKS.DB

BOOKS	Book Code	Title	Author	Year of Pu	Publisher Cod	Cost	Price	Quanti
1	ATL11	Art Through Life	Jane Rick	1994	AW30	$13.50	$22.95	*******
2	CAL28	Calculus	Henry Slate	1977	TT12	$25.40	$42.94	*******
3	ECC22	Economically Correct	Lester Dane	1974	CE03	$19.95	$32.95	*******
4	EMP19	Even More Poems	Sina Grant	1976	BP07	$12.60	$21.00	*******
5	LOP18	Lots of Poems	Sina Grant	1973	BP07	$10.80	$18.00	*******
6	LUI81	Look Up In The Sky	Bruce Tipple	1989	TT12	$17.00	$28.95	*******
7	MOR47	Modern Russian	Igora Bylov	1990	CE03	$17.00	$28.50	*******
8	MUC17	Music Composition	Eliza Smith	1985	AW30	$19.50	$32.95	*******
9	MUH16	Music Harmony	Eliza Smith	1986	AW30	$19.50	$32.95	*******
10	POG17	The Physics of Glass	Kate Rice	1993	BP07	$4.75	$7.95	*******
11	PWM51	Philosophize With Me	Whyle Jones	1975	TT12	$18.50	$30.95	*******
12	WOH23	World of History	James Dyce	1988	CE03	$20.95	$34.95	*******

Figure 1 - 16

26. Print the table by clicking the **Print** button on the toolbar. Remember to pick the **Create Horizontal Overflow Pages As Needed** option. Click the **OK** button.
27. Close the table with **FILE/Close.**
28. If you are finished with *Paradox*, exit from *Paradox* with **FILE/Exit.**
29. If you are finished with Windows, exit from Windows with **FILE/Exit Windows.**

Independent Project 1.3: The Real Estate Office

During a summer job in a real estate office the manager learns of your work with databases and asks you to create a database for the listings of commercial properties. He shows you a sample sheet that contains commercial offers; it lists 10 items of data: street address of the building, city, state, zip code, size in square feet, floor of the building, whether it is to purchase or rent, price, date it becomes available, and the code for the agency that holds the listing.

In order to include a key field, a unique code number has been created for each listing. Thus, the 11 fields should be given the names in Table 1 - 8. The data you are given to get started and test the table is shown in Table 1 - 9.

Field Name	Type	Description
Code		2 letters plus 2 digits (the only key field)
Address		
City		
State		
Zip		
Size	I (Long Integer)	Number of square feet
Floor	S (Short)	Number of the floor in the building
Purchase or Rent		The letter P or R
Price		
Available		Date available for occupancy
Agency Code		2 letters plus 2 digits

Table 1 - 8

1. Create a new table named **COMMERCL.DB** to hold the commercial real estate listings with **FILE/New/Table.** It will be a **Paradox 5.0 for Windows** table.

	Code	Address	City	State	Zip	Size	Floor	Purchase or Rent	Price	Available	Agency
1	ES52	5 Elm St.	Greenwich	CT	06830	4800	1	R	$72,000	6/1/95	SC18
2	FA28	18 Frost Ave.	Greenwich	CT	06830	3700	2	R	$52,000	8/1/95	RR11
3	GP25	12 Gedney Place	Danbury	CT	06810	8900	3	R	$105,000	7/15/95	SC18
4	LW17	1 Lewis Way	Danbury	CT	06810	12000	2	R	$140,000	7/1/95	PP24
5	MC29	Maple Court	New Canaan	CT	06840	450	1	P	$125,000	4/1/95	PP15
6	MS11	22 Main St.	Stamford	CT	06901	5500	10	R	$75,000	5/20/95	RR11
7	RP12	2 Research Park	Stamford	CT	06902	18000	1	P	$3,400,000	6/1/95	PP15
8	RP13	3 Research Park	Stamford	CT	06902	18000	1	P	$3,400,000	6/1/95	GW14
9	RP15	5 Research Park	Stamford	CT	06902	21000	1	P	$4,100,000	8/1/95	RP12
10	RR19	952 River Rd.	Stamford	CT	06901	3750	6	R	$49,000	9/1/95	PP24

Table 1 - 9

2. Fill in the Key field (Code) together with the remaining ten fields named in Table 1 - 8. Carefully choose a data type for each, and remember to set the size for each Alpha field. Examine the data in Table 1 - 9 to help decide on the sizes. Make certain that the **Size** (in square feet) field is a number field of type **Long Integer (I)** and the **Floor** field is a number field of type **Short (S)**.

3. Save the table with the name: **COMMERCL**

4. Open **COMMERCL.DB** for data entry and switch into Edit mode.

5. Enter the ten records shown in Table 1 - 9.

6. When finished, close the table.

The manager notices that the agent's name is not recorded yet and requests an addition to the table design. A field named Agent should be added to the structure. It will contain the data shown in Figure 1 - 17.

7. Open **COMMERCL** and restructure it.

8. Place the new field **Agent** on line 12. Examine the names in Figure 1 - 17 to see what type and size to make the field.

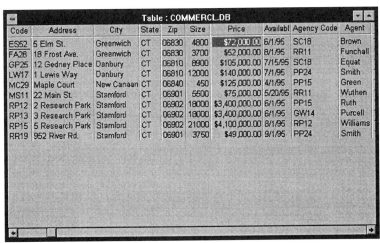

Figure 1 - 17

9. Save the design.

10. Enter the values shown in the Agent column in Figure 1 - 17.

11. Print the table.

12. Close the table.

13. If you are finished with *Paradox*, exit from *Paradox*.

14. If you are finished with Windows, exit from Windows.

Independent Project 1.4: The Veterinarian

The local veterinarian needs you to help with a database of the pets she tends. Since she likes to keep up on the names and ages of each pet she sees, the table will need to include the pet's name, date of birth (as closely as it is known), weight, color, type of animal, and owner code. She gives you the list shown in Table 1 - 10 to get started.

In this project you are to do most of the planning as well as the creating of the table. While the data is listed in Table 1 - 10, you must determine the table name, field names, and data types. In this project you will build the table for the pets; in Lesson 3 you will include a table for the owners' name and address.

To include a key field, you must create a unique code number for each pet. Whatever you call that field, it will have to be the first field in the table.

NAME	DATE OF BIRTH	WEIGHT			OWNER CODE
Homer	2/15/94	35	dark brown	dog	AS19
Fifi	9/1/89	14	yellow	cat	AS19
Wild Thing	3/5/94	22	gray	dog	AS19
Runner	10/1/91	840	brown	horse	AS19
Spot	1/1/92	49	brown	dog	DW11
Fluffy	4/1/94	15	white	cat	MU25
George	8/15/91	67	brown	dog	MU25
Kuddles	7/1/92	12	orange	cat	MU25
Sir Strut	5/1/90	915	gray	horse	TR12
Yoshi	6/1/95	0.25	brown	hamster	TR12
Clank	7/1/94	13	gray	armadillo	WE31
Lilly	2/1/93	13	black	cat	PS14
Homer	1/1/92	75	white	dog	PS14
Sneaker	5/15/90	12	orange	cat	PS14

Table 1 - 10

Carry out the following steps using *Paradox*.

1. Study Table 1 - 10 to plan the structure of the data table.

2. Create the pet table. Be sure to include a Key field.

3. Enter the data shown in Table 1 - 10.

After examining your design, the veterinarian notices that Date of Last Visit needs to be included in the table.

4. Add a field for Date of Last Visit and enter a different date for each pet, but each date must be within the last 12 months.

5. Print the table.

6. Close the table.

7. If you are finished with *Paradox*, exit from *Paradox*.

8. If you are finished with Windows, exit from Windows.

Lesson 2

Working with a Table's Data

Objectives

In this lesson you will learn how to:

- Move about within a *Paradox* table
- Size the fields in a table
- Move the fields within a table

- Edit a table's data
- Search for matching listings
- Delete records

PROJECT DESCRIPTION

In this lesson we will change the data within a table and the appearance of the table. Changing the data means editing the table. Since the data is recorded magnetically, editing it is a simple matter of typing the new values over the old data. Usually the appearance of a table will need adjusting by changing the display widths of fields, and sometimes the positions of fields.

While the editing is a straightforward task, locating the record that needs editing is often a bigger challenge. With thousands of listings in a table, you cannot read every entry searching for the desired record. The computer program must perform that task for you since it can search many times faster than a human. Thus, we will also see how to search for matching records in this lesson.

After sizing the columns, moving a column, editing some of the data, and deleting one record, the **EMPLOYES.DB** table will look like Figure 2 - 1.

Table : EMPLOYES.DB								
EMPLOYES	Employee IE	First Name	Last Name	Date Hired	Salary	Comr	Exten	Notes
1	3	Ruth	Koslow	7/5/90	$39,000.00		7903	Moved from Hawaii.
2	5	Gina	Brown	1/20/92	$32,000.00		7901	Previous job with Childr
3	8	Herman	Nutley	10/4/93	$36,000.00		7910	
4	10	Daphne	Green	3/1/94	$26,000.00		7911	Hired on a trial basis.
5	11	George	Jeffers	5/27/94	$29,000.00	Y	7904	Experience in electroni

Figure 2 - 1

MOVING ABOUT WITHIN A TABLE

Before you can change any data you must move to the position of that data within the table. There are ways to move about within a table using the mouse, the Record menu, or the keyboard. While the arrow keys may be best for navigating short distances, tables often consist of thousands of records. Moving from the first to the thousandth listing with only the arrow keys would be impractical. Thus, the following methods are important for faster and more efficient navigation.

To move about a table with the mouse:

- Click the mouse on any entry that is visible to jump to that record and field.

- The *navigation buttons* are the six buttons with triangles on their faces in the middle of the toolbar (see Figure 2 - 2). The first button jumps to the first record and the sixth button jumps to the last record. The second and fifth navigation buttons jump to the preceding and next set of records, respectively. A set of records is the number of records that fits within the table window. The third and fourth navigation buttons jump to the preceding and next records, respectively. The cursor remains in the same field during these moves.

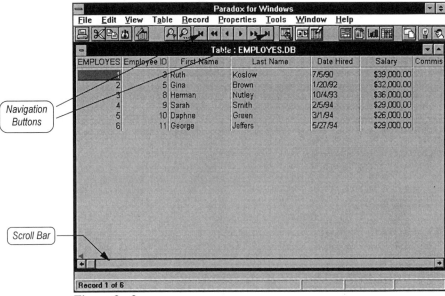

Figure 2 - 2

- The *scroll bars* at the right edge and bottom of the table window will scroll to a section of the table not currently showing in the window (see Figure 2 - 2). Each scroll bar only appears when actually needed, that is, when the table actually extends beyond the window boundary.

Activity 2.1: Navigating Within a Table with the Mouse

1. Start *Paradox*. If the Welcome to Paradox screen is showing, click on the **Paradox** button. If the Project Viewer is open, pick **FILE/Close**.

2. Make certain the Working Directory is set to the correct drive and directory.

   If the Working Directory is not correct, redo Activity 1.1 to set it.

3. Begin opening the **EMPLOYES** table with **FILE/Open/Table** or by clicking the **Open Table** toolbar button.

4. Click on **EMPLOYES.DB** and click the **OK** button.

5. Notice at the left end of the status bar that the current record number is **Record 1 of 6**.

   If the mouse pointer is on top of a toolbar button, the name of the button will show on the status bar instead. If the mouse pointer is on the menu bar or title bar, nothing will show on the left end of the status bar. If any one of those is the case, move the mouse to the middle of the table so you can see the current record number.

6. Click the **Last Record** button (sixth navigation button) to jump to the last record.

   *The status bar should now say **Record 6 of 6**.*

7. Click the **Previous Record** button (third navigation button) to jump to the preceding record.

8. Click the **First Record** button (first navigation button) to jump to record 1.

9. Click three times the **rightward pointing arrow** at the right end of the scroll bar on the bottom edge of the table's window to scroll to the right so you can see the last field in the table.

   The first column with the table name and numbers for the records is called the record number column. *Notice that you can no longer see the selection highlight in the record number column.*

10. Scroll back with the left scroll bar arrow to the first column so you can see the cursor and selection highlight in the record number column.

To move about a table with the Record menu:

- The same six choices as the navigation buttons are listed at the top of the **RECORD** menu. Click on the **RECORD** menu (see Figure 2 - 3) and pick the desired choice to jump to the **First** record, **Last** record, **Next** record, **Previous** record, **Next Set**, or **Previous Set**.

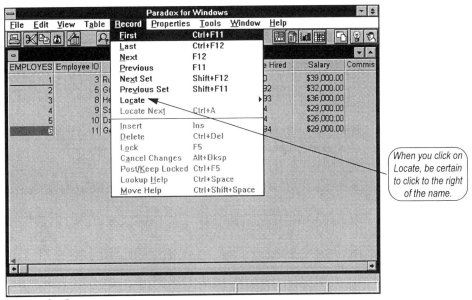

Figure 2 - 3

- Pick **RECORD/Locate/Field** to jump to any field in the table. A dialog box with the list of field names will appear. Click on the desired name and click the **OK** button (see Figure 2 - 4). (NOTE: When you click on **Locate** be careful not to click on one of the first five letters of the word as that always accidentally picks the first choice in the submenu that opens on top of the word Locate. This is a trap in *Paradox* that you must avoid.)

Figure 2 - 4

- Pick **RECORD/Locate/Record Number** to jump to a particular record. Type the number of the desired record in the dialog box and click the **OK** button (see Figure 2 - 5). (NOTE: Be careful of the same trap as described in the **RECORD/Locate/Field** menu choice.)

Figure 2 - 5

Activity 2.2: Navigating within a Table with the Record Menu

1. Pick **Last** in the **RECORD** menu to jump to the last record.

2. Choose **RECORD/Locate**. Be careful to click on the **e** of Locate (or further to the right) so as not to simultaneously pick the submenu choice that overlays it.

3. In the submenu click on **Field**.

4. In the **Locate Field** dialog box, click on **Extension** (see Figure 2 - 4) and click the **OK** button.

   *The highlight should jump to the **Extension** field without changing records.*

5. Choose **RECORD/Locate/Record Number**.

   *If the **Locate Field** dialog box opens accidentally, click the **Cancel** button and try step 5 again. Remember to click on the e of Locate or further to the right.*

6. In the **Locate Record Number** dialog box, type **2** in the **Locate Record Number** text box (see Figure 2 - 5) and click the **OK** button.

   The highlight should jump to record 2 within the same field.

7. Click on the **RECORD** menu, but do not make any choices (see Figure 2 - 3).

To move about a table with keys:

- The **ARROW KEYS** move to the preceding or next record or one field to the left or right in the direction of the arrow.

- The **ENTER** key or **TAB** key move to the next field and **SHIFT+TAB** moves to the previous field.

- **PGUP** (or **PAGE UP**) and **PGDN** (or **PAGE DOWN**) move up or down the number of records showing in the window; that is, they jump to the next screenful of records.

- **HOME** jumps to the first column (the record number column).

- **END** jumps to the last field.

- Looking at either the **RECORD** menu on your screen or Figure 2 - 3, notice that there are keys to simulate the navigation buttons. For example, **CTRL+F12** will jump to the last record. These six key assignments are probably not worth the effort of trying to remember them.

Activity 2.3: Navigating Within a Table with Keys

1. Click on the word **RECORD** in the menu bar to close the **RECORD** menu.

2. Press **HOME** to jump to the first column.

3. Press the **DOWN ARROW** to move to record **3**.

4. Press **PGUP** (or **PAGE UP**) to jump upward as many records as fit (or show) in the table window.

5. Press **ENTER** five times to move to the **Salary** field.

6. Press **END** to jump to the last field.

7. Close the table with **FILE/Close**.

SIZING FIELDS

When a table is created, each field is displayed as either its designed width in characters or the width of the field name, whichever is longer. While this is often workable, under two situations the original display width may need to be changed. If the field name is larger than the design width, you may wish to narrow the column, partially covering the field name. Alternatively, since the fonts used in *Paradox for Windows* are proportional (different characters take up different amounts of space), the display width is set for average width characters. Should you happen to type several wider than average characters in a field, the default width will be inadequate and you may need to widen the column. For whatever reason, should you want to alter the display width of a column, you drag the line at the right of the field name until the width is as desired. When you close a table whose field widths have been changed, you may either save the changes to make them permanent, or discard the changes if they were intended to be temporary.

It is important to realize that changing the display widths of the columns has no impact on the designed structure of the table. If a Last Name field was designed to be 15 characters wide, that is how many characters at most may be entered for a last name, no matter how many characters could show in the adjusted display width for the column.

To change the display width of a column:

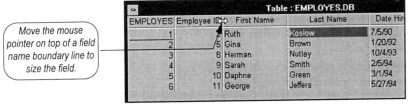

Move the mouse pointer on top of a field name boundary line to size the field.

Figure 2 - 6

- Move the mouse pointer on top of the line at the right edge of the desired field name (see Figure 2 - 6). The mouse pointer will become a double-headed left-and-right pointing arrow. Hold down the mouse button and drag the mouse to the left to narrow the column or to the right to widen it.

- When the table is closed *Paradox* will ask about saving the changed view properties (see Figure 2 - 9). If the changes are to be permanent, click the **Yes** button; if they were intended to be temporary, click the **No** button.

Activity 2.4: Sizing a Table's Fields

1. Click the **Open Table** button on the toolbar.

2. Click on the name **EMPLOYES.DB** and click the **OK** button to open that table into a window.

   A shortcut to open a table is to double-click on the table name.

3. Move the mouse pointer on top of the right edge of the field heading for the **Employee ID** field. When the mouse cursor shape is a double-headed left-and-right arrow (see Figure 2 - 6), hold down the mouse button and drag the line to the left until it is between the two letters **pl** of Employee. Release the mouse button (see Figure 2 - 7).

Figure 2 - 7

4. Increase the width of the same field so that the entire field name, **Employee ID**, shows.

   It often requires more than one try to get the desired width since you cannot see the result until you release the mouse button.

5. Narrow the width of the **First Name** field so that the field name just fits (see Figure 2 - 8).

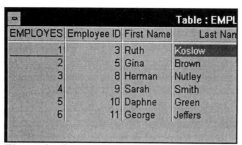

Figure 2 - 8

6. Move the mouse on top of the line at the right edge of the field selector for the **Last Name** column and narrow the column so that the field name just fits.

7. Similarly, narrow the **Date Hired** column.

8. Narrow the **Salary** field.

   If you narrow a number field too much, the values will turn into asterisks. Merely widen the column until the asterisks disappear and the numbers show again.

9. Widen the **Notes** field so that the last memo, **Experience in electronics.**, can be seen in its entirety.

10. Choose **FILE/Close** to close the **EMPLOYES.DB** table.

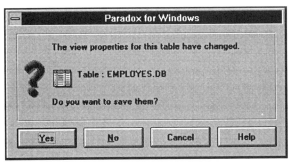

Figure 2 - 9

11. Click the **Yes** button in the dialog box to record the new widths (see Figure 2 - 9).

MOVING FIELDS

On occasion you may need one or more fields in a different position while viewing the table. Perhaps you need to see the first and last columns simultaneously. You may move fields to new positions either temporarily or permanently. Moving fields does not restructure the table; it only repositions the fields for viewing purposes. To move a field, merely position the mouse pointer on top of the field name and drag the field to a new position. When you close the table you will be asked whether or not to save the layout changes and make them permanent.

To move a field:

- Move the mouse pointer on top of the field name at the top of the desired column. The mouse pointer will change to a small rectangle (see Figure 2 - 10).

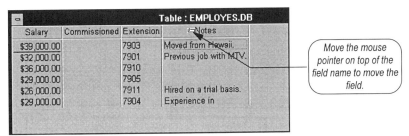

Figure 2 - 10

- Hold down the mouse button and drag the field to a new position. When you first depress the mouse button there will be a thick highlight on both sides of the current field, but, as you drag the mouse to the left or right, the highlight will jump to each line that separates one column from another. When the highlight is in the position that you want the field to occupy, release the mouse button.

Activity 2.5: Moving Fields

We will move the **Notes** field in-between **Last Name** and **Date Hired** so we can see the names and notes simultaneously.

1. Open the **EMPLOYES.DB** table.

2. Press the **END** key to jump to the **Notes** field.

3. Move the mouse pointer on top of the field name (Notes) and hold down the mouse button.

4. Drag the mouse to the left until the highlight that jumps from grid line to grid line is between **Last Name** and **Date Hired** (see Figure 2 - 11). Release the mouse button.

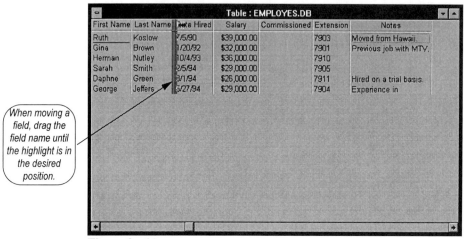

When moving a field, drag the field name until the highlight is in the desired position.

Figure 2 - 11

5. Press the **HOME** key to jump to the first field.

   Notice that you can now see the ID, names, and notes simultaneously.

6. Choose **FILE/Close** to close the table.

7. As the change of position of the **Notes** field was only intended to be temporary, answer "**The view properties for this table have changed. Table : EMPLOYES.DB Do you want to save them?**" by clicking the **No** button.

EDITING A TABLE'S DATA

To edit the data in a *Paradox* table, switch into Edit Mode with the **F9** key or the **Edit Data** button on the toolbar, move to the data that needs to be changed, and type over the old entry with a new entry. Changes to each record are automatically saved when you move to a different line. When finished editing, press the **F9** key again or click the **Edit Data** button to conclude Edit Mode.

Editing a memo field is slightly different. Since only a few characters of a memo field show in the column in the table, you must open a window in which to see and edit a memo. The Memo View key is **SHIFT+F2**. A full screen window will open for typing or editing a memo. When finished, press **SHIFT+F2** again.

To replace an entire field's entry:

• When you move to a field, the entire entry in the field will be highlighted (see Figure 2 - 12). While the entry is highlighted, the next character you type would replace the entire entry.

Table : EMPLOYES				
EMPLOYES	Employee ID	First Name	Last Name	Date Hire
1	3	Ruth	Koslow	7/5/90
2	5	Gina	Brown	1/20/92
3	8	Herman	Nutley	10/4/93
4	9	Sarah	Smith	2/5/94
5	10	Daphne	Green	3/1/94
6	11	George	Jeffers	5/27/94

Figure 2 - 12

- Should you accidentally erase an entire entry while it is highlighted, press the **ESC** key immediately. If you have already moved to another field within the same record, you can still choose **EDIT/Undo**. Undo will restore all fields within the record to the values the record contained when you began editing that record. If you have moved to a different record, it is too late; you must retype the data.

To edit a few characters within a field:

- To switch to a moveable cursor within the field, either press the **F2** Field View key, click the **Field View** button ![ab] on the toolbar, or click the mouse within the field. The right end of the status bar will show the word Field. Once the cursor is blinking within the field (see Figure 2 - 13), you may use the **LEFT** and **RIGHT ARROW** keys to move from character to character, press **BACKSPACE** or **DELETE** to remove characters, and insert new characters.

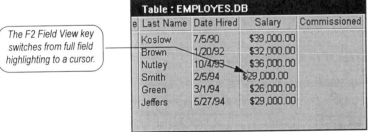

The F2 Field View key switches from full field highlighting to a cursor.

Table : EMPLOYES.DB				
e	Last Name	Date Hired	Salary	Commissioned
	Koslow	7/5/90	$39,000.00	
	Brown	1/20/92	$32,000.00	
	Nutley	10/4/93	$36,000.00	
	Smith	2/5/94	$29,000.00	
	Green	3/1/94	$26,000.00	
	Jeffers	5/27/94	$29,000.00	

Figure 2 - 13

- To exit from Field View so that the entire entry is highlighted and the table movement keys function normally, press **F2** again, click the **Field View** button on the toolbar again, or move to another field with **ENTER**, **TAB**, the **UP** or **DOWN** arrow keys, or by clicking the mouse on another field.

To edit a memo field:

- To edit a memo field, press the **SHIFT+F2** Memo View key. Editing is performed in a full screen window. When done, press **SHIFT+F2** again to return to the table. Of course, you must already be in Edit Mode when you open the memo editing window.

  While editing (or entering) data, you do not need to do anything to save the changes to the data. The moment you move to a different record, any data changes are registered. Thus, at no time is more than one record unsaved.

Activity 2.6: Editing Data

Sarah Smith has received a raise; she now makes $31,000. We need to correct her record. Also, Sarah and George Jeffers are on commission, so we need to update that field. Finally, we will add the note **Looking for a new position** to Sarah's **Notes** field.

1. Open the **EMPLOYES.DB** table.

2. Press the **F9** Edit key to switch into Edit Mode.

3. Move to the **Salary** field on the line for **Sarah Smith** by either clicking the mouse on that field or with the movement keys.

4. Click the mouse between the **$** and the **2** of Sarah Smith's **Salary** to position the cursor (see Figure 2 - 13). If the vertical insertion bar is not blinking between the **$** and **2**, press **ARROW** keys until it is.

5. Press the **DELETE** key twice to remove the **29**.

6. Type: **31** to insert the new value.

7. Press the **ENTER** key to move to the **Commissioned** field.

8. Type: **Y** in the **Commissioned** field.

9. Press the **ENTER** key twice to move to the **Notes** field.

10. Press the **SHIFT+F2** Memo View key to open the memo editing window (see Figure 2 - 14).

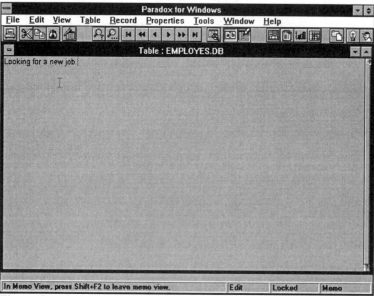

Figure 2 - 14

11. Enter: **Looking for a new position**.

12. Press **SHIFT+F2** to return to the table.

   *The word **position** may not show in the table because* Paradox *will not split words and it does not fit within the current column width even though it does not exceed the 30 characters we designated as the portion at the beginning of a memo field to show at all times. Widen the field to see the full entry.*

13. Click the mouse on the **Commissioned** field of **George Jeffers'** record.

   *If you cannot see the last name Jeffers, press **HOME** to jump to the first column, move onto the record for George Jeffers, and press **ENTER** several times to move to the **Commissioned** field.*

14. Enter: **Y**

15. Press **F9** to terminate Edit Mode.

   The changes are automatically saved.

16. Choose **FILE/Close** to close the table.

SEARCHING FOR RECORDS

While the typing of changes to the data in a table is relatively straightforward, finding the record, especially as the table gets large, can be more difficult. With hundreds or thousands of records you cannot take the time (nor would you want to) to read every name or code number looking for a matching value. The program can search much faster and doesn't tire of reading data.

To search for a value in a table:

- Choose **RECORD/Locate/Value**, click the **Locate Field Value** button ![button] on the toolbar, or press the **CTRL+Z** key.

- In the **Locate Value** dialog box, type the characters to be located into the **Value** text box.

- Check **Case-sensitive** only if you have typed correctly capitalized characters and want to restrict matches to that capitalization.

- Select one of the three options for how to match the value. Pick either **Exact Match** to require an exact match of all characters, **@ and ..** to utilize wildcard characters within the value (see the next section), or **Advanced Pattern Match** to use an extended list of wildcard characters.

- In the **Fields** list select the appropriate field to be searched.

- The **Help** command button will open the Help System to the page that explains the choices in the dialog box. Clicking the "**extended list of wildcards**" jump term on that screen will show the list of extended wildcard characters.

- When you click the **OK** button, the highlight will jump to the matching data in the table.

- As there may be multiple matches for the set of characters you are trying to locate, press the **CTRL+A** key or click the **Locate Next** button ![button] on the toolbar to find the next match. If there are no additional matches in the field, the status bar will say so.

Activity 2.7: Searching for Matching Records

We need to find the employee with Extension 7905.

1. Open the **EMPLOYES.DB** table.

2. Click the **Locate Field Value** button on the toolbar or press **CTRL+Z**.

3. In the **Value** text box type **7905**

4. Click on the **Exact Match** option.

5. Open the list of fields by clicking the drop-down arrow and pick **Extension** by clicking on that name (see Figure 2 - 15).

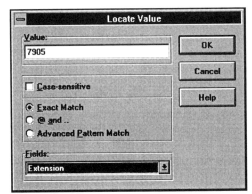

Figure 2 - 15

6. Click the **OK** button.

The highlight within the table will jump to the matching Extension in record 4.

WILDCARDS

Often you will not know the complete set of characters for a value within the table. Perhaps you are not sure how to spell the entry. Alternatively, you may not wish to match the entire value. For example, you might be searching for a Hired Date in the year 1993 regardless of the month or day. Perhaps you need to locate a word or phrase within a memo. In these situations you use *wildcard* characters in the value for which you are searching.

In *Paradox* the two wildcard characters are **..** and **@**. The .. (two periods) represents any number of characters from no characters to the maximum. Thus, **..93** would represent any date in 1993, **W..** would stand for any entry that begins with a W, and **..job..** would mean any entry with the word job somewhere within it. In the last example, the word job could begin the entry, end the entry, or be embedded anywhere within it.

The @ represents exactly one character per @ sign. For example, **@@@@@** would stand for any five character entry and 5/@@/95 means a two digit day in May of 1995.

To search with a wildcard:

- Begin a search by clicking the **Locate Field Value** button on the toolbar or pressing **CTRL+Z**.

- Enter any wildcards and characters in the **Value** text box.

- Select any other settings and options.

- Pick the field to search.

- Click the **OK** button.

Activity 2.8: Searching for matching records with wildcards

Because of an approaching project, we need to find the two employees with experience in television (with MTV) and electronics.

1. The **EMPLOYES.DB** table should still be open.

2. Click the **Locate Field Value** button on the toolbar (or press **CTRL+Z**).

3. In the **Locate Value** dialog box, type: **..mtv..** in the **Value** text box.

   The entry ..mtv.. means there may be characters in front of the mtv, there may be characters following the mtv, but there must be the three characters mtv somewhere within the field.

4. Do not check **Case-sensitive**.

5. Click the **@ and ..** option.

6. Open the list of fields and pick **Notes**.

7. Click the **OK** button.

   The dotted outline will surround the note in record 2 (see Figure 2 - 16). Notice that the MTV is in capital letters even though we typed lowercase letters.

8. Press the **CTRL+A** key to continue the search should there be a second match.

   The message "..mtv.." was not found. on the status bar shows there is no other match.

9. Press **CTRL+Z** again to begin a search for the word **electronics**.

   Paradox remembers that you searched for ..mtv.. last time in case you need to begin that search again.

Table : EMPLOYES.DB

Salary	Commissioned	Extension	Notes
$39,000.00		7903	Moved from Hawaii.
$32,000.00		7901	Previous job with MTV.
$36,000.00		7910	
$31,000.00	Y	7905	Looking for a new
$26,000.00		7911	Hired on a trial basis.
$29,000.00	Y	7904	Experience in electronics.

Figure 2 - 16

10. In the **Value** text box type: **..electronics..** to replace the earlier characters.

11. Leave **Case-sensitive** unchecked, leave the **@ and ..** option selected, and the **Field** should still be **Notes**. Click the **OK** button.

    The dotted outline will jump to Jeffers in record 6 where you should be able to see the word electronics.

12. Perhaps there is someone else with electronics experience, so press **CTRL+A**.

    The message ”..electronics..” was not found. on the status bar shows there are no other matches.

13. Press the **HOME** key to see the full name and Employee ID of the person with electronics experience.

Activity 2.9: Editing a Matching Record

After asking Gina Brown about her MTV experience, it turns out she actually worked for CTW, Childrens Television Workshop, not MTV. We need to correct the inaccurate data.

1. If the **EMPLOYES.DB** table is not still open, open it.

2. Click the **Locate Field Value** button on the toolbar or press **CTRL+Z**.

3. In the **Value** text box, replace ..electronics.. with: **..mtv..**

    Paradox remembers what you searched for the last time in case you need to repeat that search.

4. The choice for Case-sensitive should have no check and **@ and ..** should still be selected.

5. Open the list of fields and pick **Notes**.

6. Click the **OK** button.

    Record 2 (Brown) will again become the selected record and the note with MTV will be outlined.

7. Press **F9** to get into Edit Mode.

8. Press **SHIFT+F2** to switch into the memo edit window.

9. Drag the mouse across the characters **MTV** to select them.

10. Type: **Childrens Television Workshop** to replace the old characters (see Figure 2 - 17).

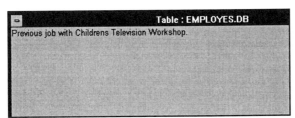

Figure 2 - 17

11. Press **SHIFT+F2** to switch out of the memo edit window.

12. To adjust the column width to show up to 30 characters of this longer note, drag the line at the right edge of the field name to widen the column (see Figure 2 - 18).

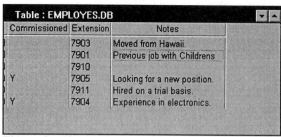

Figure 2 - 18

*The entire note cannot be seen in the table since we specified in the table design that only 30 characters should be displayed in the **Notes** column. Paradox will not split words, so only the first four words fit. Of course, you can open the memo window to see the rest of the note whenever necessary.*

13. Close the table with **FILE/Close**.

*Because you have made changes to the column width of the **Notes** field, the message for saving the view properties appears.*

14. Click **Yes** to save the changes to the column width.

DELETING RECORDS

A record can be deleted by merely moving onto the record and either pressing the **CTRL+DELETE** key or choosing **RECORD/Delete** in the menu. The table must already be in Edit Mode. When you delete records, the deletions are permanent. There is no confirmation or undo capability, so be absolutely certain you want to delete the current record.

To delete a record:

• Move onto the record to be deleted.

• Switch into Edit Mode.

• Press the **CTRL+DELETE** key or choose **RECORD/Delete** in the menu.

Activity 2.10: Deleting a Record

Sarah Smith has left the company. We need to delete her record.

1. Open the **EMPLOYES.DB** table.

2. Click the mouse anywhere on the record for Sarah Smith (record 4).

3. Press the **F9** edit key.

4. Press the **CTRL+DELETE** key.

5. Press the **F9** edit key to leave edit mode.

6. Close the table with **FILE/Close**.

SUMMARY

In this project you have made several different types of changes to a table. You have sized the fields and moved them into different positions. You have edited the data and searched for the listings that needed editing. You have deleted a record. In Lesson 3 you will work with additional tables, and in Lesson 4 you will find complete sets of matching records and work with multiple tables at one time.

KEY TERMS

Field view   Record number column
Navigation buttons   Wildcards

INDEPENDENT PROJECTS

Independent Project 2.1: The School Newspaper

This Independent Project continues the Newspaper Ad database you began in Lesson 1. In this project you will edit the table to make some changes to the data, size the fields, move a field, delete a record, and search for listings.

The following changes need to be made. When finished, the table should look like Figure 2 - 19.

- Pizza Plus has changed their ad number 2389 to a Full Page. They paid the larger fee on 5/11/95.

- The Student Grill paid for ad number 2396 on 5/12/95.

- College Movies has cancelled its ad number 2392.

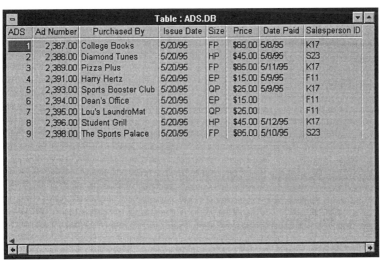

Figure 2 - 19

1. Run *Paradox*.

2. Close the Welcome to Paradox window by clicking the **Paradox** button and close the Project Viewer, if it is open, with **FILE/Close**.

3. Maximize the *Paradox* window if it does not already cover the entire screen.

4. Open the **ADS.DB** table by clicking the **Open Table** button on the toolbar, clicking on the name in the list of tables, and clicking the **OK** button.

5. To change Pizza Plus' ad number 2389 to a Full Page, begin by searching for that ad number. Press **CTRL+Z** or click the **Locate Field Value** button, type **2389** into the **Value** text box, click on the **Exact Match** option, pick **Ad Number** as the field in the **Fields** list, and click the **OK** button. The highlight should move to record 3.

6. Press **ENTER** twice to move to the **Size** field.

7. The **HP** should be highlighted, so press **F9** to enter edit mode and merely type: **FP** to replace the old value.

8. Press **ENTER** again to jump to the **Price** column and enter: **85**

9. Press **ENTER** once more and change the Date Paid to **5/11/95**. You can either retype the entire date, or press **F2** to switch into field view and change the 9 to an 11.

10. To fill in the Date Paid for the Student Grill ad number 2396, begin by searching for that ad number. Press **CTRL+Z** or click the **Locate Field Value** button, type **2396** into the **Value** text box, pick the **Ad Number** field, and click the **OK** button. The highlight should move to record 9.

11. Press **ENTER** four times to move to the **Date Paid** field.

12. The table is already in edit mode, so enter: **5/12/95**

13. To remove the College Movies ad number 2392, begin by searching for that ad number. Press **CTRL+Z** or click the **Locate Field Value** button, type **2392** into the **Value** text box, pick the **Ad Number** field, and click the **OK** button. The highlight should move to record 5.

14. Make certain you are on the correct record (College Movies, Ad Number 2392), then press the **CTRL+DELETE** key.

15. Since you are finished editing the table, press **F9** to end edit mode.

16. Press the **END** key to jump to the **Issue Date** field.

17. Move the mouse on top of the field name at the top of the column.

18. Hold down the left mouse button and drag that field to the left until the dark highlight is between **Purchased By** and **Size**. Release the mouse button to drop the field and reposition it there.

19. Press the **HOME** key to jump to the first field.

20. Resize the **Ad Number** field by moving the mouse on top of the right edge of its field name and dragging the line until it's the proper size.

21. Similarly, resize the remaining fields (see Figure 2 - 19).

22. Print the table by clicking the **Print** button on the toolbar or choosing **FILE/Print**. Print **1** copy of **All** pages with **Create Horizontal Overflow Pages As Needed** selected. Click **OK**.

23. Close the table with **FILE/Close**. Save the changes to the column widths and positions by clicking **Yes** in the view properties alert box.

24. If you need to exit from *Paradox* and/or Windows, do so properly.

Independent Project 2.2: The Bookstore

This Independent Project continues the Bookstore database you began in Lesson 1. In this project you will edit the table to make some changes to the data, size the fields, delete a record, and search for listings.

The following changes need to be made.

- The book with code ALT11 ("Art Through Life") has the wrong publisher code. Instead of AW30, it should be TT12.

- The music students have purchased their texts so that the Quantity in Stock of MUC17 ("Music Composition") has dropped from 127 to 85, and the Quantity in Stock of MUH16 ("Music Harmony") has dropped from 86 to 48.

- The Author of LUI81 ("Look Up In The Sky") is incorrect. Instead of Bruce Tipple, it should be Bruce Tiggle.

- LOP18 ("Lots of Poems") is being discontinued, so it should be deleted.

When finished, the table should look like Figure 2 - 20.

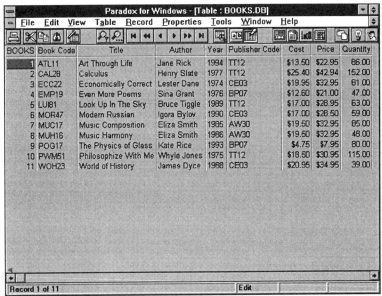

Figure 2 - 20

1. Run *Paradox*.

2. Close the Welcome to Paradox window by clicking the **Paradox** button and close the Project Viewer, if it is open, with **FILE/Close**.

3. Maximize the *Paradox* window if it does not already cover the entire screen.

4. Open the **BOOKS.DB** table by clicking the **Open Table** button on the toolbar and double-clicking on the name **BOOKS.DB**.

5. Maximize the table window by clicking the **Maximize Button**.

6. To change the publisher code for ALT11 ("Art Through Life") from AW30 to TT12, you need to locate the record. It is the first record, so you don't need to search.

7. Press **ENTER** five times to move to the **Publisher Code** field.

8. The **AW30** should be highlighted, so press the **F9** edit key and type: **TT12** to replace the old value. Be careful to type capital letters.

9. To update the Quantity in Stock for the two music texts, begin by searching for the first book's code number. Click the **Locate Field Value** button on the toolbar, type **MUC17** into the **Value** text box, and click the **Exact Match** option button. Open the list of fields and pick **Book Code**. Click the **OK** button. The highlight should move to record 8.

10. Press the **END** key to jump to the **Quantity in Stock** field.

11. The **127.00** should be highlighted and the table is already in edit mode, so merely type: **85** to replace the old value.

12. To update the Quantity in Stock for the second music text, search for the Book Code by clicking the **Locate Field Value** button on the toolbar, typing **MUH16** into the **Value** text box, choosing the **Book Code** field in the list, and clicking the **OK** button. The highlight should move to record 9.

13. Press the **END** key to jump to the **Quantity in Stock** field.

14. The **86.00** should be highlighted, so merely type: **48** to replace the old value.

15. To correct the Author's name for LUI81 ("Look Up In The Sky"), click the **Locate Field Value** button on the toolbar, type **LUI81** into the **Value** text box, choose the **Book Code** field in the list, and click the **OK** button. The highlight will jump to record 6.

16. Press **ENTER** twice to move to the **Author** field.

17. You only need to correct two letters, so press the **F2** key to get an insertion bar rather than the full field highlight.

18. Move over to the **pp** and delete those two characters. Then type: **gg** in their place so the name becomes Bruce Tiggle.

19. LOP18 ("Lots of Poems") is being discontinued and should be deleted. Since it is the preceding record (record 5), merely press the **UP ARROW** to move to the listing.

20. Make certain the highlight is on the line for LOP18 ("Lots of Poems") and press **CTRL+DELETE**.

21. Resize the **Year of Publication** field so that only the word **Year** shows. To do this, move the mouse on top of the right edge of its field name and drag that line to the left until it is at the right edge of the word Year (see Figure 2 - 20).

22. Resize the remaining fields to best fit the data (see Figure 2 - 20).

23. Print the table by clicking the **Print** button on the toolbar or choosing **FILE/Print**. Print **1** copy of **All** pages with **Create Horizontal Overflow Pages As Needed** selected. Click **OK**.

24. Close the table with **FILE/Close**. Save the changes to the column widths by clicking **Yes** in the view properties alert box.

25. If you need to exit from *Paradox* and/or Windows, do so properly.

Independent Project 2.3: The Real Estate Office

This Independent Project continues the Real Estate Office database you began in Lesson 1. In this project you will edit the table to make some changes to the data, size the fields, move a field, delete a record, and search for listings.

The following changes need to be made.

- Property MC29 will take longer to prepare than was originally estimated, so the date when it will be available should be 5/15/95 instead of 4/1/95.

- The rental price on 1 Lewis Way, Danbury has been lowered to $125,000.

- MS11 has been leased and should be deleted.

When finished, the table should look like Figure 2 - 21.

1. Run *Paradox* and maximize the window.

2. Open the **COMMERCL.DB** table.

3. Switch into edit mode.

4. Change the **Available** date for MC29 (Maple Court, New Canaan) from 4/1/95 to **5/15/95**.

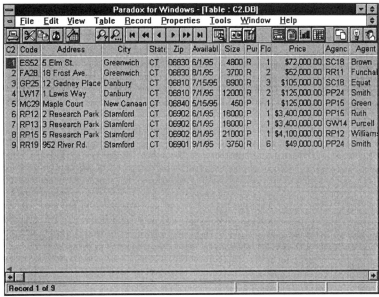

Figure 2 - 21

5. Locate **1 Lewis Way** in Danbury and change its **Price** to **$125,000**.

6. To remove the listing for **MS11** (22 Main St., Stamford), click anywhere on it and press **CTRL+DELETE**.

7. Leave edit mode by pressing **F9**.

8. Resize **Purchase or Rent** so that only **Pur** shows in the title (see Figure 2 - 21).

9. Resize all other fields to the best fit for each field (see Figure 2 - 21). You can resize the record number column, too. Feel free to cover over part of the long field names.

10. Move the **Available** field between Zip and Size.

11. Print the table.

12. Close the table. Save layout changes.

13. If you need to exit from *Paradox* and/or Windows, do so properly.

Independent Project 2.4: The Veterinarian

This Independent Project continues the veterinarian database you began in Lesson 1. In this project you will edit the table to make some changes to the data, size the fields, move a field, delete a record, and search for listings.

Make the following changes.

• Wild Thing's weight has increased to 30 pounds.

• Spot is much older than his family thought; change his date of birth to 1/1/88.

• The owner of Sir Strut has sold the horse to a breeder several hundred miles away. Delete that record from the table.

• Set the width of each field in the table to fit the data as closely as possible.

• Move the field that contains the type of animal (dog, cat, etc.) immediately to the right of the name field.

Lesson 3

Alternative Views of One or More Tables

Objectives

In this lesson you will learn how to:

- Use the Project Viewer
- View more than one table at a time
- Index a table

- Design a multiple table system
- Create a form
- Use a form

PROJECT DESCRIPTION

In this lesson we will begin to explore the need for multiple tables to hold the data that a typical business generates. Usually it is neither efficient nor desirable to combine all of the data into a single table. Since we have only created the single **EMPLOYES.DB** table, we will use several other tables that are supplied on the student diskette. We will see how the tables fit together in a system of tables, a Relational Database System. We will also create and use forms, an alternative way to view and work with data in either a single table or multiple, related tables. To facilitate our work with multiple tables, we will make use of the Project Viewer and secondary indexes.

When this lesson concludes, the Project Viewer will contain several listings for forms we have created (see Figure 3 - 1).

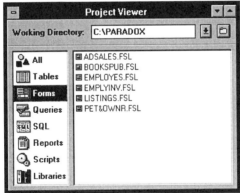

Figure 3 - 1

THE PROJECT VIEWER

Each time you have run *Paradox*, the Project Viewer has probably automatically opened onto the desktop. In the previous lessons you closed it, but the Project Viewer can be a useful shortcut, not only for opening the existing tables, reports, and other designed objects, but also for creating new designs.

The top section of the Project Viewer allows you to pick the working directory just like the **FILE/Working Directory** menu choice. Unlike the menu, however, the Project Viewer will remember in its list the last ten directories used, making it easier to switch in and out of several different working directories. The left section of the Project Viewer lets you select the category of designed object you want to open or create. The list box on the right side shows the names of the existing objects of the selected type. By merely double-clicking on the name of the object you wish to open, it will open into a window on the desktop so that you can work on it.

To begin a new design in one of the listed categories, click the **right** mouse button on top of the category name. When you right-click on an icon, button, or object, you *inspect* the item and a *self-contained menu* will open. A *self-contained menu* is a shortcut menu with only the choices that apply to the current item. All icons, buttons, or objects in *Paradox for Windows* have self-contained menus. We will begin using these self-contained menus more in this and the following lessons.

If the Project Viewer is not open when you run *Paradox*, or to jump back to it when a window is covering it, click the **Open Project Viewer** button on the toolbar or pick **TOOLS/Project Viewer** in the menu. To have the Project Viewer open automatically when you run *Paradox*, make certain the Project Viewer is open on the desktop, then choose **Project** in the **PROPERTIES** menu and check the box next to "Open Project Viewer on Startup." The next time you run *Paradox*, the Project Viewer will open onto the desktop automatically.

To inspect an icon, button, or object:

- Click the **right** mouse button on top of the item. (There are two other methods for inspecting items, but they only work on certain types of items and, thus, are not recommended. They are pressing the **F6** key and picking **PROPERTIES/Current Item** in the menu when the object's name is highlighted.)

To open the Project Viewer:

- Click the **Open Project Viewer** button on the toolbar or pick **TOOLS/Project Viewer** in the menu.

To use the Project Viewer:

- Choose the desired Working Directory.

- In the list of object types, click on the desired category.

- If you are opening an existing object, double-click on the name of the object in the list at the right, or click once on the name and press the **ENTER** key.

- If you want to create a new design for the selected category, inspect (right-click on) the category name and choose **New** from the self-contained menu.

Activity 3.1: Using the Project Viewer

We will open the Project Viewer and use it to open a table.

1. Run *Paradox*.

2. Click the **Paradox** button on the Welcome to Paradox screen if it is open.

3. If the Project Viewer is not already open, click the **Open Project Viewer** button on the toolbar.

4. Choose the desired Working Directory by clicking on the drop-down arrow and choosing from the list in the top section of the Project Viewer.

5. Click on the **Tables** category in the list on the left side of the Project Viewer (Figure 3 - 2).

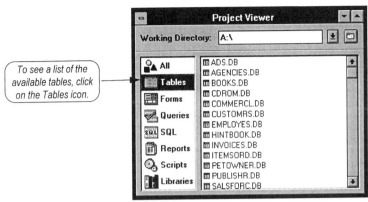

To see a list of the available tables, click on the Tables icon.

Figure 3 - 2

The EMPLOYES.DB table and several others should now be listed in the list box on the right side of the Project Viewer (see Figure 3 - 2).

6. Double-click on the name **EMPLOYES.DB** to open the **EMPLOYES** table.

7. Click the **Open Project Viewer** button on the toolbar to make it the active window, as well as to bring it back on top of the table window.

OPENING MULTIPLE TABLES

You may open additional tables, as needed, so that you have multiple tables open at one time. With multiple tables open on the desktop, move from one to another with either the **CTRL+F6** key or by clicking on the desired table window name in the list at the bottom of the **WINDOW** menu.

To see multiple tables arranged on the desktop, pick either **WINDOW/Tile** or **WINDOW/Cascade**, or drag the window frame lines and title bars yourself.

To open multiple tables:

- If you are using the Project Viewer, double-click on each additional table name that should be opened.

- If you are using the **Open Table** dialog box that you get when you choose **FILE/Open/Table**, click on the first name then hold down the **CTRL** key and click on each additional name of a table that you want opened. When you click the **OK** button, all of the highlighted tables will open one after another.

To make a different open window the active window:

- Press **CTRL+F6** until the desired window appears or choose the desired window name at the bottom of the **WINDOW** menu.

- Alternatively, if you can see any portion of the desired window on the desktop, you may also click the mouse on it to switch to that window.

Activity 3.2: Opening Additional Tables

We will open multiple tables and arrnge them on the desktop.

1. Double-click on **CDROM.DB** to open that table as well.

   If the CDROM.DB table does not show in the listing at the right side of the Project Viewer, you must get a copy of the files on the Student Data Diskette. The table names AGENCIES.DB, CDROM.DB, CUSTOMRS.DB, HINTBOOK.DB, INVOICES.DB, ITEMSORD.DB, PETOWNER.DB, PUBLISHER.DB, and SALSFORC.DB should be available to you. The other names showing in Figure 3 - 2 come from the Independent Projects, which you may or may not have completed.

2. Click the **Open Project Viewer** button on the toolbar to bring it back on top.

   Two tables are now open on the desktop and the Project Viewer is in a third window.

3. Choose **FILE/Close** to close the Project Viewer.

4. Pick **WINDOW/1 Table : EMPLOYES.DB** to switch to the **EMPLOYES** table.

   The CTRL+F6 key will also switch windows.

5. Click on the **WINDOW** menu and choose **Tile**.

   The two tables should be sized and positioned side by side (see Figure 3 - 3).

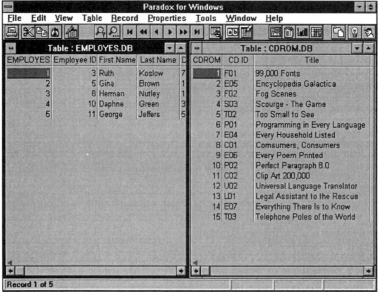

Figure 3 - 3

6. After seeing the new arrangement (see Figure 3 - 3), close both tables with **WINDOW/Close All**.

7. Select **FILE/Open/Table** or click the **Open Table** toolbar button.

   *The **Open Table** dialog box (see Figure 3 - 4) will list the same tables you saw in the Project Viewer.*

8. Click the left mouse button **once** on the name **CUSTOMRS.DB** to highlight that name.

9. Hold down the **CTRL** key and click on the name **INVOICES.DB** to highlight that name as well.

10. Hold down the **CTRL** key and click on the name **ITEMSORD.DB** so that three names are highlighted (see Figure 3 - 4).

11. Click the **OK** button.

    All three tables open onto the desktop.

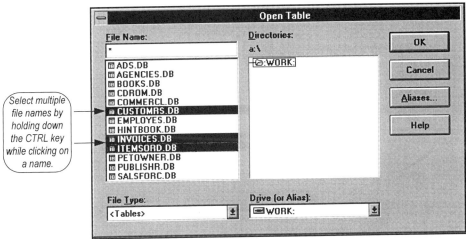

Figure 3 - 4

12. Press **CTRL+F6** to activate the next table window.

13. Press **CTRL+F6** again to activate the third and final table window.

14. Press **CTRL+F6** a third time to activate the first table window.

15. Pick **WINDOW/Tile** to arrange the three tables side by side (see Figure 3 - 5).

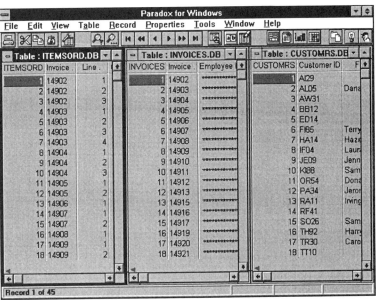

Figure 3 - 5

16. Close the three tables with **WINDOW/Close All**.

17. Open the Project Viewer again by clicking the **Open Project Viewer** button.

ORDERING THE RECORDS

Usually the order of the records in a table is determined by a key field, which keeps the selected field(s) in alphabetical, numeric, or date order. If there is no key field, the records will be recorded in the order in which they were typed. Even if the records were originally typed in order according to the values in some field, after editing and adding new records, the table will soon be out of order. To reorder a table with no key, or to order any keyed table in some alternative order, either sorting or indexing can be used.

Sorting rearranges the order of the records into the desired alphabetical, numeric, or date order by moving the records around so that they are recorded in the desired order. Indexing merely makes a list of how the records should be shown so that they will appear in the desired order. It does not move any records. When the index is deactivated, the table will appear in typed in order again. Usually, tables will have a key field for a permanent order; in this case use indexes to temporarily obtain some other order.

While everyone has sorted a paper list at some time, in *Paradox* sorting is not common. Sorting has too many restrictions and difficulties.

- The moment editing occurs or new records are entered, the previous sort is out of date and the table needs to be resorted. Sorting can take a long time for large tables.

- If there is a key field in the original table, you can only sort to a new copy of that table since the sorted order would contradict the key order.

- If you sort to a new copy of the table, you cannot edit the new table and make any impact on the original table.

Indexing is the preferred way to order a table's records for the following reasons.

- Indexes are usually assigned the option of being automatically maintained. Thus, they are immediately updated by *Paradox* when editing changes or new records alter a table.

- Indexes can coexist with key fields; in fact, a key field is a *primary index* and any other indexes that are created for the table are *secondary indexes*. The secondary index can temporarily override the key field order.

- An index is applied to the original table. Thus, any editing that happens while an index is in effect alters the data in the actual table.

Indexing is also required for multiple table operations, like the multi-table form we will create at the end of this lesson.

INDEXING THE RECORDS

Indexes are created during the design of a table or the restructuring of a table. The dialog boxes for those two operations have a list of Table Properties. One of the Table Properties is Secondary Indexes. That selection opens the **Define Secondary Index** dialog box (see Figure 3 - 6) where the fields to be used are assigned and options are selected.

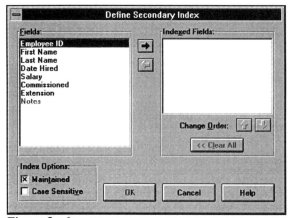

Figure 3 - 6

An index can be based on a single field or multiple fields. Examples of multiple field indexes would be Last Name together with First Name, or State plus City plus Date Hired. Both types of memo fields, graphic, OLE, logical, binary, and byte fields are not allowed in the definition of an index. The two options are Maintained and Case Sensitive (see Figure 3 - 6). Maintained means that *Paradox* will keep the index up to date at all times, rather than only when the index is actually used. Maintained is highly preferable, but can be selected only when the table already has a key field. The Case Sensitive option orders uppercase letters ahead of lowercase. Case Sensitive is usually not desirable.

Once an index has been created, it can be activated with the **TABLE/Filter** menu choice. The **Filter Tables** dialog box that opens contains the list of indexes. Clicking on the name of the desired index and clicking the **OK** button will order the records in the table by the index.

To define a secondary index:

- Open the table.

- Choose **TABLE/Restructure Table** or click the **Restructure** toolbar button.

- In the **Restructure** dialog box click on the drop-down arrow for the **Table Properties** list.

- Pick **Secondary Indexes** from the list.

- Click the **Define** button.

- In the **Define Secondary Index** dialog box click on the most important field for the index and click the right-pointing arrow button to copy that field name to the **Indexed Fields:** list.

- Pick a second most important field for the index, if there is one. Pick any additional fields for the index, as well.

- Pick any options. If **Maintained** is available (if the table has a key field), check it. You probably do not want to check the **Case Sensitive** option.

- Click the **OK** button.

- Type the name for the index.

- Click the **Save** button in the **Restructure** dialog box.

To erase a secondary index:

- Open the table.

- Choose **TABLE/Restructure Table**.

- In the **Restructure** dialog box click on the drop-down arrow for the **Table Properties** list.

- Pick **Secondary Indexes** from the list.

- Click on the name of the index to be removed.

- Click the **Erase** button at the bottom right corner of the dialog box.

- Click the **Save** button in the **Restructure** dialog box.

Activity 3.3: Creating a Secondary Index

We will create two secondary indexes for the **EMPLOYES.DB** table. The first will be based on the **Extension** field. The second will use the Last Name together with the First Name.

1. Open the **EMPLOYES.DB** table.

2. Select **TABLE/Restructure Table** or click the **Restructure** toolbar button.

3. In the **Restructure** dialog box, click on the drop-down arrow for **Table Properties** (see Figure 3 - 7).

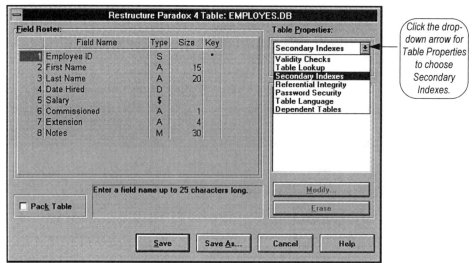

Figure 3 - 7

4. Click on **Secondary Indexes**.

5. Click the **Define** button.

6. In the **Define Secondary Index** dialog box, click on **Extension** and click the arrow button that points to the right to copy the field name to the **Indexed Fields:** list (see Figure 3 - 8).

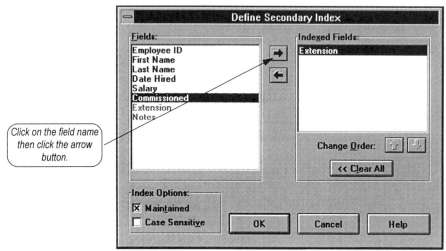

Figure 3 - 8

7. Make certain the **Maintained** option box is checked and the **Case Sensitive** option is *not* checked as shown in Figure 3 - 8.

8. Click the **OK** button to return to the **Restructure** dialog box.

9. In the **Save Index As** dialog box type **Phone Extension** as the name for the index (see Figure 3 - 9).

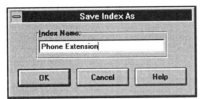

Figure 3 - 9

The names for indexes follow the same rules as the names for fields. While you might be tempted to name a single field index with the field name itself, Paradox will not allow that unless it is a Case Sensitive index. Since ours is not, rather than the field name Extension, we will name it Phone Extension.

10. Click the **OK** button.

*The new name will appear in the list immediately below the **Define** button.*

11. Click the **Define** button again.

12. In the **Define Secondary Index** dialog box, click on **Last Name** and click the arrow button that points to the right to copy the field name to the **Indexed Fields:** list.

13. Click on **First Name** and click the arrow button that points to the right to copy that field name to the **Indexed Fields:** list (see Figure 3 - 10).

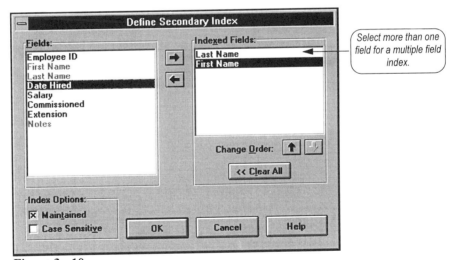

Figure 3 - 10

14. Make certain the **Maintained** option is checked and the **Case Sensitive** option is *not* checked.

15. Click the **OK** button to return to the **Restructure** dialog box.

16. Enter the name **Last and First Name** in the **Save Index As** dialog box and click **OK**.

*That name will join Phone Extension in the list at the right side of the **Restructure** dialog box (see Figure 3 - 11).*

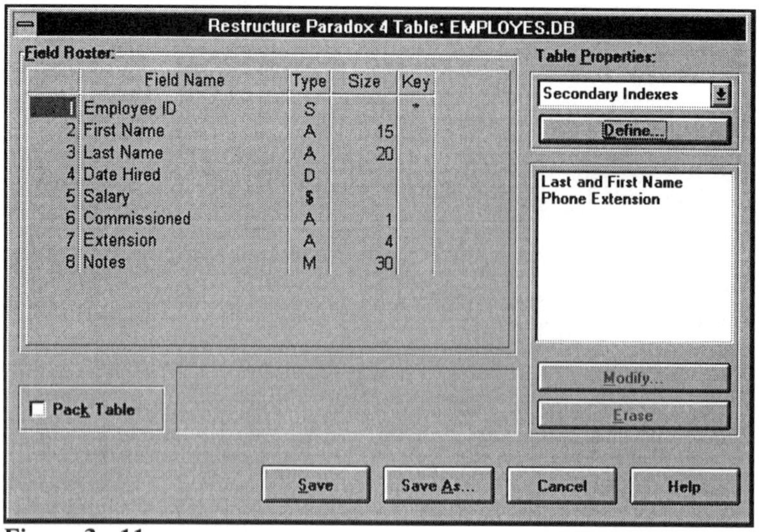

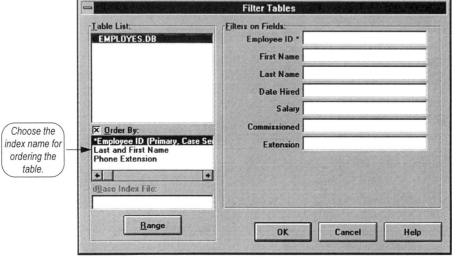

Figure 3 - 11

17. Click the **Save** button to save both index definitions as part of the table properties.

To activate an index:

- Open the table.

- Pick **TABLE/Filter**.

- In the **Filter Tables** dialog box (see Figure 3 - 12), click on the name of the index by which to order the table.

Figure 3 - 12

- Click the **OK** button.

Activity 3.4: Activating a Secondary Index

We will apply each of the two secondary indexes to the **EMPLOYES.DB** table in turn.

1. **EMPLOYES.DB** should still be open on the desktop.

2. Pick **TABLE/Filter**.

3. In the **Filter Tables** dialog box click on the name **Phone Extension**.

4. Click the **OK** button.

   The order of the records should change into the order of the Extensions as shown in Figure 3 - 13.

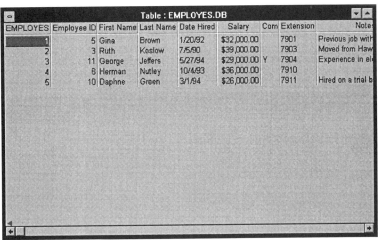

Figure 3 - 13

5. Pick **TABLE/Filter** again.

6. In the **Filter Tables** dialog box click on the name **Last and First Name**.

7. Click the **OK** button.

   The order of the records should change to name order as shown in Figure 3 - 14.

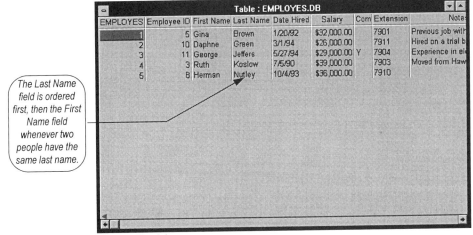

Figure 3 - 14

8. Close the table with **FILE/Close**.

An index is in effect only while the table remains open. Once you close the table, you need to specifically activate the index again the next time you open the table.

A RELATIONAL SYSTEM OF TABLES

As you gain experience developing tables of data, you will encounter situations that cause various design problems. For example, suppose the CDROM company asks you to design a table to record customer purchases. You might try a single table like Figure 3 - 15, but, when you begin filling in the data, an immediate problem occurs. Data begins to get duplicated. Redundant data usually signals a poor design and taxes the system in the following five ways.

- A data entry person is wasting time and effort retyping every character that is duplicate data.

- Disk space is wasted recording the redundant data.

- Inconsistencies will occur among the duplicated data when changes are made, as some of it will get updated and some may not.

- *Paradox* will slow down as it works its way through more data than is necessary.

- Typing errors will proliferate since more data entry is being done than is required.

A poor design because of the duplication.

Customer	Employee	Last Name	Invoice #	Quantity Sold	Title	Price
Arrow Way Freight	Daphne	Green	14902	20	99,000 Fonts	$99.00
Arrow Way Freight	Daphne	Green	14902	100	Every Household Listed	$299.00
Arrow Way Freight	Daphne	Green	14902	25	Comsumers, Consumers	$299.00
Edible Delights	Daphne	Green	14903	20	Comsumers, Consumers	$299.00
Edible Delights	Daphne	Green	14903	5	99,000 Fonts	$99.00
Edible Delights	Daphne	Green	14903	10	Every Household Listed	$299.00
Edible Delights	Daphne	Green	14903	5	Perfect Paragraph 8.0	$795.00
AreaWide Insurance	George	Jeffers	14904	55	Every Household Listed	$299.00
AreaWide Insurance	George	Jeffers	14904	3	Perfect Paragraph 8.0	$795.00
AreaWide Insurance	George	Jeffers	14904	100	Comsumers, Consumers	$299.00
Your Trip Travel	George	Jeffers	14905	10	Clip Art 200,000	$109.00
Your Trip Travel	George	Jeffers	14905	5	Comsumers, Consumers	$299.00
Timed Travel, Inc	George	Jeffers	14906	2	Every Household Listed	$299.00
Jerome	George	Jeffers	14907	1	Too Small to See	$49.00
Jerome	George	Jeffers	14907	1	Every Poem Printed	$149.00
Arrow Way Freight	Daphne	Green	14908	125	Every Household Listed	$299.00
Yorko	George	Jeffers	14909	1	Everything There Is to Know	$129.00
Yorko	George	Jeffers	14909	1	Every Poem Printed	$149.00
Yorko	George	Jeffers	14909	1	Fog Scenes	$9.99
Yorko	George	Jeffers	14909	1	Encyclopedia Galactica	$499.00
Regent Foods	Daphne	Green	14910	30	Perfect Paragraph 8.0	$795.00
Balloon Bonanza	Daphne	Green	14911	5	Every Household Listed	$299.00
Balloon Bonanza	Daphne	Green	14911	2	Perfect Paragraph 8.0	$795.00
Harrington	George	Jeffers	14912	1	Every Poem Printed	$149.00
Oradelio	Daphne	Green	14913	1	Too Small to See	$49.00
Arrow Way Freight	Daphne	Green	14915	50	Comsumers, Consumers	$299.00

Figure 3 - 15

To eliminate data duplication, divide some of the data into separate tables. While entire books are devoted to this topic, there are two fundamental situations which, with experience, you can begin to recognize.

- When an indeterminate number of items needs to be recorded.

- When data items will occur over and over again.

As an example of the first situation, suppose you need to record customer purchases of CDROMs. You will need to record the customer's name and address, of course, but how many CDROMs will the customer purchase at a time? There is no way of telling. Therefore, you cannot design a table based on the customer, with a separate column for each CDROM ordered (see Figure 3 - 16). You don't know how many columns to create. If you create too few columns, the remainder of the order will not fit, and if you create too many fields, every order for a single CDROM will waste the space reserved in each additional column. Such a design fails either way.

On the other hand, and as an example of the second situation where data will repeat over and over, you might try to record each CDROM ordered in a separate record (see Figure 3 - 15). But then, if you keep track of the customer's name and address, a customer who orders ten CDROMs will have ten records with his or her name and address repeated on every line! That design fails because of redundancy.

Customer	Street	State	Title1	Qty1	Title2	Qty2	Title3	Qty3
Arrow Way Freight	2395 E. Third Ave.	GA	Comsumers, Consu	25	Every Household L	100	99,000 Fonts	20
Edible Delights	781 Outrigger St.	CO	Perfect Paragraph	5	Every Household L	10	99,000 Fonts	5
AreaWide Insurance	778 Mid-Town Rd.	CA	Comsumers, Consu	100	Perfect Paragraph	3	Every Household L	55
Your Trip Travel	1290 Joshua Dr.	CO	Comsumers, Consu	5	Clip Art 200,000	10		
Timed Travel, Inc	1000 Flying Cloud D	NY	Every Household L	2	Every Poem Printed	1		
Jerome	82 Marlow Ln.	NH	Too Small to See	125				
Arrow Way Freight	2395 E. Third Ave.	GA	Every Household L	125				
Yorko	546 Troddle St.	IL	Encyclopedia Gala	1	Everything There Is	1	Every Poem Printed	1
Regent Foods	6990 Industrial Blvd.	NC	Perfect Paragraph	30				
Balloon Bonanza	11114 80th Street	IL	Every Household L	5	Perfect Paragraph	2		
Harrington	12093 Brighton Dr.	IL	Every Poem Printed	1				
Oradelio	90 South Main	FL	Too Small to See	1				
Edible Delights	781 Outrigger St.	CO	Clip Art 200,000	25				
AreaWide Insurance	778 Mid-Town Rd.	CA	Clip Art 200,000	50				
Fielder	Satellite Way	IL	Programming in Any	1				
Truefoe	10204 Elm Rd.	GA	Everything There Is	1	Encyclopedia Gala	1		
Ifalo	4529 Garrett Ave.	MA	Fog Scenes	1				
Thompson	19 Memory Lane	CA	Too Small to See	1	Encyclopedia Gala	1	Scourge - The Gam	1
Packard	Saleno Court	WI	Every Household L	110				
Udarell	Heather Lane	CA	Fog Scenes	1				
Killian	89 Harvard Place	NJ	Encyclopedia Gala	1				
Allington	89 Canter Rd.	NY	Legal Assistant to th	1				
Sorbite	9 Allison Way	TX	Programming in Any	1				
						0		0

A poor design because you cannot predict how many CD titles the customer will order.

Figure 3 - 16

The solution to both design problems is to split the data into separate tables (Figure 3 - 17). Record each customer only once in a separate customer table. Do not enter the CDROM order there, but give each customer a code number and enter that code on each order. Since the code number will be very short, we will not mind typing it on each order, even if the same customer orders over and over so that his or her code is repeated many times.

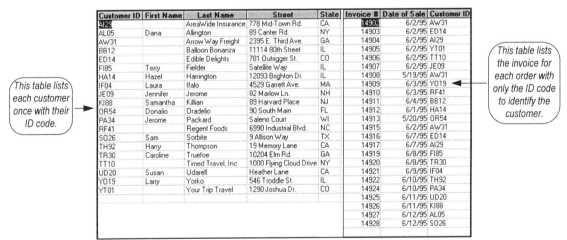

This table lists each customer once with their ID code.

Customer ID	First Name	Last Name	Street	State
AI29		AreaWide Insurance	778 Mid-Town Rd.	CA
AL05	Dana	Allington	89 Canter Rd.	NY
AW31		Arrow Way Freight	2395 E. Third Ave.	GA
BB12		Balloon Bonanza	11114 80th Street	IL
ED14		Edible Delights	781 Outrigger St.	CO
FI85	Terry	Fielder	Satellite Way	IL
HA14	Hazel	Harrington	12093 Brighton Dr.	IL
IF04	Laura	Ifalo	4529 Garrett Ave.	MA
JE09	Jennifer	Jerome	82 Marlow Ln.	NH
KI88	Samantha	Killian	89 Harvard Place	NJ
OR54	Donalio	Oradelio	90 South Main	FL
PA34	Jerome	Packard	Saleno Court	WI
RF41		Regent Foods	6990 Industrial Blvd.	NC
SO26	Sam	Sorbite	9 Allison Way	TX
TH92	Harry	Thompson	19 Memory Lane	CA
TR30	Caroline	Truefoe	10204 Elm Rd.	GA
TT10		Timed Travel, Inc	1000 Flying Cloud Drive	NY
UD20	Susan	Udarell	Heather Lane	CA
YO19	Larry	Yorko	546 Troddle St.	IL
YT01		Your Trip Travel	1290 Joshua Dr.	CO

Invoice #	Date of Sale	Customer ID
14902	6/2/95	AW31
14903	6/2/95	ED14
14904	6/2/95	AI29
14905	6/2/95	YT01
14906	6/2/95	TT10
14907	6/2/95	JE09
14908	5/19/95	AW31
14909	6/3/95	YO19
14910	6/3/95	RF41
14911	6/4/95	BB12
14912	6/1/95	HA14
14913	5/20/95	OR54
14915	6/2/95	AW31
14916	6/7/95	ED14
14917	6/7/95	AI29
14919	6/8/95	FI85
14920	6/8/95	TR30
14921	6/9/95	IF04
14922	6/10/95	TH92
14924	6/10/95	PA34
14925	6/11/95	UD20
14926	6/11/95	KI88
14927	6/12/95	AL05
14928	6/12/95	SO26

This table lists the invoice for each order with only the ID code to identify the customer.

Figure 3 - 17

Since we cannot anticipate how many items will be on an order, make one table for the customer's order as a whole (an invoice with order number, date, sales person, etc.—each item that has a predetermined number of entries), and a separate table that lists the items on the order with one item in each record (see Figure 3 - 18). To know which order an item belongs to, record the order number along with each item. Since the order number will be short, we won't mind if it is repeated on each of the ten lines of an order for ten items.

To test your understanding of these two database design problems, try determining which problem each of the following examples resembles.

- A design to keep track of the computer equipment each employee is using. How many pieces of equipment (computer, printer, screen, mouse, etc.) would each employee have?

- One or more tables to keep track of the publisher's name and address for each CDROM title, where many CDROMs may come from the same publisher.

- A list of the people who are contacts at each publisher. Could there be more than one contact?

- A design for the family members (dependents) of each employee. Could a family have 10 members? 12? 14?

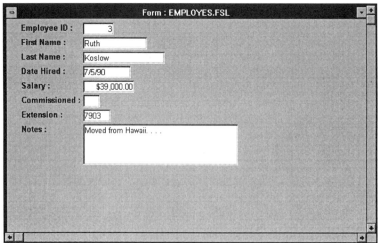

Invoice #	Employee ID	Date of Sale	Customer ID		Invoice #	Line #	Quantity	CD ID	Back Ordered
14902	10	6/2/95	AW31		14902	1	20	F01	N
14903	10	6/2/95	ED14		14902	2	100	E04	N
14904	11	6/2/95	AI29		14902	3	25	C01	N
14905	11	6/2/95	YT01		14903	1	20	C01	N
14906	11	6/2/95	TT10		14903	2	5	F01	N
14907	11	6/2/95	JE09		14903	3	10	E04	N
14908	10	5/19/95	AW31		14903	4	5	P02	N
14909	11	6/3/95	YO19		14904	1	55	E04	N
14910	10	6/3/95	RF41		14904	2	3	P02	N
14911	10	6/4/95	BB12		14904	3	100	C01	N
14912	11	6/1/95	HA14		14905	1	10	C02	N
14913	10	5/20/95	OR54		14905	2	5	C01	N
14915	10	6/2/95	AW31		14906	1	2	E04	N
14916	10	6/7/95	ED14		14907	1	1	T02	Y
14917	11	6/7/95	AI29		14907	2	1	E06	N
14919	10	6/8/95	FI85		14908	1	125	E04	N
14920	11	6/8/95	TR30		14909	1	1	E07	N
14921	11	6/9/95	IF04		14909	2	1	E06	N
14922	11	6/10/95	TH92		14909	3	1	F02	N
14924	10	6/10/95	PA34		14909	4	1	E05	N
14925	11	6/11/95	UD20		14910	1	30	P02	N
14926	11	6/11/95	KI88		14911	1	5	E04	N
14927	10	6/12/95	AL05		14911	2	2	P02	N
14928	11	6/12/95	SO26		14912	1	1	E06	N
	0				14913	1	1	T02	Y
					14915	1	50	C01	N

This table lists each invoice.

This table lists each item on the invoices.

Figure 3 - 18

Now that you understand the necessity for multiple tables, we will actually use multiple tables in the next sections with forms, as well as in most of the remaining lessons.

CREATING A FORM

A form is an alternative arrangement for the fields in a table (see Figure 3 - 19). Rather than the straight columns and rows of a table, a form may have any field placed anywhere you please. Normally a form displays only one record at a time so the user can focus on a single listing. Because a form allows great freedom in design, you may not only arrange some or all of the fields in any order on the screen, but you may add titles, instructions, boxes and lines, colors, calculations, and graphics to enhance the design. Forms can also display more than one related table at a time.

Form : EMPLOYES.FSL

Employee ID :	3
First Name :	Ruth
Last Name :	Koslow
Date Hired :	7/5/90
Salary :	$39,000.00
Commissioned :	
Extension :	7903
Notes :	Moved from Hawaii. . . .

Figure 3 - 19

Designing a form from scratch would be a lengthy and tedious process as you would need to place every field and every label individually, adjust the appearance and alignment of those items, and add any other details you wanted. Fortunately *Paradox* can perform most of the tedious work for you. *Paradox* offers a number of options and then creates the form for you based on your choices. This will save a great deal of time and effort.

To create a form:

- Pick **FILE/New/Form**. Alternatively, **right**-click the **Open Form** toolbar button ⊞ or **right**-click the **Forms** icon in the Project Viewer and pick **New** from the self-contained menu.

- Click the **Data Model/Layout Diagram** button for a speedy form with relatively few questions and options or the **Form Expert** button for dozens of options in a more lengthy, but flexible, process. Avoid the **Blank** button as you would end up doing all of the design and layout work yourself.

- If you chose the **Form Expert** button, complete each of the up to eight sets of questions and options and the *Form Expert* will create your design.

- If you chose the **Data Model/Layout Diagram** button, type the table name in the **File Name** text box or select a table from the list. Click the **OK** button.

- Choose the Style of form, the Field Layout, whether you want to Label Fields, and the Style Sheet. Click the **OK** button.

- Click the **View Data** button ⚡ to see the form.

- Save the design.

Activity 3.5: Creating a Form

We will create a standard form (see Figure 3 - 19) for the **EMPLOYES.DB** table that includes all eight fields.

1. Right-click the **Forms** icon in the left section of the Project Viewer to open its self-contained menu (see Figure 3 - 20).

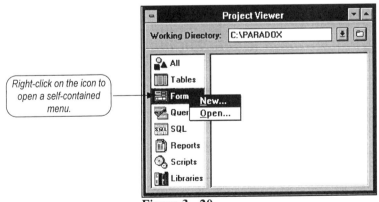

Right-click on the icon to open a self-contained menu.

Figure 3 - 20

2. Select **New** from the menu. (Alternatively, you could pick **FILE/New/Form**.)

3. In the **New Form** dialog box click on the **Data Model/Layout Diagram** button (see Figure 3 - 21).

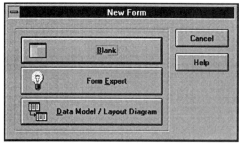

Figure 3 - 21

4. Click on the table name **EMPLOYES.DB** (see Figure 3 - 22).

   *The table name will appear in the gray panel at the right side of the **Data Model** dialog box (see Figure 3 - 22).*

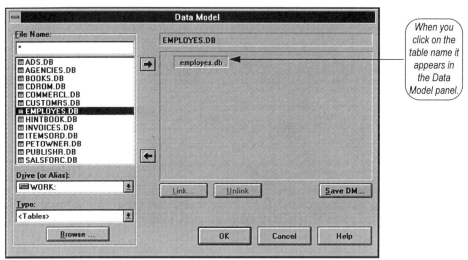

Figure 3 - 22

5. Click the **OK** button.

   *The **Design Layout** dialog box appears with the basic design showing (see Figure 3 - 23).*

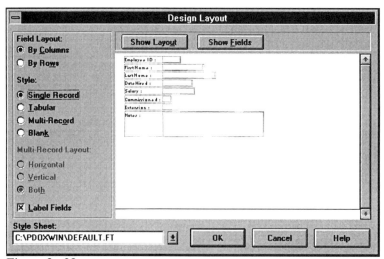

Figure 3 - 23

6. If the left panel of the **Design Layout** dialog box does not show the layout options like Figure 3 - 23, click the **Show Layout** button at the top of the dialog box.

7. Click on the **Single Record** option for **Style** if it is not already selected, so that only one record will show on the form at a time.

8. Click on the **By Columns** option for the **Field Layout** if it is not already selected, so that the fields will be organized in a single column rather than multiple columns.

9. The **Label Fields** check box should be checked so that each field will be labeled.

10. Click on the drop-down arrow for **Style Sheet** and click on **CONTRL3D.FT** (Figure 3 - 24).

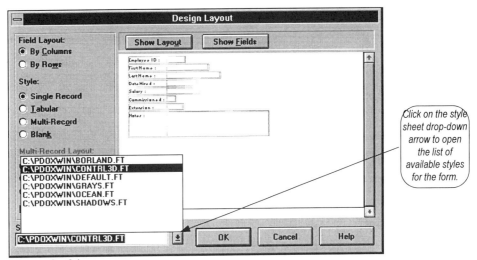

Figure 3 - 24

The appearance of the design should change to reflect a 3-D look to the boxes. While the style of a form is often a matter of taste, the 3-D style clearly defines the data entry boxes.

11. Click the **OK** button.

*The **Form Design** window will open (see Figure 3 - 25).*

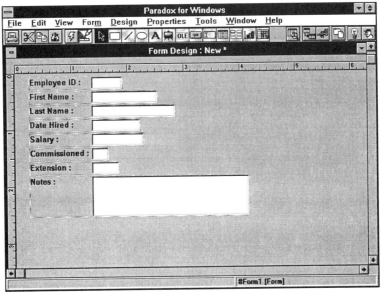

Figure 3 - 25

12. To save the design, choose **FILE/Save As**, type the name **Employes**, and click **OK** (see Figure 3 - 26).

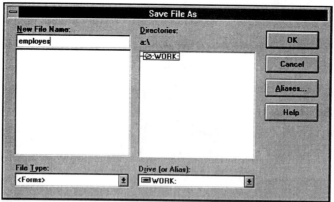

Figure 3 - 26

13. Click the **View Data** button on the toolbar to switch from the design to the form with data showing in it (see Figure 3 - 19).

14. Do *not* close the form.

USING A FORM

You work with this form the same way you do with a table, except that the movement is mostly vertical instead of horizontal. The data is the same; editing is the same; searching is the same. It's the same table of data, just reorganized visually.

To use a form:

- Open the form.

- View the data, edit the existing data, or type new data.

- The single difference between data entry in a table and a form concerns a memo field. In a table, when you press **SHIFT+F2** to enter Memo View, an editing window opens for the memo. In a form, when you press the **Memo View** key, you edit within the box on the form.

- The form may be printed.

- Close the form.

Activity 3.6: Using a Form

A form is used to view or edit the data, or to enter new data. A form may also be printed. We will view the existing listings in **EMPLOYES.DB**, then enter a new record on the form.

1. If the **EMPLOYES.FSL** form is not already open on the screen from the previous activity, double-click on **EMPLOYES.FSL** in the list of forms in the Project Viewer.

   The current record number at the left end of the status bar should say 1 of 5.

2. View record 2 by pressing the **PGDN** (or **PAGE DOWN**) key.

3. View record 3 by clicking the **Next Record** navigation button.

4. Jump to the last record by clicking the **Last Record** navigation button.

5. Press the **F9** key to enter Edit Mode.

6. To begin a new record, press the **PGDN** key or click the **Next Record** button.

   *The status bar should show **Empty record**, and empty typing boxes should be displayed (see Figure 3 - 27).*

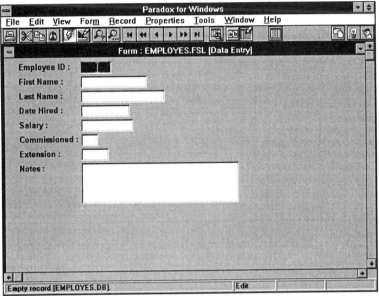

Figure 3 - 27

7. For the **Employee ID**, enter: **12** and press **ENTER** to move to the next field.

8. Fill in the **First Name** by typing: **Gary** and press **ENTER**.

9. For **Last Name**, type: **Lamp** and press **ENTER**.

10. His **Date Hired** is: **2/1/95**.

11. Enter: **28,000** for **Salary**.

12. For **Commissioned** type: **Y** since he is on commission. Press **ENTER** to continue.

13. The **Extension** is: **7905**

14. In the **Notes** field press the **SHIFT+F2** Memo View key and enter: **Previous experience in marketing.**

15. Press **SHIFT+F2** to end Memo View.

    In a form you may type a memo without entering Memo View, but then you cannot enter tabs or carriage returns. Also, when there are already characters in the memo field, if you just begin typing without Memo View, you will replace any previous entry. With Memo View you may add to the previous characters.

16. As this is the only new employee, we are finished (see Figure 3 - 28). Press **F9** to end Edit Mode.

17. Close the form with **FILE/Close**.

    *The new form **EMPLOYES.FSL** will be listed in the Project Viewer.*

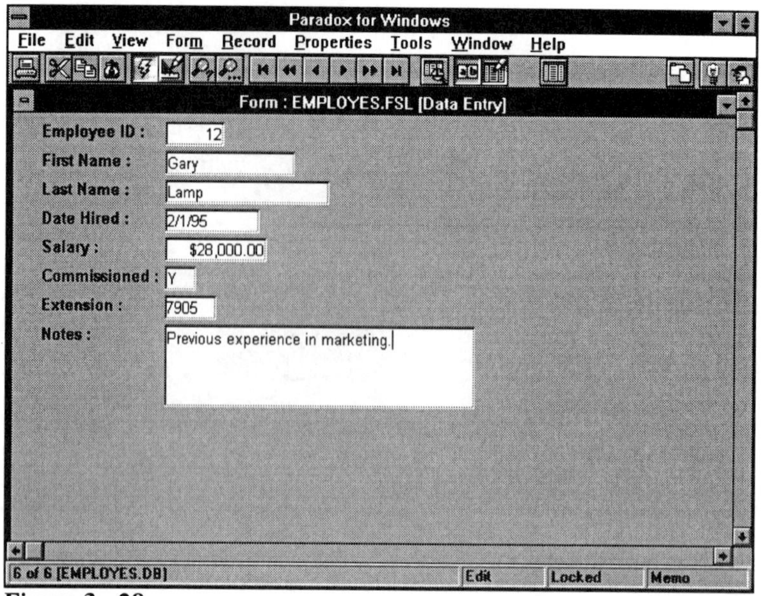

Figure 3 - 28

A MULTI-TABLE FORM

Two or more tables can be displayed on the same form design. The main table is called the *master table*; the secondary table is the *detail table* (see Figure 3 - 29). The two tables are related by a field that is common to both tables. That common field is the basis of the link or relationship between the pair of tables. Once there is such a link, *Paradox* will display only the records from the detail table that go with the current record in the master table. *Paradox* figures out which records go together (are related) and displays them on the form simultaneously.

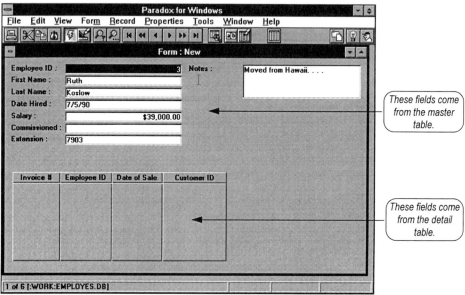

Figure 3 - 29

Remembering the discussion of relational tables two sections ago, we will create a form with data from both the Employees and the Invoices tables. Both tables contain the linking field Employee ID. Employees will be the master table and a subform listing Invoices will be embedded on it (see Figure 3 - 29).

The requirements for multi-table forms where matching records must show are:

- The **detail table** must have either a primary index (key field) or a secondary index on the common field

- The field types and sizes of the common fields must be identical in the two tables.

While the Data Model/Layout Diagram can be used for a multi-table form, the *Form Expert* is considerably easier. It asks a sequence of up to eight questions and options, and then designs the form for you, including multi-table forms. [Note: There appears to be a problem in *Paradox* with having a primary index (key field) as the index in the detail table. The *Form Expert* rejects such a link, whereas the Data Model/Layout Diagram method accepts a primary index for the link. Secondary indexes do not present any problems.]

To create a Multi-table form:

- Make certain the detail table has an index on the common field. If it does not, create a primary index (key field) or secondary index on that field.

- Pick **FILE/New/Form**. Alternatively, right-click the **Open Form** toolbar button or right-click the **Forms icon** in the Project Viewer and pick **New** from the self-contained menu.

- Click the **Form Expert** button for the easiest method to create a multi-table form. (The **Data Model/Layout Diagram** button can also be used, but the method is not as obvious.) Avoid the **Blank** button.

- If you chose the **Form Expert** button, answer each of the up to eight sets of questions and options.

- Click the lightning bolt button to complete the design.

- Save the design.

Activity 3.7: Creating a Multi-table Form

We need to work with the employees and the invoices they have sold, so we will create a multi-table form where **EMPLOYES.DB** is the master table and **INVOICES.DB** is the detail table (or *embedded form*). This form will display the employees one at a time, with the invoices they sold in the embedded portion on the same form.

Since a requirement for the linking of **INVOICES.DB** and **EMPLOYES.DB** is an index on the common field in the detail (embedded) table, we will create a secondary index on the **Employee ID** field in **INVOICES.DB**.

Table : INVOICES.DB				
INVOICES	Invoice #	Employee ID	Date of Sale	Customer ID
1	14902	10	6/2/95	AW31
2	14903	10	6/2/95	ED14
3	14904	11	6/2/95	AI29
4	14905	11	6/2/95	YT01
5	14906	11	6/2/95	TT10
6	14907	11	6/2/95	JE09
7	14908	10	5/19/95	AW31
8	14909	11	6/3/95	YO19
9	14910	10	6/3/95	RF41
10	14911	10	6/4/95	BB12
11	14912	11	6/1/95	HA14
12	14913	10	5/20/95	OR54
13	14915	10	6/2/95	AW31
14	14916	10	6/7/95	ED14
15	14917	11	6/7/95	AI29
16	14919	10	6/8/95	FI85
17	14920	11	6/8/95	TR30
18	14921	11	6/9/95	IF04

Figure 3 - 30

1. Open the **INVOICES.DB** table, which is supplied on the Student Data Diskette (see Figure 3 - 30).

    *Notice in **INVOICES.DB** that there are no names of the employees who sold the invoices; there are only Employee ID numbers. To determine who each salesperson was, you have to look at the Employee ID, transfer to the **EMPLOYES.DB** table, and search for the matching ID number. This matching of ID numbers is what Paradox will do for you on a multi-table form.*

2. Since an index (either primary or secondary) is a requirement, begin creating a secondary index on the **Employee ID** field in **INVOICES.DB** by clicking the **Restructure** button on the toolbar.

3. In the **Table Properties** section of the **Restructure** dialog box, click on the drop-down arrow to open the list of properties. Click on **Secondary Indexes** (see Figure 3 - 31).

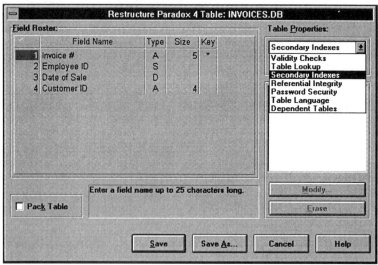

Figure 3 - 31

4. Click the **Define** button that is immediately below the **Table Properties** list.

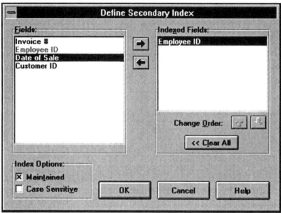

Figure 3 - 32

5. In the **Define Secondary Index** dialog box click on **Employee ID** in the **Fields:** list and click the arrow button that points to the right (see Figure 3 - 32) to copy the field name into the **Indexed Fields:** list.

6. **Maintained** should be checked. **Case Sensitive** should *not* be checked. Click **OK**.

7. In the **Save Index As** dialog box type the name: **EmpID** (see Figure 3 - 33) and click **OK**.

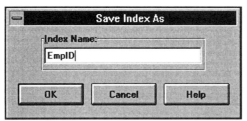

Figure 3 - 33

The secondary index name, EmpID, will appear in the list below the Define button.

8. Click the **Save** button.

9. Close the table with **FILE/Close**.

10. Right-click on the **Forms** icon in the left section of the Project Viewer.

11. Pick **New**.

12. Click the **Form Expert** button (see Figure 3 - 21).

13. In Step 1 of 8 (see Figure 3 - 34) click on the **4. View one master record and multiple detail records. Detail records display in a table format.** option.

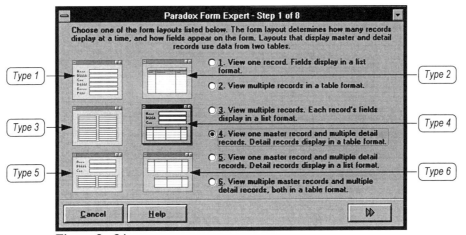

Figure 3 - 34

14. Click on the **double-arrowhead** button (>>) that points to the right to continue.

15. Pick **EMPLOYES.DB** as the Master Table Name in Step 2 and click the >> button (see Figure 3 - 35).

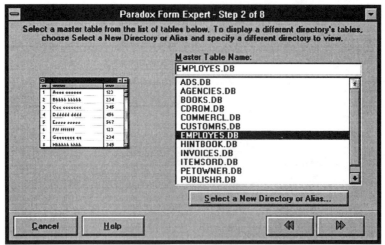

Figure 3 - 35

16. Select **INVOICES.DB** as the Detail Table Name in Step 3 and click the >> button (see Figure 3 - 36).

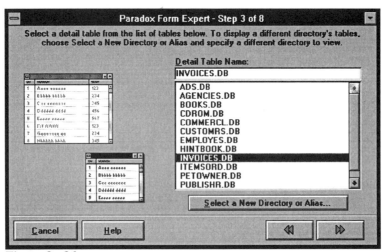

Figure 3 - 36

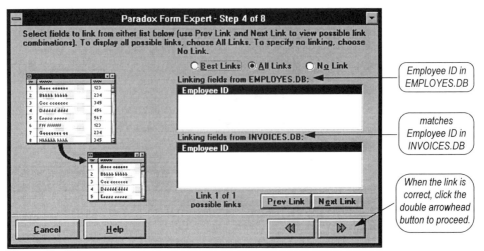

Figure 3 - 37

*Because of the secondary index on the **Employee ID** field, the Form Expert figures that **Employee ID** in **EMPLOYES.DB** matches **Employee ID** in **INVOICES.DB** and has already selected the correct linking fields (see Figure 3 - 37).*

17. The link is already correct in Step 4, so click the >> button.

18. We want all eight fields from **EMPLOYES.DB**, so everything is correct in Step 5 (see Figure 3 - 38). Click the >> button.

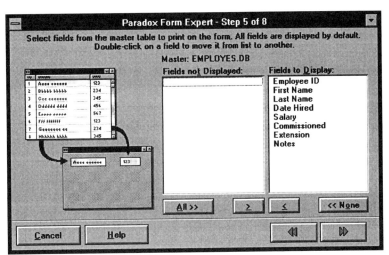

Figure 3 - 38

19. We want all four fields from **INVOICES.DB**, so everything is correct in Step 6 (see Figure 3 - 39). Click the >> button.

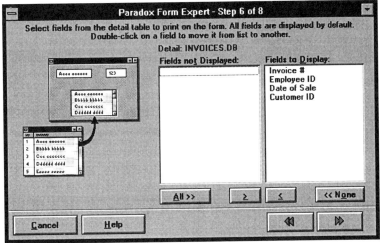

Figure 3 - 39

*The Target Output for the Form is the **Video Screen**. The Available Page Size will probably be **VGA: 640 x 480**, but if there is any problem with that choice or if that choice is not showing, ask your instructor or lab assistant what the Page Size should be on the computer you are using.*

20. Make certain **Video Screen** and **VGA: 640 x 480** are the selected choices in Step 7 (see Figure 3 - 40), then click the >> button.

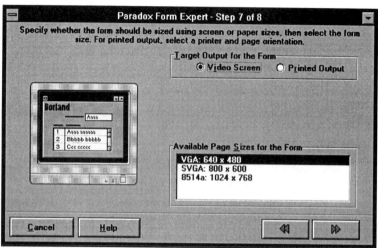

Figure 3 - 40

21. In Step 8 click on each of the six styles in the **Style Sheet** list (see Figure 3 - 41) to examine them. Then, pick **Control 3D style** and click the **lightning bolt** button.

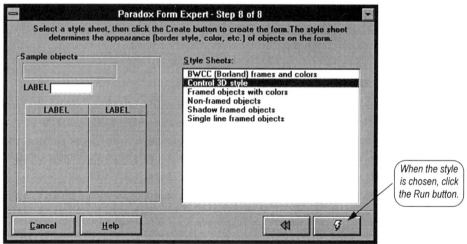

Figure 3 - 41

*The lightning bolt is the **Finish** button. There will be a short wait while the **Form Expert** creates the design.*

22. When the message "The form you specified is complete..." appears, click the **Yes** button to run it so you can see the resulting form with data displayed in it (see Figure 3 - 42).

*The first employee, Ruth Koslow, doesn't have any invoice sales, so the secondary form below the **Extension** field is empty. The next two employees are not salespeople, either.*

23. Press **PGDN** (or **PAGE DOWN**) three times to get to **Daphne Green** (see Figure 3 - 43).

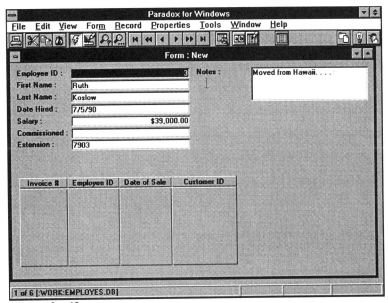

Figure 3 - 42

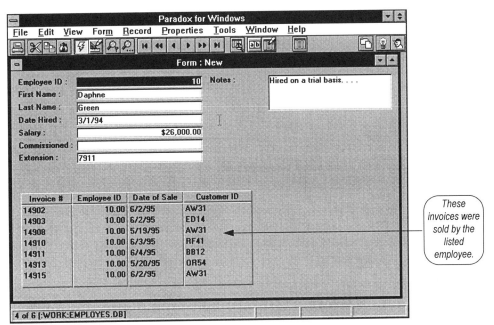

Figure 3 - 43

As Daphne is a salesperson, she has invoices associated with her Employee ID number. Notice that her number, 10, is listed on every one of the invoices that shows in the embedded form.

24. Press **PGDN** (or **PAGE DOWN**) once to get to **George Jeffers**. He is in sales and has many invoices listed.

25. Press **PGDN** (or **PAGE DOWN**) once more to get to **Gary Lamp**. He is in sales, but so new he doesn't have any sales yet.

26. Begin to close the form with **FILE/Close**.

27. We do want to save the design, so click the **Yes** button in the **"Newly created document: Do you want to save it?"** dialog box (see Figure 3 - 44).

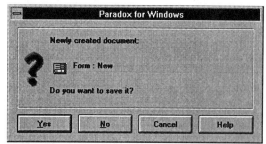

Figure 3 - 44

28. Type the name: **Emplyinv** in the **Save File As** dialog box (see Figure 3 - 45) and click the **OK** button.

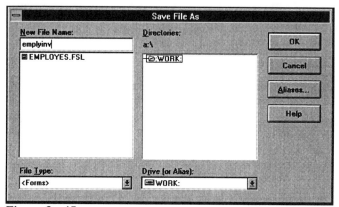

Figure 3 - 45

Operations with multiple tables like this multi-table form are much simpler if you name the matching fields in each table the exact same thing. In this past example, the *Paradox Form Expert* figured out that Employee ID was the common field partly because of the index on Employee ID and partly because the field name was the same in both tables. You are not required to make the names identical, but it makes many operations with multiple tables much simpler.

SUMMARY

In this lesson we have begun to work with multiple tables. We utilized the Project Viewer and opened multiple tables at a time onto the desktop. We created secondary indexes and used the Data Model to design a single table form. We discussed the need for a relational system of tables rather than a single table for the data in a system. We examined the need for common fields between pairs of tables and used the *Form Expert* to create a form that displayed data from two tables simultaneously.

In the next two lessons we will carry the multiple table idea one step further by seeing how to join separate, but related, tables. We will also learn how to select subsets of the data in a table based on matching specified values.

KEY TERMS

Detail table	Inspect	Relational Database System
Embedded form	Master table	Secondary index
Form Expert	Primary index	Self-contained menu

INDEPENDENT PROJECTS

Independent Project 3.1: The School Newspaper

This Independent Project continues the Newspaper Ad database from Independent Project 2.1. In this project you will examine the table containing the salespersons' names and create a form that includes both the salespersons' names and the sales data on one screen. Finally, you will use that form to enter a new ad.

The table of names was typed by someone else who works for the newspaper and saved as **SALSFORC.DB** (short for Sales Force) on the Student Data Diskette. You might ask why are the salespersons' names in a separate table? Why not include them right in the **ADS.DB** table? Because the same salespeople sell many ads, and their names would be repeated over and over in **ADS.DB**. In **SALSFORC.DB** each salesperson is entered just once and given a code number. Only the short code number is included on each ad. Of course, to combine both **SALSFORC.DB** and **ADS.DB** on the same form, the matching code numbers must be in the **ADS.DB** table, too.

The two requirements for creating a multi-table form are that there must be either a primary (key field) or secondary index on the **Salesperson ID** field in the detail (embedded) table, and the **Salesperson ID** field must have the same data type and size in both tables. You can check both tables to make certain the data type and size are the same.

The table of names looks like Figure 3 - 46. The finished form should resemble Figure 3 - 47.

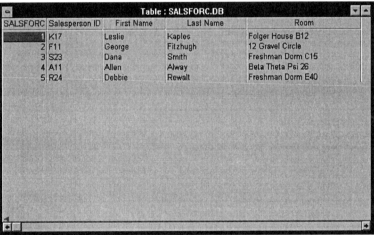

Figure 3 - 46

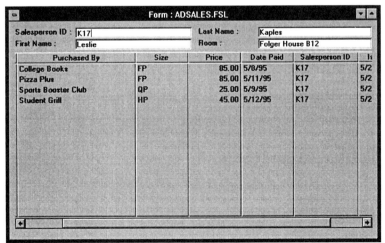

Figure 3 - 47

1. Run *Paradox*.

2. Click the **Paradox** button to close the Welcome to Paradox screen if it is open.

3. Maximize the *Paradox* window if it does not already cover the entire screen.

4. Click the **Open Project Viewer** button on the toolbar if it is not already open. Check that you are in the correct working directory.

5. Double-click the name **ADS.DB** to open the table.

6. To create a secondary index on **Salesperson ID**, click the **Restructure** button on the toolbar.

7. Click on the drop-down list for **Table Properties** and pick **Secondary Indexes**.

8. Click the **Define** button.

9. Click on **Salesperson ID** in the **Fields:** list and click the arrow button to copy the name to the **Indexed Fields:** list. **Maintained** should be checked, but not **Case Sensitive**.

10. Click the **OK** button.

11. Enter the name **Salesperson ID Index** and click the **OK** button. Remember, you may not duplicate the field name, so we added the word **Index**.

12. Click the **Save** button.

13. Close **ADS.DB** by picking **FILE/Close**.

14. Begin creating the form by right-clicking on (inspecting) the **Forms** icon in the left column of the Project Viewer.

15. Pick **New**.

16. Click the **Form Expert** button.

17. In the panel of form types, click option **4. View one master record and multiple detail records. Detail records display in a table format.** and click the >> button.

18. For the Master Table Name, click on **SALSFORC.DB**. Then click the >> button.

19. For the Detail Table Name, click on **ADS.DB**. Click the >> button.

20. The *Form Expert* should find the linking fields and list **Salesperson ID** for both tables. Click the >> button to continue.

21. Accept all four fields from **SALSFORC.DB** by clicking the >> button with all four fields in the **Fields to Display:** list.

22. Accept all seven fields from **ADS.DB** by clicking the >> button with all seven fields in the **Fields to Display:** list.

23. Make certain **Video Screen** is the chosen option and pick the Page Size for the computer you are working on (probably **VGA: 640 x 480**). Click the >> button.

24. Pick **Control 3D style** and click the **lightning bolt (Finish)** button.

25. Click the **Yes** button to run the form instead of staying on the form design screen.

26. When the form appears, press the **PAGE DOWN** key to move to record 2. The ads sold by George Fitzhugh should appear in the embedded form.

27. Press the **PAGE DOWN** key three times, pausing between each press to examine the data. Notice that two salespersons have no sales (records 4 and 5). The other three should have sales.

28. Press **PGUP** to jump to record 4, the record for **Debbie Rewalt**. She has made a sale!

29. Click the mouse in the column below **Ad Number** in the embedded form.

30. Press the **F9** Edit key.

31. Enter Ad Number **2399**. Notice that the **Salesperson ID** field is immediately filled in with the matching code.

32. The ad was purchased by **College Movies** as a **QP** (Quarter Page Size) at **$25** and was paid on **5/12/95**. Enter each data item in the apropriate field.

33. Press **ENTER** twice to jump to **Issue Date** and type: **5/20/95**

34. Close the form with **FILE/Close**.

35. Save the form design by clicking the **Yes** button and entering the form name **Adsales**. Click the **OK** button.

36. If you need to exit from *Paradox* and/or Windows, do so properly.

Independent Project 3.2: The Bookstore

This Independent Project continues the Bookstore database from Independent Project 2.2. In this project you will examine the table containing the publishers' names and create a form that includes both the book data and the publishers' names on one screen. Finally, you will use that form to enter a new book and a new publisher.

The table of publishers was typed by a clerk at the bookstore and saved as **PUBLISHR.DB** (short for Publishers) on the Student Data Diskette. You might ask why are the publishers' names in a separate table? Why not include them right in the **BOOKS.DB** table? Because the same publishers supply many books, and their names would be repeated over and over in the **BOOKS.DB** table. In PUBLISHR.DB each publisher is entered just once and given a code number. Only the short code number is included on each book listing. Of course, to combine both **PUBLISHR.DB** and **BOOKS.DB** on the same form, the matching code numbers must be in the **BOOKS.DB** table, too. You can check **BOOKS.DB** to make certain they are.

The two requirements for creating a multi-table form are that there must be either a primary (key field) or secondary index on the **Publisher Code** field in the detail (embedded) table, and the **Publisher Code** field must have the same data type and size in both tables. You can check both tables to make certain they are the same.

The table of publishers' names looks like Figure 3 - 48. When finished with the form, it should resemble Figure 3 - 49.

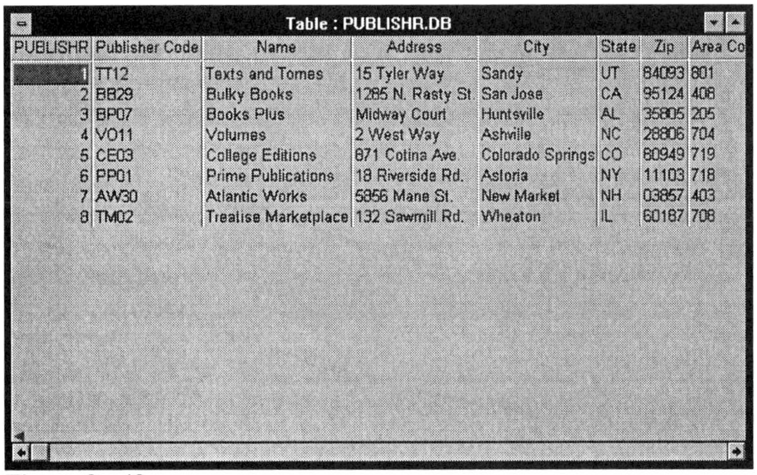

PUBLISHR	Publisher Code	Name	Address	City	State	Zip	Area Co
1	TT12	Texts and Tomes	15 Tyler Way	Sandy	UT	84093	801
2	BB29	Bulky Books	1285 N. Rasty St	San Jose	CA	95124	408
3	BP07	Books Plus	Midway Court	Huntsville	AL	35805	205
4	VO11	Volumes	2 West Way	Ashville	NC	28806	704
5	CE03	College Editions	871 Cotina Ave	Colorado Springs	CO	80949	719
6	PP01	Prime Publications	18 Riverside Rd.	Astoria	NY	11103	718
7	AW30	Atlantic Works	5856 Mane St.	New Market	NH	03857	403
8	TM02	Treatise Marketplace	132 Sawmill Rd.	Wheaton	IL	60187	708

Table : PUBLISHR.DB

Figure 3 - 48

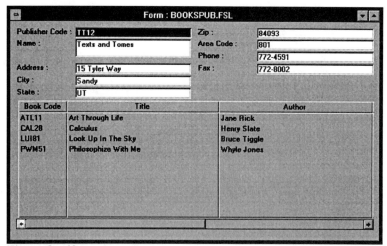

Figure 3 - 49

1. Run *Paradox*.

2. Click the **Paradox** button to close the Welcome to Paradox screen if it is open.

3. Maximize the *Paradox* window if it does not already cover the entire screen.

4. Click the **Open Project Viewer** button on the toolbar if it is not already open. Check that you are in the correct working directory.

5. Double-click the name **BOOKS.DB** to open the table.

6. To create a secondary index on **Publisher Code**, click the **Restructure** button on the toolbar.

7. Click on the drop-down list for **Table Properties** and pick **Secondary Indexes**.

8. Click the **Define** button.

9. Click on **Publisher Code** in the **Fields:** list and click the **arrow** button to copy the name to the **Indexed Fields:** list. **Maintained** should be checked, but not **Case Sensitive**.

10. Click the **OK** button.

11. Enter the name **Publisher Code Index** and click the **OK** button. Remember, you may not duplicate the field name, and so we added the word **Index**.

12. Click the **Save** button.

13. Close **BOOKS.DB** by picking **FILE/Close**.

14. Begin creating the form by right-clicking on (inspecting) the **Forms** icon in the left column of the Project Viewer.

15. Pick **New**.

16. Click the **Form Expert** button.

17. In the panel of form types, click option **4. View one master record and multiple detail records. Detail records display in a table format.** and click the >> button.

18. For the Master Table Name, click on **PUBLISHR.DB** and click the >> button.

19. For the Detail Table Name, click on **BOOKS.DB** and click the >> button.

20. The *Form Expert* should find the linking fields and list **Publisher Code** for both tables. Click the >> button to continue.

21. Accept all nine fields from **PUBLISHR.DB** by clicking the >> button with all nine fields in the **Fields to Display:** list.

22. Accept all eight fields from **BOOKS.DB** by clicking the **>>** button with all eight fields in the **Fields to Display:** list.

23. Make certain **Video Screen** is the chosen option and pick the Page Size for the computer you are working on (probably **VGA: 640 x 480**). Click the **>>** button.

24. Pick **Control 3D style** and click the **lightning bolt (Finish)** button.

25. Click the **Yes** button to run the form instead of staying on the form design screen.

26. Press the **PAGE DOWN** key seven times, pausing between each press to examine the data. Notice that four publishers have no books in the **BOOKS.DB** table yet. The other four have from two to four each.

27. To make sure the form works, you will enter one new book and one new publisher. To start the new book, you must search for the correct publisher. Click the **Locate Field Value** button on the toolbar, enter: **BB29** (the code for Bulky Books) in the **Value:** text box, and click on the **Exact Match** option. Make certain the field is **Publisher Code** in the **Fields:** list and do not check Case Sensitive. Click the **OK** button.

28. Click the mouse in the **Book Code** column in the embedded form.

29. Press the **F9** Edit key.

30. Enter Book Code **CHC18**. The Title is **Chemical Compendium**. There is no Author. Type in the Year of Publication as **1995** and skip over the Publisher Code as that is already filled in. The Cost is **34.50** and the Price is **49.95**. Enter **0** for the Quantity in Stock.

31. To enter the new publisher, click the mouse on the current **Publisher Code**, click the **Last Record** navigation button on the toolbar to jump to the final record, and press **PAGE DOWN** for a new record.

32. Type: **AA15** for the Publisher Code, press the **DOWN ARROW** and enter **Authors Away** as the Name. Also, type **415** for the Area Code, **326-8899** in the Phone field, and **326-9988** for the Fax number.

33. Close the form with **FILE/Close**.

34. Save the form design by clicking the **Yes** button and entering the form name **Bookspub**. Click the **OK** button.

35. If you need to exit from *Paradox* and/or Windows, do so properly.

Independent Project 3.3: The Real Estate Office

This Independent Project continues the Real Estate Office database from Independent Project 2.3. In this project you will examine the table containing the agencies' names and create a form that includes both the properties and the agencies' names on one screen. Finally, you will use that form to enter a new commercial real estate listing and a new agency.

The table of agencies was typed by a colleague at the real estate office and saved as **AGENCIES.DB** on the Student Data Diskette. You might ask, why are the agencies' names in a separate table? Why not include them right in the **COMMERCL.DB** table? Because the same agency supplies many commercial listings, and their names would be repeated over and over in the **COMMERCL.DB** table. In **AGENCIES.DB** each office and its associated data are entered just once and given a code number. Only the short code number is included on each commercial property listing. Of course, to combine both **AGENCIES.DB** and **COMMERCL.DB** on the same form, the matching code numbers must be in the **COMMERCL.DB** table, too.

The two requirements for creating a multi-table form are that there must be either a primary (key field) or secondary index on the **Agency Code** field in the detail (embedded) table, and the **Agency Code** field must have the same data type and size in both tables. You can check both tables to make certain they match.

The table of agencies' names looks like Figure 3 - 50. When finished with the form, it should resemble Figure 3 - 51.

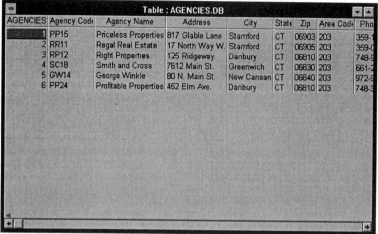

Figure 3 - 50

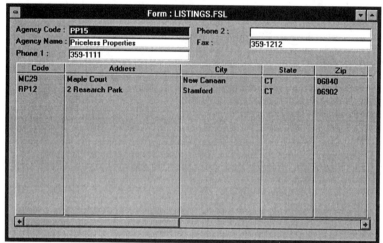

Figure 3 - 51

1. Run *Paradox*, close the Welcome to Paradox screen, and maximize the window.

2. Open the Project Viewer.

3. Open **COMMERCL.DB**.

4. Use the **Restructure** button to open the **Restructure** dialog box and create a secondary index based on the **Agency Code** field. Name it **Agency Code Index**.

5. Save the new structure for **COMMERCL.DB**.

6. Close **COMMERCL.DB**.

7. Begin creating the form by inspecting the **Forms** icon on the left side of the Project Viewer and picking **New**.

8. Use the *Form Expert* to create a type **4** form.

9. **AGENCIES.DB** will be the master table.

10. **COMMERCL.DB** will be the detail table.

11. Accept the link on **Agency Code**.

12. From **AGENCIES.DB** keep only the **Agency Code, Agency Name, Phone 1, Phone 2**, and **Fax** fields. Send the others back to the **Fields not Displayed:** list by clicking on each name and clicking the button with the arrowhead that points to the left.

13. For the embedded form (the detail table) include all fields from **COMMERCL.DB**.

14. Make certain **Video Screen** is the chosen option and pick the Page Size for the computer you are working on (probably **VGA: 640 x 480**).

15. Pick **Control 3D style**.

16. Run the form.

17. Press the **PAGE DOWN** key five times, pausing between each press to examine the data.

18. A new listing at 6 Research Park, Stamford has been announced. The listing agent will be RP12, Right Properties. Locate that real estate agency in the top portion of the form, then enter the new listing from the data shown in Table 3 - 1 into the embedded portion of the form. You will need to scroll across the embedded form to see all of the fields.

Field Name	Data
Code	RP16
Address	6 Research Park
City	Stamford
State	CT
Zip	06902
Size	19,000
Floor	1
Purchase or Rent	P
Price	$3,900,000
Available	10/1/95
Agency Code	RP12
Agent	Williams

Table 3 - 1

19. To enter the new real estate agency, click on the **Agency Code** field in the agency part of the form, move to the final record (PP24), and press **PAGE DOWN** for a new record.

20. Type **CP19** for the Agency Code, **Colonial Properties** as the Agency Name, **359-8372** for Phone 1, and **359-0573** in the Fax field.

21. End Edit Mode.

22. Close the form with **FILE/Close**.

23. Save the form design with the name **Listings**.

24. If you need to exit from *Paradox* and/or Windows, do so properly.

Independent Project 3.4: The Veterinarian

This Independent Project continues the veterinarian database from Independent Project 2.4. In this project you will examine the table containing the owners' names and create a form that includes both the pets and the owners' names on one screen. Finally, you will use that form to enter a new owner and his pet.

The table of owners is already typed and has been saved as **PETOWNER.DB** on the Student Data Diskette. Be sure you can answer the question as to why the owners' names are in a separate table rather than included right in the pets table.

Complete the following tasks.

1. Open **PETOWNER.DB** and examine the data in it.

2. Create a secondary index in the pets table for the owner code field.

3. Use the *Form Expert* to create a type **4** form for the **PETOWNER.DB** table that will include the pets table as the embedded form (detail table). It should match the form illustrated in Figure 3 - 52, except that the embedded form will have the field names you made up and the Code and Date of Last Visit fields will have the values you entered.

*IMPORTANT: This will only work if you made the field with the codes for the owners in the pets table an **Alpha** field of Size **4**. If you did not, you must restructure the pets table before you can create this form.*

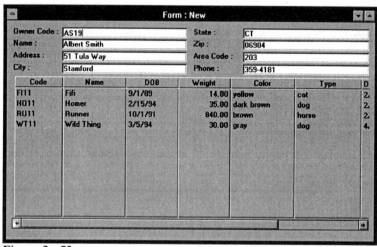

Figure 3 - 52

4. Use the form to enter a new pet for Dan Wilson. The pet is a black horse named Wilhelm that weighs 940 pounds. It was born about 6/15/90.

5. Use the form to enter a new owner. He is Monty Wright and he lives at 56 Wildwood Terrace, Stamford, CT, 06905. His phone number is (203) 359-4415.

Queries

Objectives

In this lesson you will learn how to:

- Set up a query
- Select the fields to be included
- Sort the query result
- Specify single criteria for selecting records

PROJECT DESCRIPTION

A *query* is a search for all of the records within a table that contain a specific value. For example, you might need a list of all of your customers who ordered a particular CDROM title.

In this lesson we will run several queries based on the **CDROM.DB** table in order to extract various groups of listings, check inventory levels, and gather other pertinent information. We will match a single value at a time in this lesson. In the next lesson we will use queries with multiple matching values, as well as multiple tables to access data from more than one source.

QUERYING A TABLE

During editing we searched for matching listings one at a time; with queries you get the complete set of matching records all at once. A query also allows sorting the resulting listings, as well as selecting which fields will be included. Once designed, a query may be saved, or merely used temporarily and discarded. Since the result of a query is a separate table containing just the matching data, reports can be printed for the table that results from a query.

Paradox uses what is called *Query by Example*. This means that, rather than type out a lengthy instruction in words, in *Paradox* you merely fill in a diagram (see Figure 4 - 1) by giving an example of the value you want matched. For example, to get a listing of only records of customers who live in New York, you would type the example "NY" in the **State** field. The example that you want matched is also called the *criterion*.

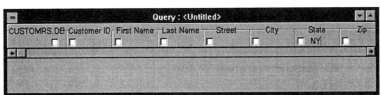

Figure 4 - 1

The table that results from a query is always named **ANSWER.DB**. Since that name is used over and over for each query, **ANSWER.DB** is a *temporary table. Temporary* means that *Paradox* may erase the table whenever necessary. **ANSWER.DB** (as well as the 13 other table names like **LIST.DB** and **INSERT.DB** that *Paradox* creates itself and are thus temporary) will be erased in three situations:

- If you run another query.

- When you exit from *Paradox*.

- When you change the directory or drive where the temporary tables are recorded.

If you want to make the resulting **ANSWER.DB** table permanent, rename the table. To rename a table, pick **TOOLS/Utilities/Rename** and fill in the dialog box.

A SINGLE TABLE QUERY

In our first query we will produce a list of each CDROM Title and its Quantity in Stock. We begin by opening the **Query** window.

To set up a Query:

- Pick **FILE/New/Query**. Alternatively, right-click (inspect) the **Queries** icon in the list at the left side of the Project Viewer or the **Open Query** button [icon] on the toolbar and pick **New**.

- Choose the table from the **Select File** dialog box and click **OK**.

Activity 4.1: Setting up a Query

The first step is to initiate the query and choose the table whose data will be the basis of the search.

1. The Project Viewer should be open in *Paradox*.

2. Right-click on (inspect) the **Queries** icon (see Figure 4 - 2) and pick **New** in the self-contained menu.

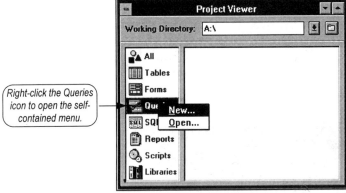

Figure 4 - 2

3. Since we are interested in selected data from the **CDROM.DB** table, when the **Select File** dialog box opens, click on **CDROM.DB** (see Figure 4 - 3) and click the **OK** button.

    *The **Query** window opens with the **CDROM.DB** query table in it (see Figure 4 - 4).*

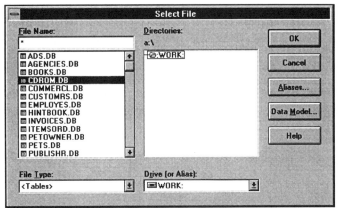

Figure 4 - 3

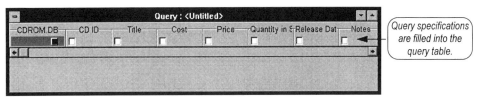

Figure 4 - 4

SELECTING THE FIELDS

Each column in the query table has a check box which, if checked, will include that field in the resulting answer table. If a column is not checked the field will be omitted from the answer.

To select the fields to be included in the result:

- The first column contains the name of the table that is being queried. If you click its check box, all fields will be checked.

- Click on any individual field's check box to check just that single column.

- Once a field is checked, clicking its check box a second time removes the check.

- To remove all checks, move the mouse pointer on top of the check box under the table name in the first column and hold down the mouse button. A list of available check marks will appear (see Figure 4 - 5). Drag the mouse down to the second line that shows no check mark and release the mouse button.

- Instead of clicking the check boxes, you can also move to the column and press the **F6** key.

To run a query:

- Click the **Run Query** button [⚡] on the toolbar, press **F8**, or pick **VIEW/Run Query** in the menu.

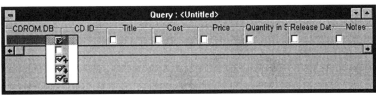

Figure 4 - 5

Activity 4.2: Selecting the Desired Fields and Viewing the Result

Since we need only the Title and Quantity in Stock, we will select only those two fields.

1. Click the mouse on the check box in the **Title** field.

    A check mark will appear in the check box and the highlight moves to this column.

2. Click the mouse on the check box in the **Quantity in Stock** field (see Figure 4 - 6).

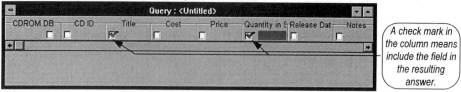

Figure 4 - 6

*The **Run Query** button on the toolbar is the button with the lightning bolt symbol.*

3. Click the **Run Query** button on the toolbar to view the result.

    All 15 records are listed, but only the two fields are included (see Figure 4 - 7). Notice that the titles are sorted. This resulting table is named ANSWER.DB.

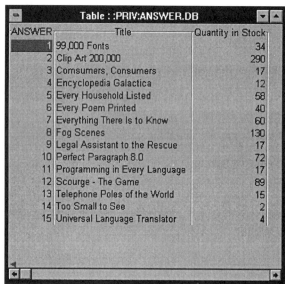

Figure 4 - 7

4. Close the **ANSWER.DB** table with **FILE/Close** to return to the query design.

5. Do *not* close the **Query** window.

SORTING THE ANSWER

A query can sort the resulting answer table in ascending or descending order based on the selected fields. Which check mark you choose determines whether **ANSWER.DB** is sorted at all, as well as whether ascending or descending order will be used. Table 4 - 1 shows the three types of check marks and their meanings. (There is a fourth check mark that groups by sets; it is beyond the scope of this book.) If sorted in this way, **ANSWER.DB** will be ordered by the values in the left-most field, then the second field whenever the first field contains identical values, and so on across all columns.

The check mark also determines whether duplicates will be included in the answer. For example, you might want a list of the states that customers live in. You would not want more than one of each state name for such a list, so duplicates should not be included. The regular check mark eliminates duplicates from the answer. On the other hand, you might need a list of the names of customers who have placed orders. Should two customers happen to have the same name, you would still want to see the two identical names. Check Plus includes duplicates. To decide which check mark to use, ask yourself whether duplicates would be an issue in the current query, then select Check Plus only if the answer is yes. Check Plus is not used as much as the regular check mark since most queries include some type of code number (Customer ID, Product Code, etc.) in the answer, which distinguishes one listing from another so that duplicates cannot occur.

Check Mark	Name	Description
✔	Check	Do not include duplicates. Sort in ascending order.
✔↓	Check Descending	Do not include duplicates. Sort in descending order.
✔+	Check Plus	Include duplicates. Do not sort. A single Check Plus in any column makes the entire query a Check Plus query.

Table 4 - 1

We will see how to sort by fields other than the left-most fields two sections hence.

Activity 4.3: Sorting by CD ID

Rather than Title order, perhaps the CD IDs should be the order for the answer. By including the **CD ID** field in the **ANSWER.DB** table, it will appear in its designed position to the left of the Titles and control the sort order.

1. Since the **CD ID** field is not yet included in the answer, click the mouse on the check box in the **CD ID** column.

2. Click the **Run Query** button on the toolbar to see the result (see Figure 4 - 8).

ANSWER	CD ID	Title	Quantity in Stock
1	C01	Comsumers, Consumers	17
2	C02	Clip Art 200,000	290
3	E04	Every Household Listed	58
4	E05	Encyclopedia Galactica	12
5	E06	Every Poem Printed	40
6	E07	Everything There Is to Know	60
7	F01	99,000 Fonts	34
8	F02	Fog Scenes	130
9	L01	Legal Assistant to the Rescue	17
10	P01	Programming in Every Language	17
11	P02	Perfect Paragraph 8.0	72
12	S03	Scourge - The Game	89
13	T02	Too Small to See	2
14	T03	Telephone Poles of the World	15
15	U02	Universal Language Translator	4

Figure 4 - 8

All 15 records are still listed, but they are now sorted into order by CD ID.

Also notice that this result is named ANSWER.DB, the same as the last result. The table name ANSWER.DB is used over and over by Paradox. The first ANSWER.DB that we saw in the previous activity has been erased to allow this result to be named ANSWER.DB.

3. Close the **ANSWER.DB** table with **FILE/Close**.

4. Move the mouse pointer on top of the check box in the **CD ID** field and hold down the mouse button. In the drop-down list of check marks that opens, drag down to **Check Descending** (see Table 4 - 1) and release the mouse button.

*The **Check Descending** mark appears in the **CD ID** column (see Figure 4 - 9).*

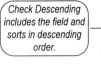

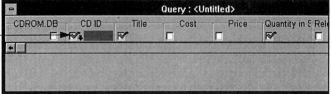

Check Descending includes the field and sorts in descending order.

Figure 4 - 9

5. Click the **Run Query** button on the toolbar to view the result.

The ANSWER.DB table contains all 15 records in descending order of CD ID.

6. Close the **ANSWER.DB** table with **FILE/Close**.

7. Move the mouse pointer on top of the check box in the **CD ID** field and hold down the mouse button. In the drop-down list of check marks that opens, drag down to **Check Plus** (see Table 4 - 1) and release the mouse button (see Figure 4 - 10).

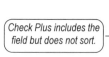

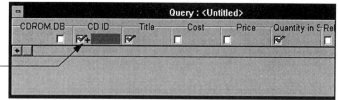

Check Plus includes the field but does not sort.

Figure 4 - 10

8. Click the **Run Query** button on the toolbar to view the result.

The ANSWER.DB table contains all 15 records in unsorted order. The order is the same as the current order in the CDROM table.

9. Close the **ANSWER.DB** table with **FILE/Close**.

10. Do *not* close the **Query** window.

SORTING THE ANSWER BY OTHER FIELDS

A query can also sort the resulting answer table by any field or combination of fields desired. In the previous example, sorting by the Quantity in Stock field would not have been possible since it was not the left-most field. The **Sort Answer Table** button on the toolbar or **PROPERTIES/Answer Sort** in the menu opens a dialog box with choices for sorting by any field or combination of fields.

To sort a query by interior fields or a combination of fields:

• Click the **Sort Answer Table** button ▦ on the toolbar or pick **PROPERTIES/Answer Sort** in the menu to open the **Sort Answer** dialog box.

- Click on the name of the most important field by which to sort in the **Available Fields:** list. Then click the right pointing arrow button to transfer the field name to the **Sort By:** list.

- Do the same for the second most important field.

- Similarly, pick any other fields for sorting.

- Click the **OK** button. When the query is run the sort order will be applied.

Activity 4.4: Sorting by Quantity in Stock

We will sort the answer table into order by the **Quantity in Stock** field.

1. Click the **CD ID** field's check box once to uncheck it, then again to restore the regular check mark.

2. Run the query by clicking the **Run Query** button on the toolbar.

3. Examine the current **ANSWER.DB** table and notice that the values in the **Quantity in Stock** field are not in order. The IDs are in order since that is the left-most field.

4. Close the table with **FILE/Close**.

5. Click the **Sort Answer Table** button on the toolbar to open the **Sort Answer** dialog box (see Figure 4 - 11).

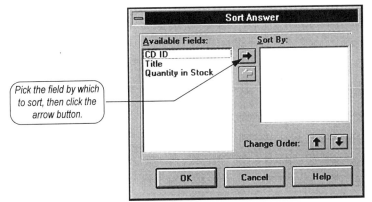

Figure 4 - 11

6. Click on the name **Quantity in Stock** in the **Available Fields:** list.

7. Click the arrow button that is pointing to the right to transfer the field name to the **Sort By:** list (see Figure 4 - 12).

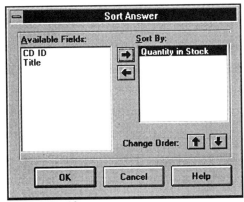

Figure 4 - 12

8. Click the **OK** button.

9. Run the query by clicking the **Run Query** button on the toolbar.

    The Quantity in Stock values should be in order (see Figure 4 - 13).

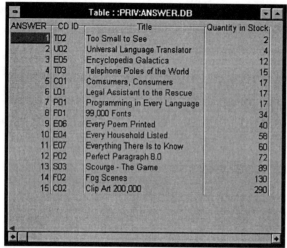

Figure 4 - 13

10. Close the **ANSWER.DB** table with **FILE/Close**.

11. Close the **Query** window with **FILE/Close**.

12. In the alert box for saving the query design (see Figure 4 - 14), click the **No** button.

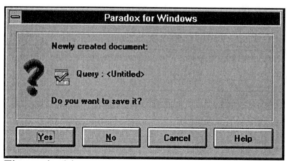

Figure 4 - 14

SAVING A QUERY DESIGN

While a query is often used to temporarily view a result, sometimes the answer is important or useful enough to save the query so it can be rerun whenever needed.

To save a query:

*   Choose **FILE/Save As**. (Alternatively, close the **Query** window and click the **Yes** button when asked about saving.)

*   Type the desired name (up to 8 characters without spaces) in the **Query Name** text box of the **Save As** dialog box. The extension **.QBE** will automatically be added.

*   Click **OK**.

Activity 4.5: Saving the Query

1. The Project Viewer should be open.

2. Right-click on (inspect) the **Queries** icon to open the self-contained menu and pick **New**.

3. Click on the name **CDROM.DB** in the **File Name:** list and click the **OK** button.

4. Click the mouse on the check box in the **Notes** column to get a regular check mark.

   *Sometimes when the column is partly off screen, the first click will only move to the column rather than check the box. If that happened with the **Notes** field, click the check box again to check it.*

5. Click the **Run Query** button on the toolbar to see the result (see Figure 4 - 15).

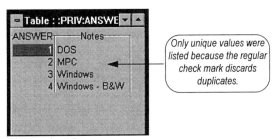

Figure 4 - 15

Although we know there are 15 records in the table, only four values are listed in the answer. Since we used a regular check mark, the duplicate values were not included.

6. Choose **FILE/Close** to get **ANSWER.DB** out of the way and back to the **Query** window.

   When the answer table is the active window, there is no choice for saving in the FILE menu since the table is already recorded. You must be in the query design window in order to save the query design.

7. With the **Query** window the active window, choose **FILE/Save As**.

8. In the **Save File As** dialog box, type the name: **CD-Types** and click **OK** (see Figure 4 - 16).

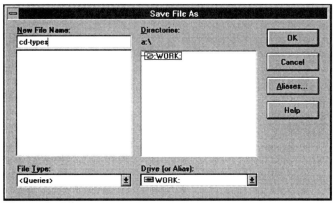

Figure 4 - 16

9. Choose **FILE/Close**.

*The name will appear in the Queries list of the Project Viewer with a **.QBE** extension (Query By Example), and could be reopened and run any time that query result was needed again. Of course, if the data in the table has changed, the next time you run the query, you will get an up-to-date answer.*

SELECTING MATCHING RECORDS WITH A QUERY

Perhaps the most valuable ability of a query is to select only those records that match some criterion that you specify. You specify the value(s) to be matched by typing an example of it (thus Query By Example). You type the example in the column in the Query table that would actually contain the matching values.

In this lesson we will search for matching values in a single field. In the next lesson we will use multiple criteria.

To select records with matching values through a query:

- Open the query window and choose a table as discussed previously.

- Check the desired fields.

- Enter the example of the value to be matched in the column that would contain that value.

- Click the **Run Query** button to see the resulting **ANSWER.DB** table.

Activity 4.6: Using Numerical Criteria in a Query

We need a listing of the CDROMs that cost $179.

1. The Project Viewer should be open.

2. Right-click on (inspect) the **Queries** icon to open the self-contained menu and pick **New**.

3. Click on the name **CDROM.DB** in the **File Name:** list and click the **OK** button.

4. Check the **Title** field by clicking the mouse on the check box in that column.

5. Check the **Cost** field.

6. Check the **Quantity in Stock** field.

7. Click back on the **Cost** column and type: **179** (see Figure 4 - 17).

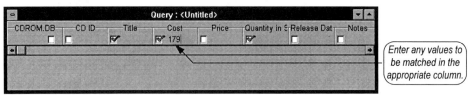

Figure 4 - 17

*Do not type a dollar sign or any commas in numbers in a criterion. If you should get an **Error** alert box, click the **OK** button, check your typing very carefully, and correct the entry.*

8. Click the **Run Query** button on the toolbar to view the result (see Figure 4 - 18).

   Examine the values for Cost. They should both be 179.00.

9. Close the **ANSWER.DB** table with **FILE/Close**. Do *not* close the **Query** window.

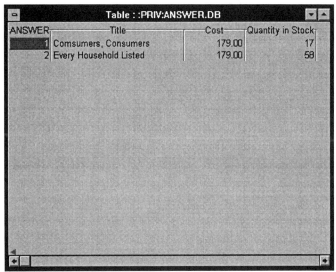

Figure 4 - 18

THE INEQUALITY SYMBOLS IN QUERIES

Paradox interprets a single value in a column as requiring an exact match, that is, the value in the table must *equal* the example. While you could type the equal sign, it is always optional. Other *operators* are allowed besides an equal sign. These inequality symbols are listed in Table 4 - 2.

Symbol	Meaning with Numbers	Meaning with Dates	Meaning with Text
>	greater than	after	alphabetically after
<	less than	before	alphabetically before
>=	greater than or equal to	on or after	alphabetically after or equal to
<=	less than or equal to	on or before	alphabetically before or equal to
not	not equal to	not on	not equal to

Table 4 - 2

To search for a range of values:

- Set up the query as we have done previously.
- Enter the inequality symbol and value in the column that would contain those values.
- Click the **Run Query** button to see the result.

Activity 4.7: Using a Numerical Range in a Query

We need a listing of any CDROMs that have dropped below the reorder point of 20 pieces in stock.

1. The previous query should still be open.

   If the previous query is not still open, follow steps 1-6 from Activity 4.6 and proceed to step 4 in this activity.

2. Erase the **179** in the Cost column. If it is highlighted, press the **DELETE** key. If the cursor is blinking next to the value, press the **BACKSPACE** key three times.

3. Press the **ENTER** key twice to move to the **Quantity In Stock** column.

   *You may, of course, use the mouse to move to a column in the **Query** table. Click the mouse to the right of the check box and below the column name.*

4. Type: **<20** (see Figure 4 - 19).

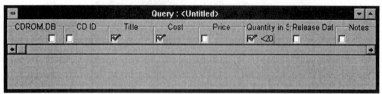

Figure 4 - 19

5. Click the **Run Query** button on the toolbar to view the result (see Figure 4 - 20).

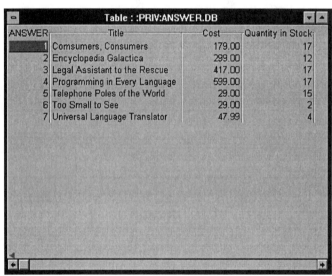

Figure 4 - 20

Examine the quantities. All seven should be less than 20.

6. Do ***not*** close the answer table.

PRINTING A QUERY RESULT

Since a reorder list could be extremely valuable, you might want to print the **ANSWER.DB** table. The toolbar contains a **Print** button. Printing **ANSWER.DB** is no different from printing any other table.

To print the ANSWER.DB table:

- Click the **Print** button ⬛ on the toolbar or pick **FILE/Print** while viewing the table.
- Choose the **Create Horizontal Overflow Pages As Needed** option.
- Click the **OK** button.

Activity 4.8: Printing ANSWER.DB and Saving the Query

So we would not have to remember the reorder list, we could print that result.

1.   Click the **Print** button on the toolbar while **ANSWER.DB** is the active table.

2.   Choose the **Create Horizontal Overflow Pages As Needed** option.

3.   Click the **OK** button.

4.   Close the **ANSWER.DB** table with **FILE/Close**.

5.   Close the **Query** window with **FILE/Close**.

6.   Click the **Yes** button in the save alert box.

7.   Enter: **reorder** as the name by which to save the query design and click **OK**.

TEXT CRITERIA IN A QUERY

The only difference between searching for matching text in Alpha fields and numeric values is that the criteria for alpha fields occasionally need to be typed between quotation marks. You could type the quotes all the time as in **"NY"** for the abbreviation for the state of New York. However, the quotes are always optional in *Paradox* unless there is a word or symbol in the characters you are trying to match that means something to *Paradox*. For example, the word **or** in "Wet or Dry Vacuum," the word ***not*** in the title "Not for Hire at Any Price," or the comma in "Westway Developers, Inc." would cause problems and would necessitate quotation marks. These occurrences are relatively uncommon, however.

Queries in *Paradox* are totally case sensitive. That is, each of the four following examples is completely different from the other three: NY, ny, Ny, and nY. You must be aware of the case of the characters for which you are searching and type an exact match. (In the next lesson we will see how to use wildcard characters to circumvent this case sensitivity.)

To search for matching text:

*   Set up the query as we have done previously.

*   Enter the example of the text value to be matched in the column that would contain that value. Type quotes at the beginning and end of the set of characters if there is a character or word that *Paradox* would misunderstand. The common words that would require quotation marks are: NOT, OR, BLANK, AS, and TODAY. The most common characters that would require quotes are the three in the following parenthesis (! , @).

*   Click the **Run Query** button to see the result.

Activity 4.9: Searching for Matching Text

We need to look up the price of the "Too Small to See" CDROM.

1.   The Project Viewer should be open.

2.   Right-click on (inspect) the **Queries** icon to open the self-contained menu and pick **New**.

3.   Click on the name **CDROM.DB** in the **File Name:** list and click the **OK** button.

   A shortcut is to double-click on the table name.

4.   Check the **CD ID** field by clicking the mouse on the check box in that column.

5.   Similarly, check **Title** and **Price**.

6. Click in the **Title** column and enter: **Too Small to See** (see Figure 4 - 21). No quotes are needed in this example (as in 99% of all queries), but the case must match exactly.

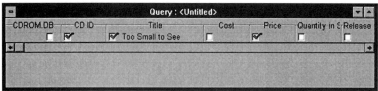

Figure 4 - 21

The column in the query table will widen automatically if more space is needed for typing.

7. Click the **Run Query** button on the toolbar to view the result (see Figure 4 - 22).

Figure 4 - 22

If the ANSWER.DB table is empty, close it to return to the query design and check the capitalization and spelling of Too Small to See. They must match exactly. When you find the discrepancy, run the query again.

Since ANSWER.DB is a table, you may change the column widths and anything else you know how to do to a table.

8. We don't need to print the $49 price, so close the answer table with **FILE/Close**.

9. Do *not* close the query table.

DATE CRITERIA IN A QUERY

In a query, enter dates to be matched in slash format. For example, July 4, 1995, would be represented as **7/4/95**. No special marks of any kind are needed.

To search for a matching date:

- Set up the query as we have done previously.

- Enter the example of the date value to be matched as M/D/YY in the column that would contain that value.
- Click the **Run Query** button to see the result.

Activity 4.10: Searching for Matching Dates

We need to look up the titles of the CDROMs that were released before 5/2/95. Since we do not need the **Price** field and do not want the title "Too Small to See," we could erase those two, or it might be easier to simply clear the entire row of the query table and start with a fresh row.

To clear the current row of a Query table:

- While on the row, press **CTRL+DELETE**.

1. Press **CTRL+DELETE** to remove all specifications from the current row of the query table.
2. Check the **CD ID** and **Title** fields.
3. Check the **Release Date** field.
4. In the **Release Date** column enter: **<5/2/95** (see Figure 4 - 23).

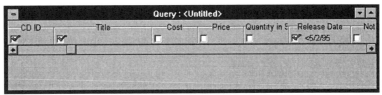

Figure 4 - 23

5. Click the **Run Query** button (see Figure 4 - 24).

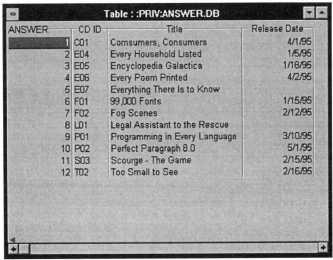

Figure 4 - 24

Twelve titles were released before 5/2/95 or have no release date. An empty date field is considered to be prior to any specified date.

6. Close the **ANSWER.DB** table with **FILE/Close** to return to the query design.

7. Add an equal sign to change the criterion to: **<=5/2/95**

8. Click the **Run Query** button to view the result (see Figure 4 - 25).

   Fourteen titles were released on or before 5/2/95 or have no release date.

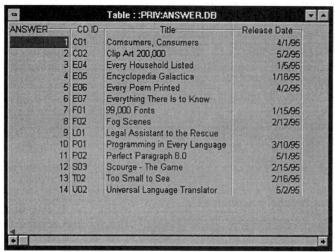

Figure 4 - 25

9. Print the table by clicking the **Print** button on the toolbar, select the **Create Horizontal Overflow Pages As Needed** option, and click the **OK** button.

10. Close the **ANSWER.DB** table with **FILE/Close** to return to the query design.

11. Choose **FILE/Close** to close the **Query** window. Click **No** in answer to saving the query design.

SUMMARY

In this lesson we have explored single criterion queries. We practiced opening the **Query** window, selecting the desired fields, sorting by various fields, and matching a criterion. The criteria we used were of numerical, text, and date types. We used the inequality symbols for ranges of values. In the next lesson we will use multiple criteria and multiple tables in queries.

KEY TERMS

Criterion	Query	Temporary table
Operator	Query By Example	

INDEPENDENT PROJECTS

Independent Project 4.1: The School Newspaper

This Independent Project continues the Newspaper Ad database from Independent Project 3.1. The newspaper's business manager has requested two lists. The first is a listing of all the Full Page (FP) ads in order of the Date Paid. The Issue Date and the Salesperson ID fields are not important for this list, so those two will be left out of the result. The second is a list of all ads sold by Leslie Kaples. It should be sorted by Price, but should only include the Ad Number, Purchased By, Price, and Date Paid fields.

The result of the first query should look like Figure 4 - 26. The result of the second should resemble Figure 4 - 27.

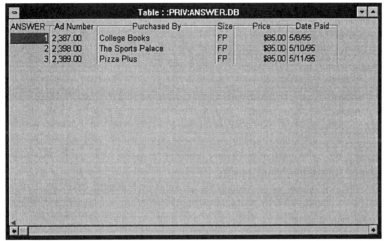

Figure 4 - 26

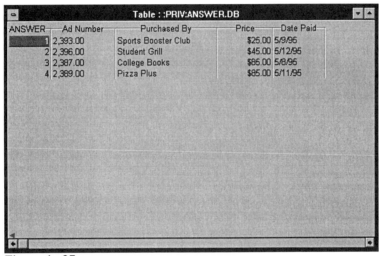

Figure 4 - 27

1. Run *Paradox*.

2. Click the **Paradox** button to close the Welcome to Paradox screen if it is open.

3. Maximize the *Paradox* window if it does not already cover the entire screen.

4. Click the **Open Project Viewer** button on the toolbar if it is not already open. Check that you are in the correct working directory.

5. Right-click on (inspect) the **Queries** icon on the left side of the Project Viewer.

6. Click **New** in the self-contained menu to start a new query.

7. Click on the name **ADS.DB** in the list of tables and click the **OK** button to open the **Query** window.

8. Click on the check box in the **Ad Number** column to check that field.

9. Similarly, check **Purchased By**, **Size**, **Price**, and **Date Paid**.

10. Click in the **Size** column and enter: **FP** for Full Page. The two letters must be capitals.

11. Click the **Run Query** button on the toolbar to see the three resulting listings. They still need to be sorted.

12. Close the answer table with **FILE/Close** to return to the query design.

13. Click the **Sort Answer Table** button on the toolbar.

14. Click on the name **Date Paid** and click the right-pointing arrow button to transfer the name to the **Sort By:** column.

15. Click **OK**.

16. Click the **Run Query** button on the toolbar to see the three resulting listings in sorted order (see Figure 4 - 26).

17. Print the result by clicking the **Print** button, picking the **Create Horizontal Overflow Pages As Needed** option, and clicking **OK**.

18. Close the **ANSWER.DB** table with **FILE/Close**.

19. Save the query as **FullPage** by picking **FILE/Save As**, entering the name, and clicking the **OK** button.

20. Close the query with **FILE/Close**.

21. To begin the second query, right-click on the **Queries** icon on the left side of the Project Viewer and pick **New**.

22. Double-click on the name **ADS.DB** in the list of tables.

23. Check the **Ad Number** field.

24. Similarly, check **Purchased By**, **Price**, and **Date Paid**.

25. Press **ENTER** to move to the **Salesperson ID** field and enter: **K17**

26. Since the business manager did not want to see the Salesperson ID, we will *not* check the check box.

27. Click the **Sort Answer Table** button on the toolbar.

28. Click on the name **Price** and click the right-pointing arrow button to transfer the name to the **Sort By:** column.

29. Click **OK**.

30. Click the **Run Query** button on the toolbar to see the resulting listings in sorted order (see Figure 4 - 27).

31. Print the result by clicking the **Print** button, picking the **Create Horizontal Overflow Pages As Needed** option, and clicking **OK**.

32. Close the **ANSWER.DB** table with **FILE/Close**.

33. We do not need to save this query, so close it with **FILE/Close**. When the alert box asks about saving, click the **No** button.

34. If you need to exit from *Paradox* and/or Windows, do so properly.

Independent Project 4.2: The Bookstore

This Independent Project continues the Bookstore database from Independent Project 3.2. The owner has requested two lists. The first is a listing of the books that have fewer than 50 copies in stock. This listing should include the Book Code, Title, Publisher Code, and Quantity in Stock. Since this will be needed repeatedly as a check on books to be reordered, this query will be saved. The second is a list of all books sold by Texts and Tomes (code TT12) sorted by Year of Publication and including the Book Code, Title, Author, Year of Publication, and Publisher Code fields. This is a temporary query and will be printed, but not saved.

The result of the first query should look like Figure 4 - 28. The result of the second should resemble Figure 4 - 29.

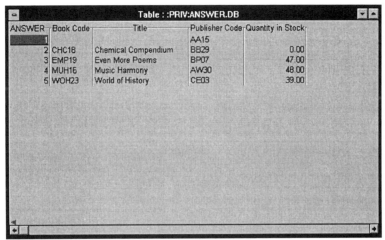

Figure 4 - 28

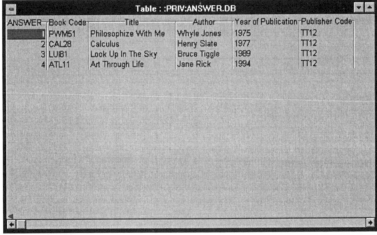

Figure 4 - 29

1. Run *Paradox*.

2. Click the **Paradox** button to close the Welcome to Paradox screen if it is open.

3. Maximize the *Paradox* window if it does not already cover the entire screen.

4. Click the **Open Project Viewer** button on the toolbar if it is not already open. Check that you are in the correct working directory.

5. Right-click on (inspect) the **Queries** icon on the left side of the Project Viewer.

6. Click **New** in the self-contained menu to start a new query.

7. Click on the name **BOOKS.DB** in the list of tables and click the **OK** button to open the **Query** window.

8. Click on the check box in the **Book Code** column to check that field.

9. Similarly, check the **Title**, **Publisher Code**, and **Quantity in Stock** fields.

10. In the **Quantity in Stock** column enter: **<50**

11. Click the **Run Query** button to see the five resulting listings (see Figure 4 - 28). For all data types, a blank field is smaller than any value. Thus, the record without a quantity is included.

12. Print the result by clicking the **Print** button, picking the **Create Horizontal Overflow Pages As Needed** option, and clicking **OK**.

13. Close the **ANSWER.DB** table with **FILE/Close**.

14. Save the query as **LowQuant** by picking **FILE/Save As**, entering the name, and clicking the **OK** button.

15. To begin the second query, press the **CTRL+DELETE** key to clear the current specifications.

16. Click on the check box in the **Book Code** column to check that field.

17. Similarly, check **Title**, **Author**, **Year of Publication**, and **Publisher Code**.

18. In the **Publisher Code** field enter: **TT12**

19. Click the **Sort Answer Table** button on the toolbar.

20. Click on the name **Year of Publication** and click the right-pointing arrow button to transfer the name to the **Sort By:** column.

21. Click **OK**.

22. Click the **Run Query** button on the toolbar to obtain the resulting answer (see Figure 4 - 29).

23. Print the result by clicking the **Print** button, picking the **Create Horizontal Overflow Pages As Needed** option, and clicking **OK**.

24. Close the **ANSWER.DB** table with **FILE/Close**.

25. We do not need to save this query, so close it without saving with **FILE/Close**. When the alert box asks about saving, click the **No** button.

26. If you need to exit from *Paradox* and/or Windows, do so properly.

Independent Project 4.3: The Real Estate Office

This Independent Project continues the Real Estate Office database from Independent Project 3.3. The office manager has requested three lists. A client has asked about commercial properties that are on the first floor of a building. This first listing should include the Code, Address, City, State, Zip, Size, Floor, Price, and Available fields and be sorted by date Available. This is a temporary query and will be printed, but not saved. The result of this first query should look like Figure 4 - 30.

ANSWER	Code	Address	City	State	Zip	Size	Floor	Price	Available
1	MC29	Maple Court	New Canaan	CT	06840	450	1	$125,000.00	4/1/95
2	ES52	5 Elm St.	Greenwich	CT	06830	4800	1	$72,000.00	6/1/95
3	RP12	2 Research Park	Stamford	CT	06902	18000	1	$3,400,000.00	6/1/95
4	RP13	3 Research Park	Stamford	CT	06902	18000	1	$3,400,000.00	6/1/95
5	RP15	5 Research Park	Stamford	CT	06902	21000	1	$4,100,000.00	8/1/95
6	RP16	6 Research Park	Stamford	CT	06902	19000	1	$3,900,000.00	10/1/95

Figure 4 - 30

The Second is a list of all properties priced below $1,000,000. Include the Code, Address, City, State, Zip, Size, Purchase or Rent, Price, Available, and Agency Code fields. Since this query is a common requirement in the office, it will be saved as well as printed. This table should match Figure 4 - 31

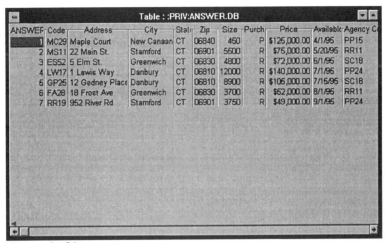

Figure 4 - 31

The third is a list of all properties that will be available on or before 8/1/95 sorted by date available. Include the Code, Address, City, State, Zip, Size, Purchase or Rent, Price, Available, and Agency Code fields. This one will be printed, but not saved. The result of this third query should resemble Figure 4 - 32.

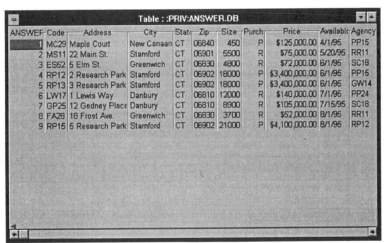

Figure 4 - 32

1. Run *Paradox*, close the Welcome to Paradox screen, and maximize the window.

2. Open the Project Viewer and confirm or pick the working directory.

3. Right-click on (inspect) the **Queries** icon and pick **New**.

4. Pick **COMMERCL.DB**.

5. Include the **Code, Address, City, State, Zip, Size, Floor, Price,** and **Available** fields.

6. Enter any criteria to limit listings to the **first floor** of a building.

7. Use the **Sort Answer Table** button to sort by date **Available**.

8. View the resulting listings (see Figure 4 - 30).

9. Print the result.

10. Close **ANSWER.DB**.

11. To begin the second query, clear the existing specifications with the **CTRL+DELETE** key.

12. Include the **Code, Address, City, State, Zip, Size, Purchase or Rent, Price, Available**, and **Agency Code** fields.

13. Enter the criterion for **Price below $1,000,000**. Be careful to type the correct number of zeros and do *not* include the $ or commas.

14. View the result (see Figure 4 - 31).

15. Print the result.

16. Close **ANSWER.DB**.

17. Save the query as **Belo1Mil**.

18. Begin setting up the third query by removing the current specifications.

19. See the list of required fields in the paragraph above step 1 and make the selections.

20. Enter the criterion for date available **on or before 8/1/95**.

21. Set the sort operator for date **Available**. (The sort may already be set up as *Paradox* has probably remembered this sort field from the first query in this project.)

22. View the result (see Figure 4 - 32).

23. Print the result.

24. We do not need to save this query, so close it without saving.

25. If you need to exit from *Paradox* and/or Windows, do so properly.

Independent Project 4.4: The Veterinarian

This Independent Project continues the veterinarian database from Independent Project 3.4. She has requested three lists. Include all fields in each query, print each result, and save each query.

- A list of all dogs.

- All animals weighing less than 20 pounds.

- Any animal born on or before 1/1/92.

Lesson

5

Multiple Criteria and Multi-Table Queries

Objectives

In this lesson you will learn how to:

- Specify multiple criteria for selecting records
- Use additional query operators

- Use wildcard characters in queries
- Join data from two or more tables with a multiple table query

PROJECT DESCRIPTION

In the previous lesson the queries needed to match only a single value. More likely, the data you are seeking must match multiple criteria. For example, you may need all of the CDROMs released before a certain date that were published by a particular publisher. The date restriction must be matched as well as the restriction on publisher. Additionally, the data you need in the answer may reside in two or more tables. With multiple tables you use a query to join the data into a single answer table.

In this lesson we will run several queries to obtain inventory information. The queries will be based on the CDROM table and use multiple criteria. Then we will query the CDROM table together with various other tables to gather additional information about the orders for CDROMs.

MULTIPLE CRITERIA

There are only two types of queries with multiple criteria: *And Queries* and *Or Queries*. An *And Query* contains two (or more) criteria, both of which must be matched simultaneously. An example would be all of the CDROMS that were released after 5/2/95 *and* are priced below $100. The resulting answer would contain only listings that satisfied both conditions.

An *Or Query* will have two or more conditions, any one of which may be matched. All of the CDROMS that were released after 5/2/95 *or* are priced below $100 is an example. The answer for this last example will have some listings released after 5/2/95 no matter what their price, some priced below $100 no matter when they were released, and possibly some records that match both parts of the criteria.

A query with multiple criteria is set up the same way a single criterion query is. Then, in the query table two or more examples to be matched are entered. The multiple criteria might be entered in different fields, or within one field. For example, all prices greater than $100 and less than $500 would place both conditions in the Price field, whereas, all items priced greater than $100 and released after 5/2/95 would put criteria in two different fields.

To query with multiple criteria:

* Begin opening the query window in the normal way with **FILE/New/Query**. Alternatively, right-click (inspect) the **Queries** icon on the left side of the Project Viewer or the **Open Query** button on the toolbar and pick **New**.

* Add the desired table from the list in the **Select File** dialog box.

* Check the desired fields.

* Enter the first criterion.

* Enter a second criterion.

* Enter any additional criteria.

* View the resulting answer.

To enter criteria for an And Query

* Type more than one criterion in the same row of the query table.

Activity 5.1: An And Query

We need a list of the CDROMs on which we might be overstocked. Any CDROM that costs more than $100 *and* of which we have more than 50 in stock is possibly overstocked.

1. Open the Project Viewer in *Paradox*.

2. Right-click (inspect) the **Queries** icon on the left side of the Project Viewer.

3. Pick **New**.

4. In the **Select File** dialog box, click on the name **CDROM.DB** and click the **OK** button.

5. Check the **Title** field.

6. Also check the **Cost** and **Quantity In Stock** fields.

7. Move to the **Cost** column and enter: **>100**

8. Move to the **Quantity In Stock** column and enter: **>50** (see Figure 5 - 1).

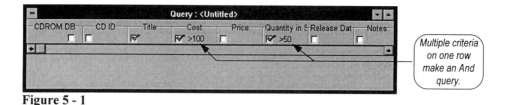

Figure 5 - 1

9. Click the **Run Query** button on the toolbar to see the resulting answer.

   Each of the two listings has a Cost above $100 as well as a Quantity greater than 50 (see Figure 5 - 2).

10. Close **ANSWER.DB** with **FILE/Close** to return to the query design. Do *not* close the query.

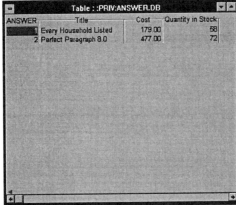

Figure 5 - 2

To enter criteria for an Or Query:

- If the criteria are based on different fields, type the first criterion on the top row of the query table, press the **DOWN ARROW** to create a second row, and type the second criterion on that second row. You *must* then check on the second row every column where there is a check mark on the first row.

- If the criteria are all in the same field, type the first criterion and a space, type the word **or**, and type a space and the second criterion.

- For more than two criteria, use additional rows in separate fields, or the word **or** additional times within a single field. If you are using separate lines, you must then check *all* subsequent rows in every column where there is a check mark on the first row.

Activity 5.2: A Multiple Field Or Query

Our manager redefines "possibly overstocked" to mean any CDROM that costs more than $100 *or* of which we have more than 50 in stock. We need a new list of the CDROMs on which we may be overstocked. This will be an important query that we will need over and over; thus we will both print and save this query.

1. Delete the **>50** from the **Quantity In Stock** column.

2. Press the **DOWN ARROW** to open a second line in the query table.

3. Click back in the **Quantity In Stock** column on the second row and enter: **>50**

4. Check the **Quantity In Stock** column on the second row.

5. Similarly, check the **Title** and **Cost** fields on the second row (see Figure 5 - 3).

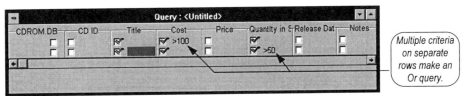

Figure 5 - 3

6. Click the **Run Query** button on the toolbar to see the resulting answer.

Of the ten listings (see Figure 5 - 4), four have only a Cost above $100, four have only a Quantity greater than 50, and two have both.

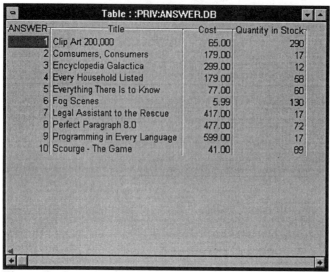

Figure 5 - 4

7. Print the result by clicking the **Print** button, picking the **Create Horizontal Overflow Pages As Needed** option, and clicking **OK**.

8. Close **ANSWER.DB** with **FILE/Close**.

9. Choose **FILE/Save As** to begin saving this query design.

10. Enter the name: **Ovrstock** and click **OK**.

11. Do *not* close the query table.

ADDITIONAL QUERY OPERATORS

An *operator* in a query is a symbol, word, or group of words that specifies the range of values to be matched. We have already used the operators =, >, and <, as well as some combinations of those. Additional operators are listed in Table 5 - 1.

Operator	Example
,	>50,<100
or	"C01" or "E04"
not	not "Windows"
blank	blank

Table 5 - 1

Activity 5.3: A Single Field Or Query

Our manager also asks for a listing of all of the data on CDROMs numbered C01, E04, or L01. Since this query is based on the same CDROM table, we do not need to begin all over. However, the currently selected fields and criteria are not what we need. Therefore, we will again use the **CTRL+DELETE** key to clear the old specifications from the query table. Since we need all data on the three CDROMs, we will include all fields in the answer.

Our manager asked for CDROMs numbered C01, E04, or L01. Since these ID numbers need to be specified in the same field, we can use the **or** operator rather than separate lines.

1.   Press **CTRL+DELETE** twice to clear all the previous specifications from both rows of the query table.

2.   To check all the fields, click the check box in the first column where the table name, **CDROM.DB**, appears. Alternatively, press the **F6** key while the highlight is in the column with the table name (see Figure 5 - 5).

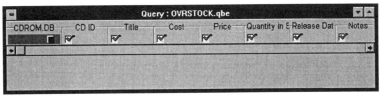

Figure 5 - 5

3.   Click in the **CD ID** column.

4.   Type: **C01 or E04 or L01**

*Be careful that you type zeros in the above criterion. The word **or** may be typed in lower or upper case, but the starting letter in each ID number must be capitalized (see Figure 5 - 6).*

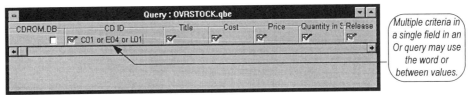

Figure 5 - 6

5.   Click the **Run Query** button to see the resulting answer.

The three ID numbers should be listed in the answer (see Figure 5 - 7).

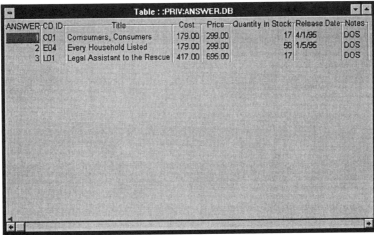

Figure 5 - 7

6.   Close the **ANSWER.DB** table with **FILE/Close**. Do *not* close the query.

ENTRIES BETWEEN TWO VALUES

When you need the data entries that fall between a starting and an ending value, you need to specify two conditions. The needed value must be greater than a starting value and less than an ending value. Since this is an And query, you will need both conditions on the same row of the query table, and they also apply to the same field. Thus, two criteria must be in a single field.

Separate multiple items in a single field with a comma. For example, to specify that a Price must be between $500 and $1000, enter the criterion **>500,<1000** in the Price field. This represents "greater than 500 and less than 1000," which means between 500 and 1000. You may, of course, use equal signs to include the starting and ending values themselves, as in **>=500,<=1000**. This means the values 500 through 1000.

To specify entries between two values:

- In the column that would contain the values, type a greater than sign and the starting value, a comma, and a less than sign with the ending value.

Activity 5.4: Querying for Entries Between Two Values

We need a list of all of the CDROMs released between 2/15/95 and 4/30/95.

1. Erase the previous criterion in the **CD ID** column.

2. Move to the **Release Date** column.

3. Enter: **>2/15/95,<4/30/95** (see Figure 5 - 8).

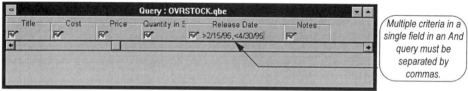

Figure 5 - 8

4. Click the **Run Query** button to see the resulting answer.

   The four dates in the answer should be between the starting and ending dates (Figure 5 - 9).

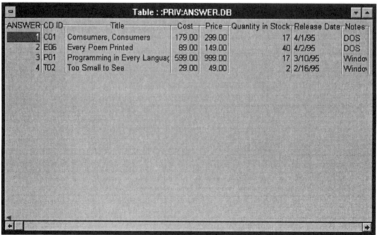

Figure 5 - 9

5. Close **ANSWER.DB** to return to the query. Do *not* close the query.

THE NOT OPERATOR

Surprisingly often in queries you know exactly what you do not want. To query for all entries that do not match a value, use the **not** operator.

To use the not operator:

- In the column that would contain the desired values, type the word **not** and a space, followed by the value to be excluded.

Activity 5.5: The Not Operator

We need a list of the CD-ROMs that are not Windows CD-ROMs

1. Erase the previous criterion.

   *If the old criterion is highlighted, merely press **DELETE** to remove it. A quick way to erase a long criterion when it is not already highlighted is to move over one column with **ENTER** and back to the original column with the **LEFT ARROW**. That move highlights the entire set of characters. Then press the **DELETE** key to erase the highlighted criterion.*

2. Move to the **Notes** column.

3. Enter: **not Windows** (see Figure 5 - 10). Remember to properly capitalize the word **Windows** since it is data. The word **not** may be in any case.

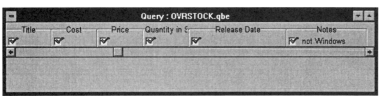

Figure 5 - 10

4. Click the **Run Query** button to see the resulting answer.

   *The eight listings in the answer (see Figure 5 - 11) will contain a variety of notes that are not **"Windows,"** although one has **"Windows - B&W."** Since **"Windows - B&W"** is not exactly **"Windows,"** it matches our criterion, too. Shortly, we will see how to eliminate this entry that includes the word **"Windows"** even though it is not exactly the same.*

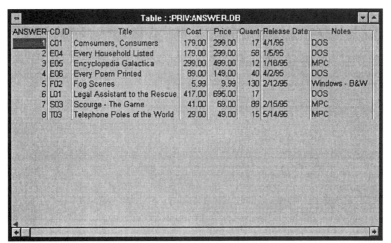

Figure 5 - 11

5. Print the result by clicking the **Print** button, picking the **Create Horizontal Overflow Pages As Needed** option, and clicking **OK**.

6. Close **ANSWER.DB** to return to the query. Do *not* close the query.

THE BLANK OPERATOR

Every time we need a set of records, we type the value to be matched. In the columns where we do not type a value, there is no restriction on the data. What if we needed the records where there was no entry in that field, that is, where the field was empty? We cannot leave the column empty since that means no restriction. The solution is the operator **blank**. Blank means empty.

To use the blank operator:

*   In the column that contains the empty entries, type the word **blank**.

*   If you want the records that are not empty, use **not blank**.

Activity 5.6: The Blank Operator

We need a list of those CDROMs that do not yet have a **Release Date** filled in.

1. Erase the previous criterion.

2. Move to the **Release Date** column and enter: **blank** (see Figure 5 - 12).

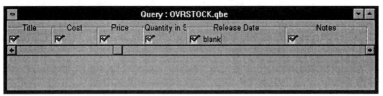

Figure 5 - 12

3. Click the **Run Query** button to see the resulting answer.

    The two listings in the answer will have empty Release Date fields (see Figure 5 - 13).

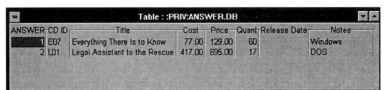

Figure 5 - 13

4. Close **ANSWER.DB** to return to the query.

5. Close the query with **FILE/Close**. Click **No** when asked about saving the query design.

WILDCARDS

Earlier, we queried for the records that did not have "Windows" in the Notes field. While most of the listings in the answer contained completely different entries, one had the entry "Windows - B&W." A portion of the entry matched, but not the whole entry. How do we match portions of entries?

Wildcard characters allow you to match a portion of the entry in a field. In *Paradox* the wildcard characters are **..** and **@**. The **..** represents any number of characters from no characters to the maximum. Thus, "**Windows**.." would represent any entry that begins with the characters "Windows" including just Windows with no more characters and Windows followed by any other set of characters. "..Windows.." would stand for any entry that contains "Windows" anywhere within it, for the wildcards stand for possible characters in front of Windows and after Windows.

The **@** represents exactly one character, no more and no less. As an example, 5/@/95 would represent any single digit day in May of 1995. 5/@@/95 would represent the two digit days. To represent any day in May of 1995, use the double dots as in 5/../95.

Equally important, when you use a wildcard in a criterion, the query is *not* case sensitive. Thus, either example with Windows (..**Windows**.. or **Windows**..) would find Windows, or WINDOWS, or windows, or even wInDoWs. Sometimes you may need to use the **..** wildcard even though you know there are no more characters just to allow for all cases.

To use wildcards in a query:

- Open the query in the normal way.

- Select fields as usual.

- Fill in criteria that include one or more wildcard characters.

Activity 5.7: Using Wildcards in the Notes Field

We need listings of every CDROM that has **Windows** anywhere within the Notes field.

1. Right-click the **Queries** icon on the left side of the Project Viewer.

2. Pick **New**.

3. In the **Select File** dialog box, click on the name **CDROM.DB** and click the **OK** button.

4. Press the **F6** key to check all fields.

5. Move to the **Notes** column and enter: **..Windows..** (see Figure 5 - 14).

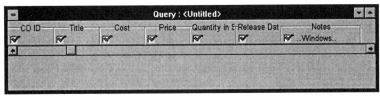

Figure 5 - 14

6. Click the **Run Query** button to see the resulting answer.

    The eight listings (see Figure 5 - 15) in the answer will have "Windows" somewhere within the Notes field. It happens they are all capitalized, but that was not necessary.

7. Print the result by clicking the **Print** button, picking the **Create Horizontal Overflow Pages As Needed** option, and clicking **OK**.

8. Close **ANSWER.DB** to return to the query. Do *not* close the query.

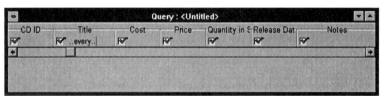

Figure 5 - 15

Activity 5.8: Using Wildcards in the Title Field

We need to see the listings of each CDROM that has the word **every** anywhere within its title. Since we only need to examine the data, we will not save this query when we are finished.

1. Erase the previous criterion.

2. Move to the **Title** column and enter: **..every..** (see Figure 5 - 16).

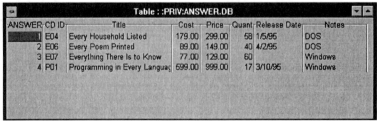

Figure 5 - 16

3. Click the **Run Query** button to see the resulting answer.

   Each of the four listings in the answer will have "every" somewhere within its title no matter what other characters are there or what the capitalization is (see Figure 5 - 17).

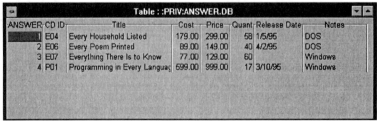

Figure 5 - 17

4. Print the result by clicking the **Print** button, picking the **Create Horizontal Overflow Pages As Needed** option, and clicking **OK**.

5. Close **ANSWER.DB** to return to the query.

6. Close the query with **FILE/Close**. Click **No** when asked about saving the query design.

MULTIPLE TABLE QUERIES

The best design for the majority of databases is to have multiple tables holding the data. For the reasons given in Lesson 3, it is usually the only way to handle the data efficiently. Yet with a multi-table design, reports and calculations will often need to access data from more than one table at a time. To join the data from multiple tables you use a *join* query.

A *join* query is merely a regular query with more than one table in the query window. When you install more than one table in the query window, you must then *link* the tables by showing *Paradox* which field (or fields) in one table is the same as a field in another table. Every table included in the query must be linked to some other table. If you do not establish the link between two tables, you will get the error message "Query appears to ask two unrelated questions."

To link the tables, you place a pair of *example elements*, one in the common field of each table. An *example element* is merely a code word, any word you want (except reserved words), but it is typed in a special way. To type an example element, press the **F5** key and type the code word. There is also a toolbar button to type example elements for you. If you click the **Join Tables** button, *Paradox* will make up the code word **join1** for the first link, **join2** for the second, etc. Since linking a pair of tables requires two example elements, using the **Join Tables** button gives you example elements in pairs. Example elements will appear in red on a color screen.

When you include more than one table in the query window and properly link the tables, you may check fields from each table. Of course, you may sort, enter criteria, and all of the normal activities we have performed with single tables when you employ multiple table queries.

To join data from multiple tables through a query:

- Begin a query in the regular way.
- Pick the first table from the list in the **Select File** dialog box.
- Choose the second table by holding down the **CTRL** key while clicking on its name.
- Choose any additional tables.
- Click the **OK** button. The **Query** window will open with a query table for each selected name in it.
- Establish the link between tables using one of the following two methods. Click the **Join Tables** button ▦ , click in the common field in the first table, and click in the matching field in the second table. Alternatively, move to the common field in the first table, press the **F5** key, type the example element, move to the matching field in the second table, press **F5**, and type the same example element.
- Link any additional tables.
- Check the desired fields.
- Enter any values to be matched in the column that would contain those values.
- Include any sorting instructions.
- Click the **Run Query** button to see the resulting join as an answer table.

Activity 5.9: Joining Multiple Tables with a Query

We need an answer table with the names of the employees who sold each invoice. Since the invoice data is in the **INVOICES.DB** table with only the Employee ID to represent the sales person, and the employees' names are in the **EMPLOYES.DB** table, we must join the needed fields from the two tables. The common field in each of the two tables is **Employee ID**.

1. Right-click the **Queries** icon on the left side of the Project Viewer.

2. Pick **New**.

3. In the **Select File** dialog box, click once on the name **EMPLOYES.DB**. Do *not* click **OK** yet.

4. Hold down the **CTRL** key and click once on the name **INVOICES.DB**.

   Both names will be highlighted (see Figure 5 - 18).

5. Click the **OK** button.

   *Both query tables will appear in a single **Query** window (see Figure 5 - 19).*

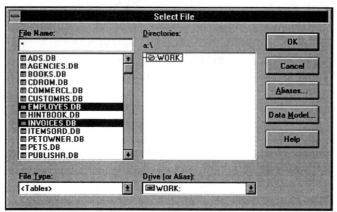

Figure 5 - 18

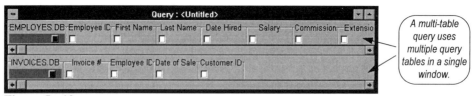

Figure 5 - 19

6. Click the **Join Tables** button on the toolbar.

   The mouse cursor becomes an arrow with a pair of tables.

7. Move the mouse pointer into the **Employee ID** field in the **EMPLOYES.DB** query table and click the left mouse button once.

   *The example element **join1** should appear in red in the field.*

8. Move the mouse pointer into the **Employee ID** field in the **INVOICES.DB** query table and click the left mouse button once.

   *The matching example element **join1** appears (see Figure 5 - 20). These two example elements establish the link between the tables.*

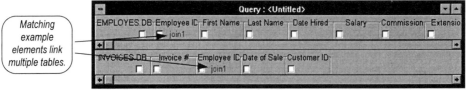

Figure 5 - 20

9. Check **First Name** in the **EMPLOYES.DB** table.

10. Check **Last Name**.

11. Check the box under the table name in **INVOICES.DB** to include (check) all of its fields (see Figure 5 - 21).

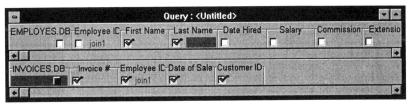

Figure 5 - 21

12. Click the **Run Query** button to see the result.

    The two sales people Daphne Green and George Jeffers are matched to the invoices they sold. Notice that the Employee ID matches the name for each invoice (see Figure 5 - 22).

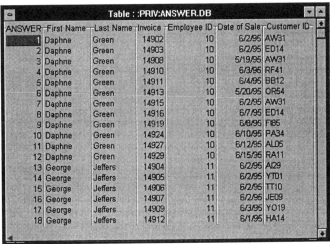

Figure 5 - 22

Also notice the Customer ID number for each invoice. Who is the customer? The next query will join the customer names to this listing by matching the Customer IDs to the **CUSTOMRS.DB** *table.*

13. Close **ANSWER.DB** to return to the query. Do *not* close the query.

Activity 5.10: Joining a Third Table into the Query

We would like the names of the customers for each invoice. We still need all of the previous data from the **EMPLOYES.DB** and **INVOICES.DB** tables, but want to add the customer names from the **CUSTOMRS.DB** table. So we need a third table, the customers table. When finished, we will save this query with the name **SALES.QBE** as we would probably need these results frequently.

1. Click the **Add Table** button on the toolbar (or pick **QUERY/Add Table** in the menu).

2. In the **Select File** dialog box click on **CUSTOMRS.DB** and click the **OK** button.

    *CUSTOMRS.DB has been added, but Paradox has not enlarged the **Query** window so you can see it. Therefore, we must increase the height of the window ourselves.*

3. Move the mouse pointer onto the bottom frame line of the **Query** window.

    The mouse pointer becomes a double-headed up-and-down arrow (see Figure 5 - 23).

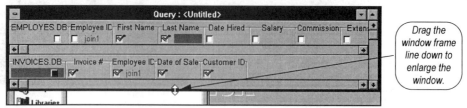

Figure 5 - 23

4. With the double-headed arrow pointer, hold down the mouse button and drag the frame line downward about an inch. Release the mouse button. If the **CUSTOMRS.DB** table does not fully show, repeat this step until it does (see Figure 5 - 24).

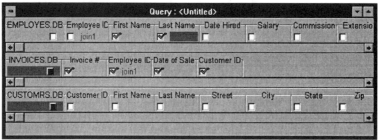

Figure 5 - 24

5. Click in the **Customer ID** field in the **INVOICES.DB** table.

    We will create the example element ourselves this time.

6. Press the **F5** key and type: **CID**

    The CID should be in red to show it is an example element. If it is not red on a color screen, erase it and try again. (On a monochrome screen it will be highlighted.)

    CID is short for Customer ID. Any single word would do for an example element (except reserved words like NOT or BLANK). The characters may be letters or digits. Spaces are illegal. They are not case sensitive. A good plan is to use the initials of the field, like CID.

7. Click in the **Customer ID** field in the **CUSTOMRS.DB** table.

8. Press the **F5** key and type: **CID** (see Figure 5 - 25)

    This CID must be in red, as well.

9. In the **CUSTOMRS.DB** table, check the **Last Name** field.

10. As we do not need to see the Customer ID any more, uncheck the **Customer ID** field in the **INVOICES.DB** table (see Figure 5 - 25).

11. Click the **Run Query** button to see the result.

    *The field name **Last Name** occurs twice, so Paradox changes the second occurrence to be **Last Name_1** (see Figure 5 - 26).*

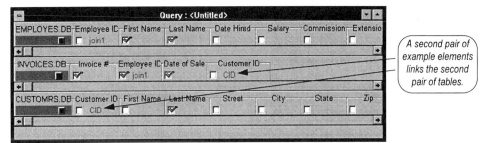

Figure 5 - 25

ANSWER	First Name	Last Name	Invoice	Employee ID	Date of Sale	Last Name_1
1	Daphne	Green	14902	10	6/2/95	Arrow Way Freight
2	Daphne	Green	14903	10	6/2/95	Edible Delights
3	Daphne	Green	14908	10	5/19/95	Arrow Way Freight
4	Daphne	Green	14910	10	6/3/95	Regent Foods
5	Daphne	Green	14911	10	6/4/95	Balloon Bonanza
6	Daphne	Green	14913	10	5/20/95	Oradelio
7	Daphne	Green	14915	10	6/2/95	Arrow Way Freight
8	Daphne	Green	14916	10	6/7/95	Edible Delights
9	Daphne	Green	14919	10	6/8/95	Fielder
10	Daphne	Green	14924	10	6/10/95	Packard
11	Daphne	Green	14927	10	6/12/95	Allington
12	Daphne	Green	14929	10	6/15/95	Razelroth
13	George	Jeffers	14904	11	6/2/95	AreaWide Insurance
14	George	Jeffers	14905	11	6/2/95	Your Trip Travel
15	George	Jeffers	14906	11	6/2/95	Timed Travel, Inc
16	George	Jeffers	14907	11	6/2/95	Jerome
17	George	Jeffers	14909	11	6/3/95	Yorko
18	George	Jeffers	14912	11	6/1/95	Harrington

Figure 5 - 26

This answer joins data from three tables. Notice some of the customer's names occur multiple times (see Figure 5 - 26). This is the very redundancy we eliminated with separate tables. We have instructed the program to temporarily show the redundant names.

12. Print the result by clicking the **Print** button, picking the **Create Horizontal Overflow Pages As Needed** option, and clicking **OK**.

13. Close **ANSWER.DB** to return to the query.

14. Choose **FILE/Save As** to save this query.

15. Type the name **SALES** in the **Save File As** dialog box and click **OK**.

16. Close the query with **FILE/Close**.

Activity 5.11: A Second Multiple Table Query

We need an answer table with the items sold on each invoice. The **INVOICES.DB** table does not contain that data since we could not predict how many items a customer would purchase. The items on each invoice are listed in the **ITEMSORD.DB** table. We will join data from the two tables based on the common field **Invoice #**.

1. Right-click (inspect) the **Queries** icon on the left side of the Project Viewer.

2. Pick **New**.

3. In the **Select File** dialog box, click once on the name **INVOICES.DB**. Do *not* click **OK** yet.

4. Hold down the **CTRL** key and click once on the name **ITEMSORD.DB**.

5. Click **OK**.

6. Click the **Join Tables** button on the toolbar.

7. Move the mouse pointer into the **Invoice #** field in the **INVOICES.DB** table and click the mouse button once to place the first of the pair of example elements.

8. Move the mouse pointer into the **Invoice #** field in the **ITEMSORD.DB** table and click the mouse button once to place the matching example element.

   A red join1 should show in both tables.

9. Check **Invoice #** in the **INVOICES.DB** table. Also check **Date of Sale**.

10. In the **ITEMSORD.DB** table, check the **Line #**, **Quantity Sold**, and **CD ID** fields (see Figure 5 - 27).

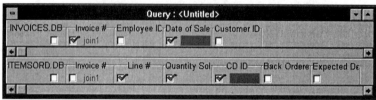

Figure 5 - 27

*You may check one of the **Invoice #** fields, both of them, or neither of them as suits your needs.*

11. Click the **Run Query** button to see the result.

    Notice that this answer shows the invoice numbers multiple times (see Figure 5 - 28), once for each item ordered on that invoice.

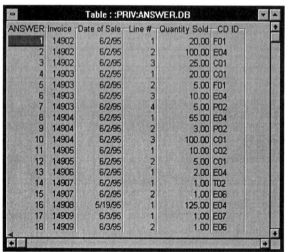

Figure 5 - 28

12. Print the result by clicking the **Print** button, picking the **Create Horizontal Overflow Pages As Needed** option, and clicking **OK**.

13. Close **ANSWER.DB**.

14. Choose **FILE/Save As** to save this query.

15. Type the name **InvItems** in the Save As dialog box and click **OK**.

16. Close the query with **FILE/Close**.

How would you add the CDROM names to this query in the place of the ID numbers? How could we add the Customers' names? How about the Employees' names?

SUMMARY

In this lesson we have used multiple criteria and multiple table queries. We used multiple criteria for And Queries and Or Queries. We also used the comma, or, not, and blank operators, as well as wildcard characters in queries. The multiple table queries joined data from more than one table into a single answer. This was achieved by linking the common field in one table to the matching field in the second table.

In the next lesson we will design reports and labels.

KEY TERMS

And Query   Link   Wildcard
Example element   Operator
Join   Or Query

INDEPENDENT PROJECTS

Independent Project 5.1: The School Newspaper

This Independent Project continues working with the Newspaper Ad database from Independent Project 4.1. The newspaper's editor needs a list of any companies with "sport" in their name to get ready for the Homecoming issue. It should include all fields. Also, the business manager wants a listing of where the sales force lives together with the businesses to whom they are selling ads. It should include the **Purchased By** field from the **ADS.DB** table, as well as the First Name, Last Name, and Room fields from the **SALSFORC.DB** table. The two tables will need to be linked by their common field, **Salesperson ID**.

The first query result should look like Figure 5 - 29. The second will correspond to Figure 5 - 30.

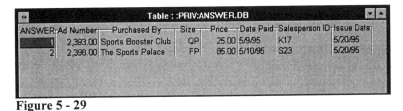

Figure 5 - 29

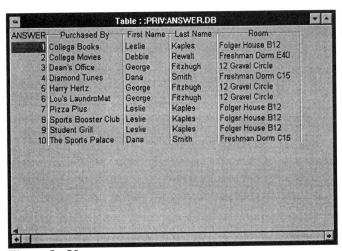

Figure 5 - 30

1. Run *Paradox.*

2. Click the **Paradox** button to close the Welcome to Paradox screen if it is open.

3. Maximize the *Paradox* window if it does not already cover the entire screen.

4. Click the **Open Project Viewer** button on the toolbar if it is not already open. Check that you are in the correct working directory.

5. Right-click on (inspect) the **Queries** icon on the left side of the Project Viewer.

6. Click **New** in the self-contained menu to start a new query.

7. Click on the name **ADS.DB** in the list of tables and click the **OK** button to open the **Query** window.

8. Click on the check box under the table name to check all fields.

9. In the **Purchased By** column enter: **..sport..**

10. Click the **Run Query** button on the toolbar to see the two resulting listings (see Figure 5 - 29).

11. Print the result by clicking the **Print** button, picking the **Create Horizontal Overflow Pages As Needed** option, and clicking **OK**.

12. Close **ANSWER.DB** with **FILE/Close**.

13. We will build the second query from the first, so clear the current selection of fields from the query table by pressing **CTRL+DELETE**.

14. To add the Sales Force table, either click the **Add Table** button on the toolbar or pick **QUERY/Add Table**.

15. Click on the name **SALSFORC.DB** in the **Select File** dialog box and click **OK**.

16. Click the **Join Tables** button on the toolbar.

17. Click once in the **Salesperson ID** field in the **ADS.DB** table, then click again in the **Salesperson ID** field in the **SALSFORC.DB** table to link the tables with example elements. The two example elements should show in red. If not, erase what did appear and try this step again.

18. Check the **Purchased By** field in **ADS.DB**.

19. Check **First Name**, **Last Name**, and **Room** in the **SALSFORC.DB** table.

20. Click the **Run Query** button to see the resulting listings (see Figure 5 - 32).

21. Print the result by clicking the **Print** button, picking the **Create Horizontal Overflow Pages As Needed** option, and clicking **OK**.

22. Close **ANSWER.DB** with **FILE/Close**.

23. Save the query as **CompRoom** by picking **FILE/Save As**, entering the name, and clicking the **OK** button.

24. Close the query with **FILE/Close**.

25. If you need to exit from *Paradox* and/or Windows, do so properly.

Independent Project 5.2: The Bookstore

This Independent Project continues working with the Bookstore database from Independent Project 4.2. The owner needs a list of books that are priced below $30 and that have between 50 and 100 in stock. It should include all fields. Since this is a one-time request, you will print, but not save, this query. She also wants a complete listing with publisher's name, title, author's name,

and year of publication. It should be sorted by publisher's name. The two tables,
PUBLISHR.DB and **BOOKS.DB**, will need to be linked by their common field, **Publisher Code**.
As this listing may be required repeatedly, this one will be saved.

    The first query result should look like Figure 5 - 31. The second will correspond to
Figure 5 - 32.

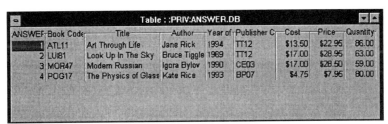

Figure 5 - 31

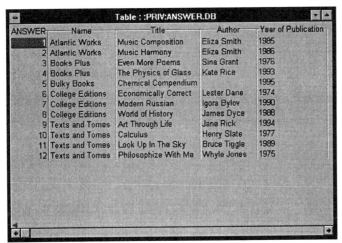

Figure 5 - 32

1. Run *Paradox*.

2. Click the **Paradox** button to close the Welcome to Paradox screen if it is open.

3. Maximize the *Paradox* window if it does not already cover the entire screen.

4. Click the **Open Project Viewer** button on the toolbar if it is not already open. Check that
   you are in the correct working directory.

5. Right-click on the **Queries** icon on the left side of the Project Viewer.

6. Click **New** in the self-contained menu to start a new query.

7. Click on the name **BOOKS.DB** in the list of tables and click the **OK** button to open the
   Query window.

8. Click on the check box under the table name to check all fields.

9. In the **Price** column enter: **<30**

10. In the **Quantity in Stock** column enter: **>=50,<=100**

11. Click the **Run Query** button on the toolbar (see Figure 5 - 31).

12. Print the result by clicking the **Print** button, picking the **Create Horizontal Overflow Pages
    As Needed** option, and clicking **OK**.

13. Close **ANSWER.DB** with **FILE/Close**.

14. You do not need to save this query, so pick **FILE/Close** and click the **No** button when asked about saving.

15. Start the second query by right-clicking the **Queries** icon in the Project Viewer and picking **New** in the self-contained menu.

16. Click on **PUBLISHR.DB** in the **Select File** dialog box and click **OK**. (We could have held down **CTRL** and clicked on **BOOKS.DB** as well. That would have placed both query tables in the **Query** window. That would have put **BOOKS.DB** above **PUBLISHR.DB** so that its fields would have appeared first in **ANSWER.DB**. However, we want the Publisher's Name first. Therefore, we will add **BOOKS.DB** as a second step to get it below **PUBLISHR.DB**.)

17. To add the **BOOKS.DB** table, either click the **Add Table** button on the toolbar or pick **QUERY/Add Table**.

18. Click on the name **BOOKS.DB** in the **Select File** dialog box and click the **OK** button.

19. Click the **Join Tables** button, click once in the **Publishers Code** field in the **PUBLISHR.DB** query table, and click again in the **Publishers Code** field in the **BOOKS.DB** table. The two example elements should show in red. If not, erase what did appear and try this step again.

20. Check the **Name** field in the **PUBLISHR.DB** table.

21. Check **Title**, **Author**, and **Year of Publication** in the **BOOKS.DB** table.

22. Click the **Run Query** button on the toolbar to see the resulting listings (see Figure 5 - 32).

23. Print the result by clicking the **Print** button, picking the **Create Horizontal Overflow Pages As Needed** option, and clicking **OK**.

24. Close **ANSWER.DB** with **FILE/Close**.

25. Save the query as **PUBBOOKS** by picking **FILE/Save As**, entering the name, and clicking the **OK** button.

26. Close the query with **FILE/Close**.

27. If you need to exit from *Paradox* and/or Windows, do so properly.

Independent Project 5.3: The Real Estate Office

This Independent Project continues working with the Real Estate Office database from Independent Project 4.3. The office manager needs a list of commercial properties that are larger than 4000 square feet in size and priced below $150,000. It should include all fields. Since this is a one time request, you will print, but not save, this query. He also wants a complete listing of properties by agency name. The **Agency Name**, **Phone 1**, and **Fax** fields from the **AGENCIES.DB** table should be included, as well as **Address**, **City**, **Size**, **Available**, and **Agent** from **COMMERCL.DB**. It should be sorted by **Agency Name**. The two tables, **AGENCIES.DB** and **COMMERCL.DB**, will need to be linked by their common field, **Agency Code**. As this listing would be needed continually, this one will be saved and printed.

The first query result should look like Figure 5 - 33. The second will correspond to Figure 5 - 34.

1. Run *Paradox*, close the Welcome to Paradox screen, and maximize the window.

2. Open the Project Viewer and confirm the working directory.

3. Right-click on the **Queries** icon and pick **New**.

4. Pick **COMMERCL.DB**.

5. Click on the check box under the table name to check all fields.

6. Enter the criteria for **Size larger than 4000** square feet in the **Size** column.

7. Enter the criteria for **Price below $150,000** in the **Price** field.

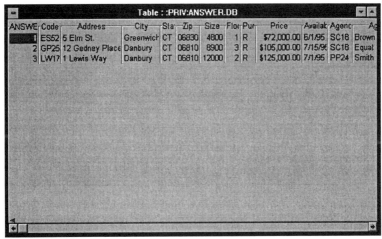

Figure 5 - 33

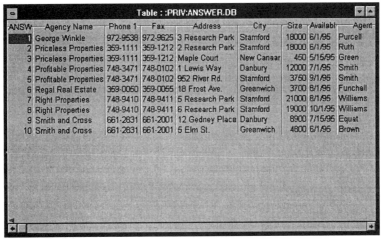

Figure 5 - 34

1. View the resulting listings (see Figure 5 - 33).

2. Print the result.

3. Close the answer table.

4. You do not need to save this query, so close the query without saving.

5. Begin a new query.

6. Pick **AGENCIES.DB** as the table.

7. Add the **COMMERCL.DB** table to the **Query** window.

8. Link the two tables on the common field **Agency Code**.

9. Place the **Agency Name**, **Phone 1**, and **Fax** fields from the **AGENCIES.DB** table.

10. Include **Address**, **City**, **Size**, **Available**, and **Agent** from the **COMMERCL.DB** table.

11. View the resulting listings (see Figure 5 - 34).

12. Print the result.

13. Close the answer table.

14. Save the query as **PROPERTY**.

15. Close the query.

16. If you need to exit from *Paradox* and/or Windows, do so properly.

Independent Project 5.4: The Veterinarian

This Independent Project continues working with the veterinarian database from Independent Project 4.4. She needs the following two lists. Include all fields, print the resulting answer, and save each query.

- A list of dogs that weigh less than 50 pounds.

- A list of animals with "er" anywhere within their given name.

She also needs a listing of the owners with their pets. Include the fields named below, print the resulting answer, and save the query.

- A list that includes **Name**, **Area Code**, and **Phone** from the owners table and the name, type of animal, and date of last visit from the pets table.

Reports

Objectives

In this lesson you will learn how to:

- Design a report using the **Data Model/Layout Diagram** method
- Design labels with the *Label Expert*

- Preview a report design
- Modify a report design
- Print a report

PROJECT DESCRIPTION

While working on the screen is ideal for editing and viewing a table's data, often a paper print-out is required to share the data with others. A typical business needs dozens of standard and special purpose reports to review such activities as sales, inventory, accounts receivable, and customer distribution, to mention just a few topics. In this lesson we will see how to design and print several varieties of reports, as well as mailing labels.

The first report will print a list of customers sorted according to the sizes of their outstanding balances, as shown in Figure 6 - 1. This report is a *tabular* design.

Customer ID	First Name	Last Name	Area Code	Phone	Credit Limit	Outstanding Balance
RF41		Regent Foods	704	523-6108	5,000.00	1,982.00
YT01		Your Trip Travel	719	380-9210	3,000.00	593.40
AW31		Arrow Way Freight	404	873-4909	5,000.00	562.00
TR30	Caroline	Truefoe	706	860-2971	200.00	129.00
JE09	Jennifer	Jerome	603	446-8021	100.00	59.10
PA34	Jerome	Packard	608	828-5512	100.00	49.00
AI29		AreaWide Insuranc	916	478-9932	10,000.00	
AL05	Dana	Allington	718	545-7609	200.00	
BB12		Balloon Bonanza	708	869-0012	3,000.00	
ED14		Edible Delights	303	669-4101	5,000.00	
FI85	Terry	Fielder	708	351-4462	0.00	
HA14	Hazel	Harrington	708	967-2091	0.00	
IF04	Laura	Ifalo	508	535-4029	0.00	
KI88	Samantha	Killian	908	753-2041	500.00	
OR54	Donalio	Oradelio	407	394-0270	0.00	
RA11	Irving	Razelroth	605	966-5080	0.00	
SO26	Sam	Sorbite	713	333-7948	0.00	
TH92	Harry	Thompson	714	833-9910	500.00	
TT10		Timed Travel, Inc	212	564-7271	3,000.00	

Thursday, March 23, 1995 — CUSTOMRS

Figure 6 - 1

The second report will use *grouping* to print the customers in groups by state, as illustrated in Figure 6 - 2.

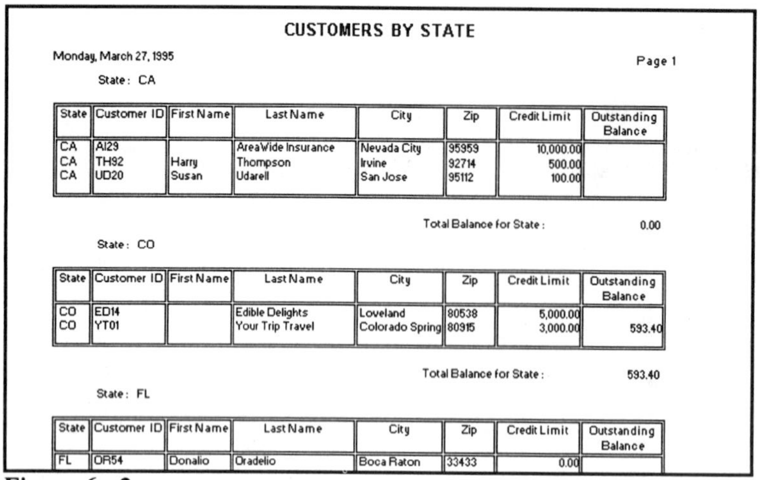

CUSTOMERS BY STATE

Monday, March 27, 1995   Page 1

State: CA

State	Customer ID	First Name	Last Name	City	Zip	Credit Limit	Outstanding Balance
CA	AI29		AreaWide Insurance	Nevada City	95959	10,000.00	
CA	TH92	Harry	Thompson	Irvine	92714	500.00	
CA	UD20	Susan	Udarell	San Jose	95112	100.00	

Total Balance for State: 0.00

State: CO

State	Customer ID	First Name	Last Name	City	Zip	Credit Limit	Outstanding Balance
CO	ED14		Edible Delights	Loveland	80538	5,000.00	
CO	YT01		Your Trip Travel	Colorado Spring	80915	3,000.00	593.40

Total Balance for State: 593.40

State: FL

State	Customer ID	First Name	Last Name	City	Zip	Credit Limit	Outstanding Balance
FL	OR54	Donalio	Oradelio	Boca Raton	33433	0.00	

Figure 6 - 2

A third report will link data from two tables to simultaneously access their records (Figure 6 - 48). The fourth report will produce *mailing labels* for the complete customer list, as illustrated in Figure 6 - 3.

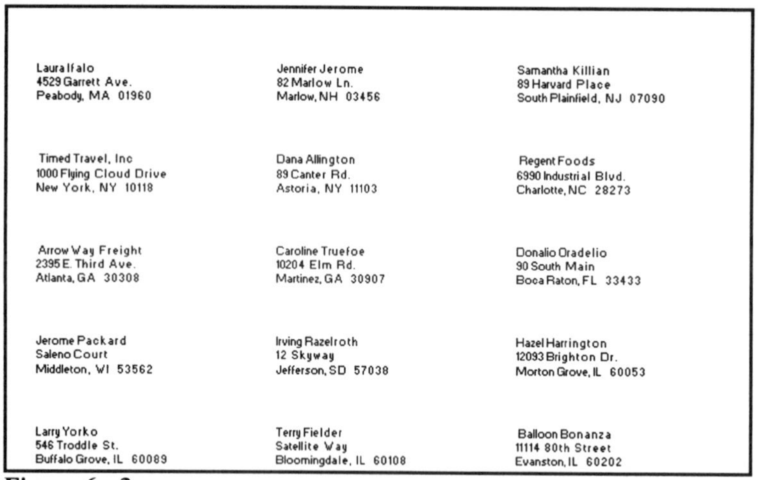

Laura Ifalo 4529 Garrett Ave. Peabody, MA 01960	Jennifer Jerome 82 Marlow Ln. Marlow, NH 03456	Samantha Killian 89 Harvard Place South Plainfield, NJ 07090
Timed Travel, Inc 1000 Flying Cloud Drive New York, NY 10118	Dana Allington 89 Canter Rd. Astoria, NY 11103	Regent Foods 6990 Industrial Blvd. Charlotte, NC 28273
Arrow Way Freight 2395 E. Third Ave. Atlanta, GA 30308	Caroline Truefoe 10204 Elm Rd. Martinez, GA 30907	Donalio Oradelio 90 South Main Boca Raton, FL 33433
Jerome Packard Saleno Court Middleton, WI 53562	Irving Razelroth 12 Skyway Jefferson, SD 57038	Hazel Harrington 12093 Brighton Dr. Morton Grove, IL 60053
Larry Yorko 546 Troddle St. Buffalo Grove, IL 60089	Terry Fielder Satellite Way Bloomingdale, IL 60108	Balloon Bonanza 11114 80th Street Evanston, IL 60202

Figure 6 - 3

DESIGNING A REPORT

The two steps in producing a designed report are to create the design, and then print the report. While designing a report is somewhat more involved than just clicking the **Print** button on the toolbar as we have done previously, it also offers far more flexibility. A report design can place fields anywhere on the page, not just in the row and column format of a table. You may select which fields you want included in the design and leave out unneeded fields. Computed results can be included, both as grand totals at the end of the report, and on each line to calculate results for each listing like a percentage of the total. Once a design is created, it can be saved and used over and over again.

The report design is divided into sections. It will usually have a *report header* (see Figure 6 - 4) at the beginning (the head) of a report to introduce the overall report and a *report footer* (see Figure 6 - 4) at the end (the foot) of the report to conclude the report by presenting any summary results. The report header might contain the title of the report, a date, or other introductory information. The report footer usually has final results like grand totals.

Each page can also have a *page header* and *page footer* (see Figure 6 - 4). *Paradox* places the current date, the name of the table, and the page number in the page header so they will print at the top of each page. A page footer typically contains the page number, although *Paradox* does not place it there.

Each header or footer is placed in its own section in the design and is separated from the neighboring sections by a line that extends across the entire design (see Figure 6 - 4). The line contains the name of the section and a pair of triangles pointing in the direction of that section. For example, the report header is the section named **Report** at the very top of the design and has triangles pointing downward toward the section. The report footer is the section named Report at the very bottom of the design. It's section line has triangles pointing upward toward it.

The section for the fields that will print each listing from the table is the *All Records* section (see Figure 6 - 4). Like the other sections, its dividing lines have its name on it with a pair of triangles pointing toward the section.

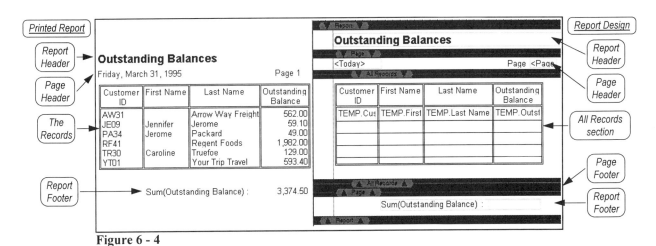

Figure 6 - 4

THE DATA MODEL/LAYOUT DIAGRAM METHOD

While it would be possible to design a report by selecting and placing each individual item onto the layout yourself, that would be very tedious. A typical report design will have 30 to 40 items that must be carefully placed and lined up with one another. A much easier solution is to employ *Paradox's* automatic report design capabilities. The **Data Model/Layout Diagram** method presents a set of choices as to which fields to include and how you want the design to look, and then produces the report design for you. This eliminates the tedium, yet allows considerable flexibility. Once the design is finished, you may, of course, alter it in any way desired in the **Report** window.

The **Data Model/Layout Diagram** method has four different basic designs from which to select (see Figure 6 - 7). A *single-record* design places the fields one below another like a form. A *tabular* design is a listing like a table (see Figure 6 - 1). A *multi-record* design places multiple copies of the chosen set of fields side by side as with labels (see Figure 6 - 3). The fourth design is a blank report where you place every item on the design.

Reports can be printed on the page in *portrait orientation* or *landscape orientation*. *Portrait* means that the printing on the page reads like this book with the pages upright. *Landscape* prints sideways on the page so that you would need to turn the paper sideways to read it. Obviously, landscape affords longer lines than portrait. We will utilize landscape when we need to fit more fields onto the width of the report than would fit on a portrait page.

When you have designed a report in either portrait or landscape orientation, *Paradox* remembers that page direction and attempts to design the next report the same way unless you set the orientation prior to beginning the next design. While switching from portrait to landscape is not a problem, switching from landscape to the narrower portrait causes *Paradox* to remove any parts of the report design that would exceed the margin. Since most of the major portions of the design will exceed the margin, Paradox erases almost everything from the design. For this reason, if you will be using portrait orientation, you must remember to set the direction to portrait before beginning the design.

To set portrait or landscape orientation prior to designing a report:

- Pick **FILE/Printer Setup**.

- Click the **Modify Printer Setup** button in the **Printer Setup** dialog box.

- Click on the option for Portrait or Landscape in the **Orientation:** section.

- Click **OK** in the printer dialog box.

- Click **OK** in the **Printer Setup** dialog box.

To design a tabular report with the *Paradox* Layout Diagram:

- Right-click (inspect) the **Reports** icon at the left side of the Project Viewer or the **Open Report** button on the toolbar and click on **New** in the self-contained menu. Alternatively, pick **FILE/New/Report** in the menu.

- Click the **Data Model/Layout Diagram** button.

- Pick the table in the **File Name:** list and click the **OK** button.

- Choose the style, field layout, and fields for the report.

- Click the **OK** button.

Activity 6.1: A Tabular Report

Management needs to see a list of the outstanding balances of the customers. We will use the **Data Model/Layout Diagram** to design a tabular report that is based on the **CUSTOMRS.DB** table. The required fields are Customer ID, First Name, Last Name, Area Code, Phone Number, Credit Limit, and Outstanding Balance. The report will be sorted by size of balance in descending order.

1. Run *Paradox*, close the Welcome to Paradox screen, and maximize the window.

2. Open the Project Viewer and confirm the working directory.

3. Right-click (inspect) the **Reports icon** at the left side of the Project Viewer.

4. Pick **New** from the self-contained menu.

5. Click on the **Data Model/Layout Diagram** button (see Figure 6 - 5).

6. In the **Data Model** dialog box (see Figure 6 - 6), click on **CUSTOMRS.DB** in the **File Name:** list and click the **OK** button.

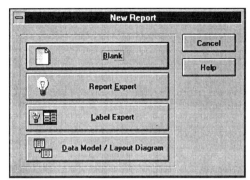

Figure 6 - 5

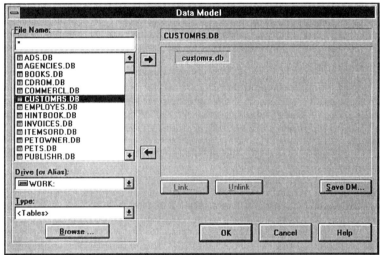

Figure 6 - 6

7. In the **Design Layout** dialog box (see Figure 6 - 7) make certain **Tabular** is the selection under **Style:**.

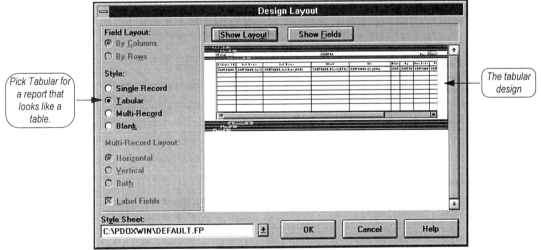

Figure 6 - 7

8. Click the **Show Fields** button at the top of the **Design Layout** dialog box to switch the left panel of the dialog box to the list of fields that will be included in the design (Figure 6 - 8).

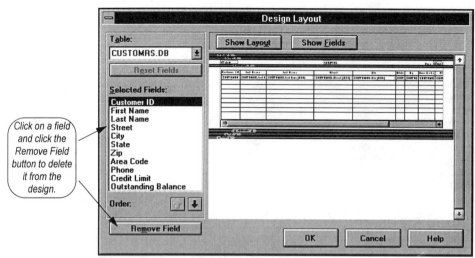

Figure 6 - 8

9. As we do not want the **Street**, **City**, **State**, or **Zip** fields, we will remove them from the design. In the list of **Selected Fields:**, click on **Street** and click the **Remove Field** button.

    Street will disappear from the list and from the tiny representation of the report design at the top right of the dialog box.

10. Click on **City** in the **Selected Fields:** list and click the **Remove Field** button.

11. Similarly, remove the **State** and **Zip** fields.

    *If you made a mistake in removing fields, click the **Reset Fields** button and begin at step 9 again.*

12. Click **OK**.

    *Paradox will assemble the report design and display it in the **Report Design** window (see Figure 6 - 9).*

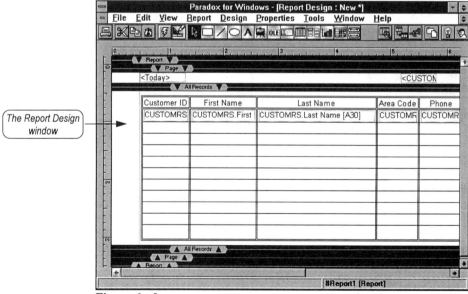

Figure 6 - 9

13. Maximize the **Report Design** window.

14. The fields we have selected will not fit on a single page width in portrait orientation. Therefore, choose **REPORT/Page Layout** and click on **Landscape** in the **Orientation:** section (see Figure 6 - 10) so that the report will be printed sideways across the width of the page. Click **OK**.

    Because we are switching to landscape we did not need to set the orientation prior to designing the report.

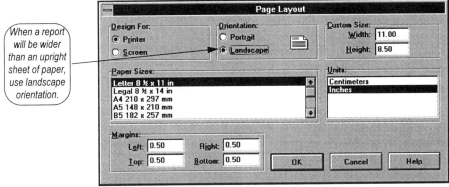

Figure 6 - 10

15. Pick **VIEW/Zoom/Fit Width** to scale the screen so the entire width of the design can be seen (see Figure 6 - 11).

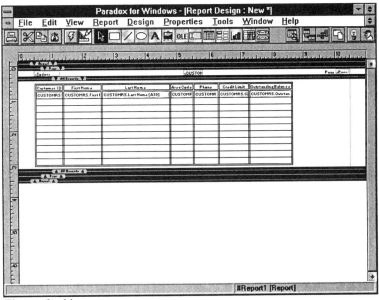

Figure 6 - 11

16. Run the report to see a preview of how it would actually print by clicking the **View Data** button on the toolbar.

    *The **Fit Width** setting is still in effect, so the full width of the report is scaled to fit on the screen (see Figure 6 - 12). It is too small to read the names, but excellent for seeing how the design fits on the overall page.*

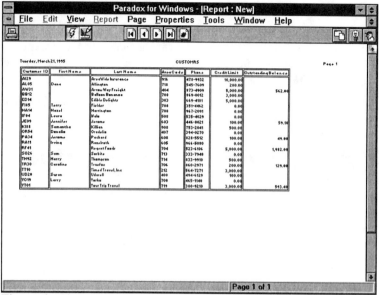

Figure 6 - 12

17. To be able to read the data, pick **VIEW/Zoom/100%** (see Figure 6 - 13).

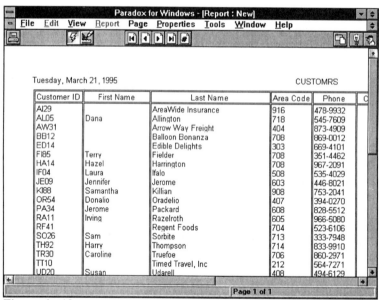

Figure 6 - 13

18. Click the right-pointing arrow at the right end of the bottom scroll bar several times to scroll to the right edge of the report so you can see the last column, **Outstanding Balance**.

    The outstanding balances are not yet sorted.

19. Return to the design by clicking the **Design** button ![Design button] on the toolbar.

SORTING THE RECORDS IN A REPORT

We need the report sorted by Outstanding Balance in descending order. To sort the records in a report, inspect the **All Records** band and pick Sort from its self-contained menu.

To sort a report:

- Inspect the All Records band.
- Pick Sort from the self-contained menu to open the **Sort Record Band** dialog box.
- Choose the fields by which to sort.
- Set the sort order for each field.
- Click **OK**.

SAVING A REPORT DESIGN

Even before the design is completed it is often a good idea to save your progress lest the power go off or the computer freeze and all of your work is lost. Always save a new design prior to printing as printing can sometimes cause problems.

- If you are on the preview screen, switch to the design screen.
- Pick **FILE/Save As**.
- Type the Filename of up to 8 characters. The extension **.RSL** will be added automatically.
- Click **OK**.

Activity 6.2: Sorting and Saving the Report

1. Click on either of the two **All Records** lines to select that section of the design.

   *Both **All Records** lines will be highlighted and they will be blue on a color screen.*

2. Position the mouse pointer on top of either of the **All Records** lines and click the **right** mouse button to inspect the section (see Figure 6 - 14).

   *If the self-contained menu does not say #Record_Band at the top, press **ESC** and try step 2 again. The mouse was not on top of the **All Records** band.*

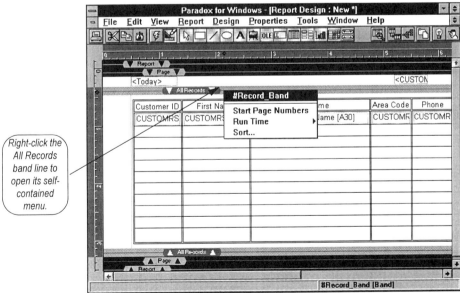

Figure 6 - 14

3. Click on **Sort** in the self-contained menu.

4. In the **Sort Record Band** dialog box, click on **CUSTOMRS.Outstanding Balances** in the **Fields:** list and click the right-pointing arrow button to transfer it to the **Sort Order:** list (see Figure 6 - 15).

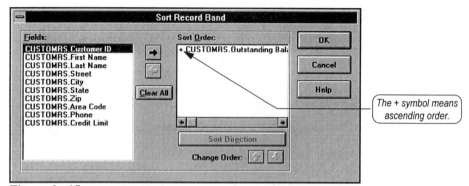

Figure 6 - 15

Notice the tiny plus sign in front of CUSTOMRS.Outstanding Balances in the Sort Order: list. That means the sort order should be ascending. We want descending order.

5. Click on the **+ CUSTOMRS.Outstanding Balances** in the **Sort Order:** list so it is highlighted and click the **Sort Direction** button at the bottom of the dialog box.

    A tiny minus sign will show instead of the plus sign to indicate descending order (see Figure 6 - 16).

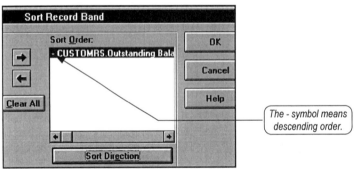

Figure 6 - 16

6. Click the **OK** button.

7. Preview the new order by clicking the **View Data** button. You will need to scroll to the right side of the report to see the **Outstanding Balance** column.

    The outstanding balances should now be sorted into descending order (see Figure 6 - 17).

8. Print the report by clicking the **Print** button on the toolbar. Since you know this design fits on a single page width, you do not need to pick **Create Horizontal Overflow Pages As Needed**. Click the **OK** button.

9. Return to the design by clicking the **Design** button.

10. Save this design by picking **FILE/Save As**, entering the name **BALANCES** in the **New File Name:** text box, and clicking **OK**.

11. Close the design with **FILE/Close**.

```
┌─────────────────────────────────────────────────────────────┐
│ ▬          Paradox for Windows - [Report : New]       ▼  ▲   │
│ □  File  Edit  View  Report  Page  Properties  Tools  Window  Help │
│ ┌──┐      ┌─┐┌─┐   ┌─┐┌─┐┌─┐┌─┐┌─┐                    ┌─┐┌─┐┌─┐│
│ │🖶│      │⚡││✓│   │◄││◄││►││►││↻│                    │  ││  ││  ││
│ └──┘      └─┘└─┘   └─┘└─┘└─┘└─┘└─┘                    └─┘└─┘└─┘│
│                                                               ▲ │
│                         CUSTOMRS                              │ │
│  ┌──────────────────┬──────────┬────────┬────────────┬─────────────────┐ │
│  │    Last Name     │Area Code │ Phone  │Credit Limit│Outstanding Balance│ │
│  ├──────────────────┼──────────┼────────┼────────────┼─────────────────┤ │
│  │ Regent Foods     │ 704      │523-6106│   5,000.00 │      1,982.00   │ │
│  │ Your Trip Travel │ 719      │380-9210│   3,000.00 │        593.40   │ │
│  │ Arrow Way Freight│ 404      │873-4909│   5,000.00 │        562.00   │ │
│  │ Truefoe          │ 706      │860-2971│     200.00 │        129.00   │ │
│  │ Jerome           │ 603      │446-8021│     100.00 │         59.10   │ │
│  │ Packard          │ 608      │828-5512│     100.00 │         49.00   │ │
│  │ AreaWide Insurance│ 916     │478-9932│  10,000.00 │                 │ │
│  │ Allington        │ 718      │545-7609│     200.00 │                 │ │
│  │ Balloon Bonanza  │ 708      │869-0012│   3,000.00 │                 │ │
│  │ Edible Delights  │ 303      │669-4101│   5,000.00 │                 │ │
│  │ Fielder          │ 708      │351-4462│       0.00 │                 │ │
│  │ Harrington       │ 708      │967-2091│       0.00 │                 │ │
│  │ Ifalo            │ 508      │535-4029│       0.00 │                 │ │
│  │ Killian          │ 908      │753-2041│     500.00 │                 │ │
│  │ Oradelio         │ 407      │394-0270│       0.00 │                 │ │
│  │ Razelroth        │ 605      │966-5080│       0.00 │                 │ │
│  │ Sorbite          │ 713      │333-7948│       0.00 │                 │ │
│  │ Thompson         │ 714      │833-9910│     500.00 │                 │ ▼ │
│  │ Timed Travel, Inc│ 212      │564-7271│   3,000.00 │                 │ │
│  └──────────────────┴──────────┴────────┴────────────┴─────────────────┘ │
│ ◄│                                     │                    │►  │
│                                          │ Page 1 of 1 │        │
└─────────────────────────────────────────────────────────────┘
```

Figure 6 - 17

CHANGING THE OBJECTS IN A REPORT DESIGN

Many changes can be made to a report design in *Paradox*. Changes are made in the **Report** window. The existing design is divided into the sections that were discussed earlier, namely the Report header, Page header, All Records section, Page footer, and Report footer. Each section is separated from the next by the bar containing its name that extends across the design window.

Each item included in the sections of the design is an *object*. The design can be changed by altering the objects and sections. Clicking on an object will produce *handles* at each corner and the middle of each side. They are the sizing handles (see Figure 6 - 18).

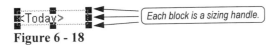

Figure 6 - 18

In a *Paradox* report design, there are usually objects within objects. For example, the overall table object (see Figure 6 - 19) in the **All Records** band contains the field objects and the column heading objects within it (see Figure 6 - 20). To select an outer object, click once on the object (see Figure 6 - 19). To select inner objects, click a second (or third, etc.) time on the specific object until the handles surround the specific item you need to work on (see Figure 6 - 20).

To select an object on a report design:

- Click on the object. If it is part of a larger, outer object, the outer object will be selected first. Click repeatedly on the inner object, until the specific inner item is selected.

To change an object on a report design:

- Select the object.

- Drag the appropriate sizing handle to change its size.

- Move the mouse pointer inside the frame line of the selected object, hold down the mouse button, and drag the object to a new position on the report.

- Once it is selected, click again within a label to get the vertical line cursor (insertion bar) and edit the label's characters by typing and deleting. To split the label onto two (or more) lines, press **SHIFT+ENTER** where you want the split to occur.

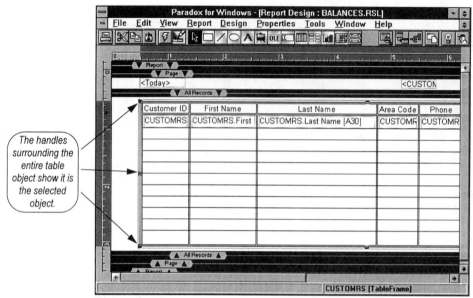

Figure 6 - 19

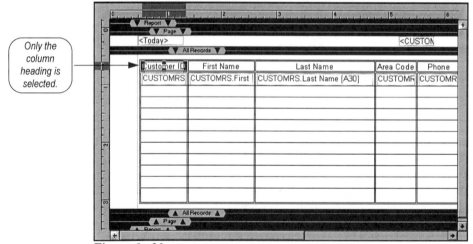

Figure 6 - 20

To change a column's width:

- Click on the table object to select the entire table in the **All Records** section. Handles will surround the entire table.

- Move the mouse pointer on top of the right frame line of the desired field name. The pointer will become a double-headed arrow (see Figure 6 - 24). Hold down the mouse button and drag the column width to the desired size. (Once the table object is selected, this is the same as the method we used on tables.)

Activity 6.3: Changing a Report Design

Management would like a report that shows which states the various customers come from. The report should list their State, Customer ID, First Name, Last Name, City, Zip Code, Credit Limit, and Outstanding Balance. (Ultimately, the report will be grouped by state in Activity 6.5.)

1. Pick **FILE/Printer Setup**.

2. Click the **Modify Printer Setup** button.

3. Click the **Portrait** option in the **Orientation** section and click **OK**.

4. Click **OK** in the **Printer Setup** dialog box.

    Because we will be using portrait orientation, we must set the direction prior to designing the report.

5. Click on the **Reports** category on the left side of the Project Viewer if it is not already selected.

6. Right-click (inspect) the **Reports** icon and pick **New** from the self-contained menu.

7. Click on the **Data Model/Layout Diagram** button in the **New Report** dialog box.

8. In the **Data Model** dialog box, click on **CUSTOMRS.DB** in the **File Name:** list and click the **OK** button.

9. In the **Design Layout** dialog box make certain **Tabular** is the selection under **Style:**.

10. Click the **Show Fields** button at the top of the **Design Layout** dialog box.

11. As we do not want the **Street**, **Area Code**, or **Phone** fields, we will remove them from the design. In the list of **Selected Fields:**, click on **Street** and click the **Remove Field** button.

12. Click on **Area Code** and click the **Remove Field** button.

13. Similarly, remove the **Phone** field. Do *not* click **OK** yet.

14. The **State** field should be the first column since the report will be grouped by state, so click on **State** in the **Selected Fields:** list and click the upward-pointing arrow button that is to the right of **Order:** four times to move **State** to the top of the list of fields (see Figure 6 - 21).

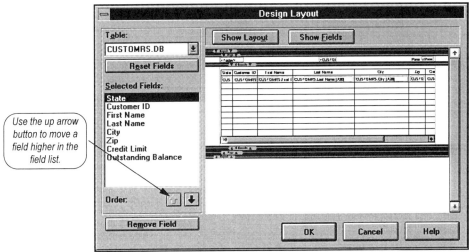

Figure 6 - 21

15. Click **OK**.

16. Maximize the **Report Design** window.

    Paradox will beep to indicate that some of the design will not fit on a single page width yet.
    Also, notice in Figure 6 - 22 that the states are not yet grouped (or even in order).

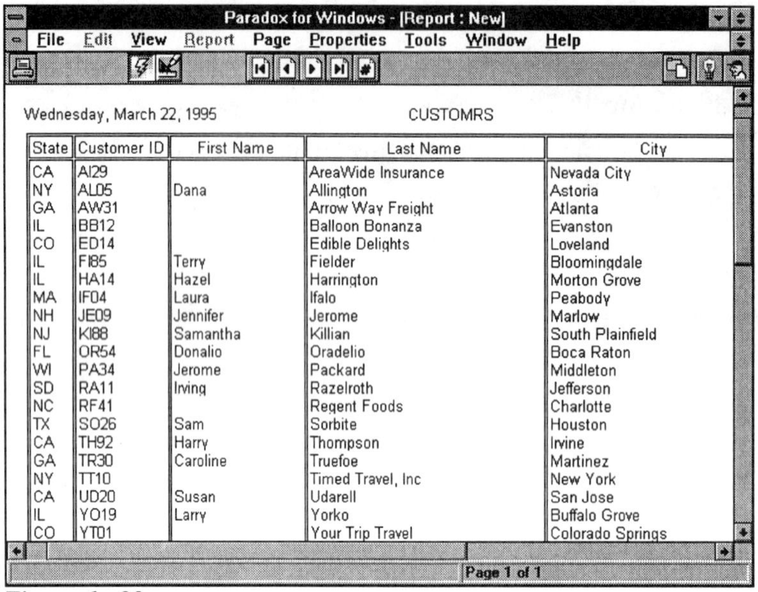

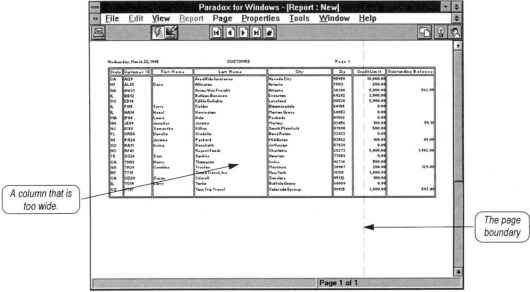

Figure 6 - 22

17. To see by how much the design is exceeding the page width, pick **VIEW/Zoom/Fit Width**.

    The dotted line on the right side of the report is the right margin (see Figure 6 - 23).
    Anything to the right of that line will not fit. Notice that several columns are wider than they
    need to be, so we will narrow some of the columns to try to get the report to fit.

A column that is too wide.

The page boundary

Figure 6 - 23

18. Click the **Design** button to return to the design.

19. To see the columns better, pick **VIEW/Zoom/100 %**.

20. Click the mouse on the table grid in the **All Records** section to select the table object.

21. Move the mouse pointer on top of the line at the right side of the column heading for **First Name** (see Figure 6 - 24). The pointer will become a double-headed arrow.

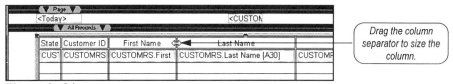

Figure 6 - 24

22. Hold down the mouse button and drag the frame line toward the left to narrow the column. Watch the dot on the horizontal ruler at the top of the design window. Drag the frame line to the 2 □ inch mark on the ruler.

    When you view the report, you will see that that width is about right. It was determined by trial and error.

23. Similarly, drag the **Last Name** frame line to the 4-inch mark on the ruler to narrow that column.

24. Drag the **City** frame line to the 5-inch mark to narrow that column.

25. Scroll to the right side of the design window and click on the **Outstanding Balance** column heading. Click a second time to specifically select just the column heading, as shown in Figure 6 - 25.

    Only the frame for the column heading should have selection handles around it.

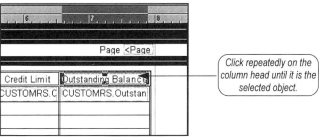

Figure 6 - 25

26. Click the mouse yet again between the two words *Outstanding* and *Balance* to place the vertical insertion bar there (see Figure 6 - 26).

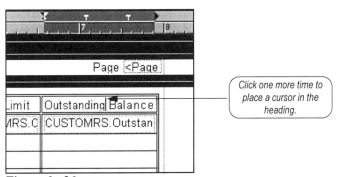

Figure 6 - 26

27. Press **SHIFT+ENTER** to split the heading onto two lines (see Figure 6 - 27).

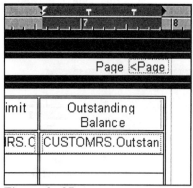

Figure 6 - 27

The column heading boxes will grow to two lines tall to accommodate the two-line title.

28. Click on any one of the band lines to change the selection away from the column heading, and then click on the table grid again to select the entire table. (An alternative method that some prefer is to press the **ESC** key once to switch the selection back to the entire heading, press **ESC** a second time to select the entire group of headings, and press **ESC** a third time to select the entire table.)

29. With the entire table grid selected, move the mouse pointer on top of the right frame line for the **Outstanding Balance** field, and drag it to 7½ on the ruler.

30. Click the **View Data** button on the toolbar to examine the current report.

31. After noticing the narrowed **First Name**, **Last Name**, and **City** columns, scroll to the right edge of the report to see the two line heading for the **Outstanding Balance** field.

32. Click the **Design** button to return to the design.

33. Save this design by picking **FILE/Save As**, entering the name **ByState** as the Report Name, and clicking **OK**.

34. Close the design with **FILE/Close**.

OPENING AN EXISTING REPORT DESIGN

Any report designs that are saved can be reopened and altered to satisfy current requirements.

To open an existing report design:

- Right-click (inspect) the name of the report in the list on the right side of the Project Viewer and pick **Design** from the self-contained menu. (Alternatively, choose **FILE/Open/Report** in the main menu or click the **Open Report** button on the toolbar, click on the report name in the **File Name:** list, pick **Design** from the **Open Mode:** options, and click **OK**.)

To remove objects from a report design:

- Click on the object and press **DELETE**.

To add a label or title to a report design:

- Click on the **Text Tool** button, move the mouse pointer to the desired place for the upper left corner of the label on the report design, and drag the mouse to size the new object.

- Type the desired text and press **ESC**.

To change the size of a section:

- Select the section by clicking on its line. That line (and the other line in the pair) will be highlighted.

- When you move the mouse pointer on top of the line you will get a double-headed arrow. For lines above the **All Records** band, the double-headed arrow appears when the mouse pointer is on the top half of the band line. Lines below the **All Records** band will show the double-headed arrow when the mouse pointer is on the bottom half of the band line. Hold down the mouse button and drag the line.

- It is crucial to realize that, no matter which line you drag, you can only change the size of the currently selected section. Therefore, to increase the space above any objects in a band that is above the **All Records** band, move onto the top half of the band line and drag it upward. To increase the space below any objects in a section that is above the **All Records** band, move onto the top half of the next lower band line and drag it downward. Reverse the direction of dragging to decrease the section's size.

- For a section below the **All Records** band, move onto the bottom half of the band line and drag it downward to increase the space below any objects in the section. To increase the space above any objects in a section that is below the **All Records** band, move onto the bottom half of the next higher band and drag it upward. Reverse the direction of dragging to decrease its size.

- You cannot make a section smaller than the objects in that section.

To add a new label to a report design:

- View the section of the design where you wish to add the label.

- Click the **Text Tool** button ![A] on the toolbar.

- Move the mouse pointer to the position for the upper left corner of the new object.

- Hold down the left mouse button and drag out the size of the box.

- Type the label.

- Press the **ESC** key.

Activity 6.4: Opening the Existing Report Design

We need to delete the table name, **CUSTOMR.DB**, from the page header and add the report title **CUSTOMERS BY STATE** in the report header.

1. Right-click (inspect) the name **BYSTATE.RSL** in the list.

2. Click on **Design** in the self-contained menu (see Figure 6 - 28).

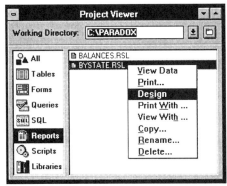

Figure 6 - 28

3. Press **CTRL+HOME** to jump to the left edge of the design.

4. In the Page header, click on the **<CUSTOMRS.DB>** object (see Figure 6 - 29).

   Probably only the first half of the table name actually shows in the box. Handles will appear on the object (see Figure 6 - 29).

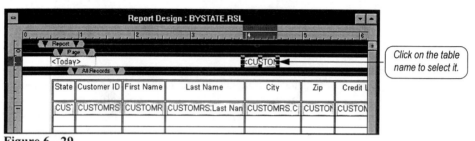

Figure 6 - 29

5. Press the **DELETE** key.

   The object will disappear from the design.

6. Click the **View Data** button on the toolbar and compare the current design to Figure 6 - 22 to see that the table name that was in the middle of the page header above the **City** field is gone.

7. Click the **Design** button to return to the design.

8. Press **HOME** to jump to the very top of the design.

9. Click the mouse on the **Report** band to select that section.

10. To open the **Report** section so there is room for a title, move the mouse cursor onto the top half of the **Page** band line. When the mouse cursor is a double up-and-down arrow, hold down the mouse button and drag that line down about half an inch as measured on the ruler at the left side of the screen (see Figure 6 - 30).

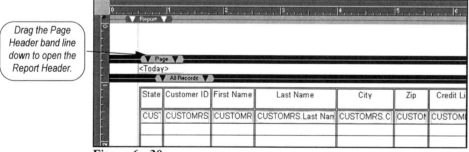

Figure 6 - 30

11. As the object we will place on the design needs to stretch across the full width of the design, pick **VIEW/Zoom/Fit Width**.

12. Click the **Text Tool** button on the toolbar.

    The mouse cursor will become a cross with a large A.

13. Move the cross to the left margin at about 1/8 inch on the vertical ruler (see Figure 6 - 31).

14. Hold down the mouse button and drag the dotted-lined box all the way across the design to the right margin and down to about 3/8 inch on the vertical ruler (see Figure 6 - 32). Release the mouse button.

    By making the text box the full report width it will be easy to center the title.

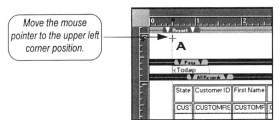

Move the mouse pointer to the upper left corner position.

Figure 6 - 31

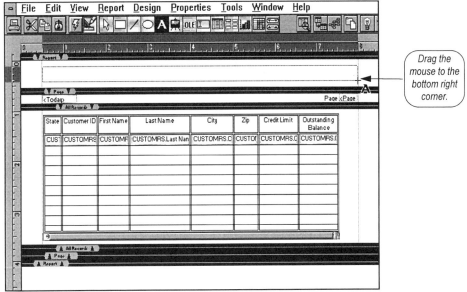

Drag the mouse to the bottom right corner.

Figure 6 - 32

15. The cursor is blinking in the new text box. Type the title: **CUSTOMERS BY STATE**

16. Press the **ESC** key to conclude typing and switch the selection back to the entire text box.

17. Position the mouse cursor on top of the text box and right-click (inspect) the title (Figure 6 - 33).

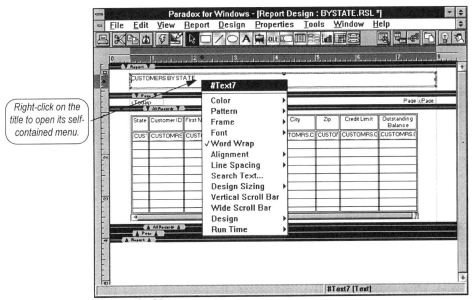

Right-click on the title to open its self-contained menu.

Figure 6 - 33

18. Pick **Alignment** in the self-contained menu.

19. Click on **Center** to center the title.

20. Inspect the title again and pick **Font/Size/16**.

21. Inspect the title a third time and pick **Font/Style/Bold**.

22. Click the **View Data** button on the toolbar to see the new title (see Figure 6 - 34).

CUSTOMERS BY STATE

Thursday, March 23, 1995   Page 1

State	Customer ID	First Name	Last Name	City	Zip	Credit Limit	Outstanding Balance
CA	AI29		AreaWide Insurance	Nevada City	95959	10,000.00	
NY	AL05	Dana	Allington	Astoria	11103	200.00	
GA	AW31		Arrow Way Freight	Atlanta	30308	5,000.00	562.00
IL	BB12		Balloon Bonanza	Evanston	60202	3,000.00	
CO	ED14		Edible Delights	Loveland	80538	5,000.00	
IL	FI85	Terry	Fielder	Bloomingdale	60108	0.00	
IL	HA14	Hazel	Harrington	Morton Grove	60053	0.00	
MA	IF04	Laura	Ifalo	Peabody	01960	0.00	
NH	JE09	Jennifer	Jerome	Marlow	03456	100.00	59.10
NJ	KI88	Samantha	Killian	South Plainfield	07090	500.00	
FL	OR54	Donalio	Oradelio	Boca Raton	33433	0.00	
VI	PA34	Jerome	Packard	Middleton	53562	100.00	49.00
SD	RA11	Irving	Razelroth	Jefferson	57038	0.00	
NC	RF41		Regent Foods	Charlotte	28273	5,000.00	1,982.00
TX	SO26	Sam	Sorbite	Houston	77058	0.00	
CA	TH92	Harry	Thompson	Irvine	92714	500.00	
GA	TR30	Caroline	Truefoe	Martinez	30907	200.00	129.00
NY	TT10		Timed Travel, Inc	New York	10118	3,000.00	
CA	UD20	Susan	Udarell	San Jose	95112	100.00	
IL	YO19	Larry	Yorko	Buffalo Grove	60089	0.00	
CO	YT01		Your Trip Travel	Colorado Spring	80915	3,000.00	593.40

Figure 6 - 34

23. Click the **Design** button to return to the design.

24. Save the modified design with **FILE/Save**.

25. Do *not* close the report design.

USING GROUPING IN A REPORT

Often a report will need to be *grouped* on the entries in one or more fields. *Grouped* means that all the records with one particular value in a field are assembled into a cluster, and each additional value in that field is placed in a separate gathering. Each group is then separated from the next and given a group header section to introduce the group and a group footer section to conclude the group. The header would typically contain the name of the group and the footer often holds subtotals for the group.

Adding grouping to a report design:

- Design a new report or open an existing report design.
- In the **Report** window pick **REPORT/Add Band**.
- In the **Define Group** dialog box, choose either to group by the values in a field or by a set number of records. If you pick grouping by values, you can group either by each different value or by ranges of values.
- The grouping will place a group header above the **All Records** section and a group footer below the **All Records** section.

Activity 6.5: Adding a Grouping Band

Our report still needs to be grouped by state.

1. The **BYSTATE.RSL** report design should be open.

2. Maximize the **Report Design** window.

3. Choose **VIEW/Zoom/Fit Height**.

4. Pick **REPORT/Add Band**.

5. In the **Define Group** dialog box (see Figure 6 - 35), make certain **Group By Field Value** is selected, click on **State** in the **Field:** list, and click the **OK** button.

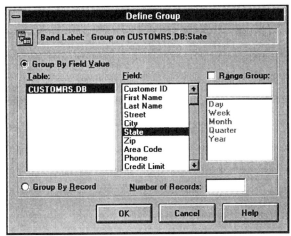

Figure 6 - 35

*Paradox will insert a grouping band with a header above and a footer below the **All Records** section. The band is named **Group on CUSTOMRS.DB.State** (see Figure 6 - 36). The grouping field, **State**, is automatically placed in the group header to introduce each group. The footer is empty, but would be where subtotals should be placed.*

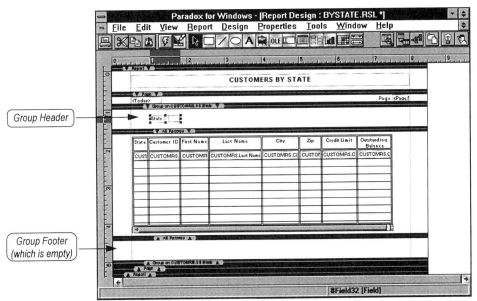

Figure 6 - 36

6. Choose **VIEW/Zoom/Fit Width** to see the group header better.

7. Click the **View Data** button on the toolbar to see the grouped report (see Figure 6 - 37).

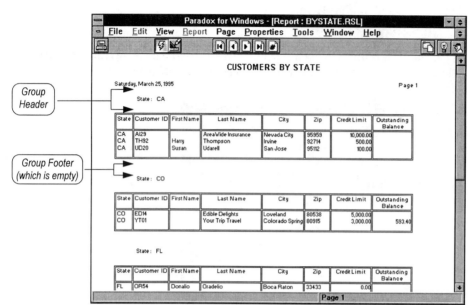

Figure 6 - 37

Notice that not only are the listings grouped by state, but the states are also sorted into order.

8. Click the **Design** button to return to the design.

9. Save the modified design with **FILE/Save**. Do *not* close the design window.

SUBTOTALS

Reports that contain groups often need to include calculations in the group footer to summarize one or more numerical fields. In our report of customers by state, we will subtotal their **Outstanding Balance** field to see what the total of all of the balances for any given state is.

Adding subtotals to the design:

*   With the report design open, click the **Field Tool** ▦ on the toolbar.

*   Move to the position in the group footer where you want the upper left corner of the subtotal to be and hold down the mouse button. Make certain you are far enough to the left to allow the full length of the field you are adding since *Paradox* will automatically size the length and height of the frame if it has enough room.

*   Drag out the approximate size of the box you want for the subtotal. The size is not critical since *Paradox* will automatically size the frame when you first define its contents.

*   Inspect the field and pick **Define Field** from the self-contained menu.

*   Choose the **...** choice at the very top of the submenu to open the Define Field Object dialog box.

*   Open the list of fields with the drop-down arrow at the right edge of the table name and pick the field that will be summarized.

- With the field name highlighted (the list does not close immediately), open the list of summary operations by clicking the drop-down arrow next to **Summary:**.

- Pick the desired summary calculation.

- Click the **OK** button.

- Click within the label for the subtotal and edit the characters to whatever label you desire.

- Drag the entire object to the desired final position on the design.

Activity 6.6: Adding Subtotals

It would be helpful to management if the sum of the **Outstanding Balance** field for each state was included on the report.

1. The **BYSTATE.RSL** report design should be open.

2. Choose **VIEW/Zoom/100 %** to see the design better.

3. Scroll down to the **Group on CUSTOMRS.DB.State** footer below the **All Records** section.

4. Scroll to the right so you can see the right edge of the table object (see Figure 6 - 38).

5. Click the **Field Tool** button on the toolbar.

   *The mouse cursor becomes a cross together with the same symbol as the **Field Tool** button.*

6. Move the mouse pointer to about 4¾ inches on the horizontal ruler and about 1/8 inch below the **All Records** band line (see Figure 6 - 38).

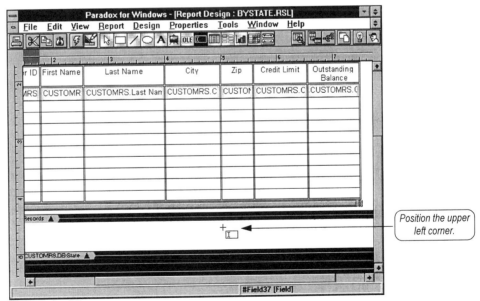

Figure 6 - 38

7. Hold down the mouse button and drag the mouse to the right to about 7½ inches on the horizontal ruler (watch the shadow on the ruler) and about ¼ inch lower on the vertical ruler (see Figure 6 - 39). Release the mouse button.

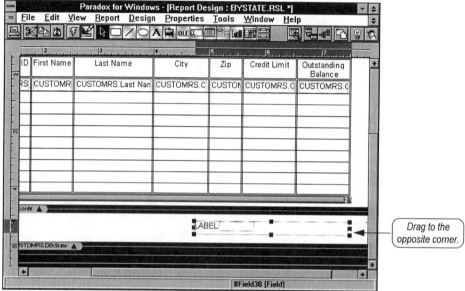

Figure 6 - 39

8. Move the mouse pointer inside the new object and inspect (right-click) it. In the self-contained menu that opens, pick **Define Field**.

9. At the very top of the submenu click on the **...** that is already highlighted (see Figure 6 - 40).

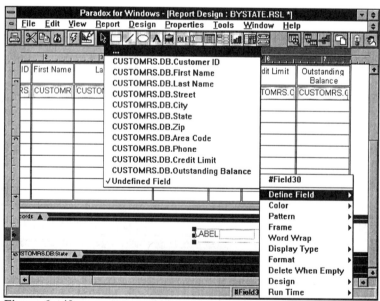

Figure 6 - 40

*The **Define Field** dialog box opens with the table name and a drop-down arrow near the top left (see Figure 6 - 41). The description in the top left panel says **Undefined Field** since we have not yet chosen what this frame will contain.*

10. Click on the drop-down arrow next to the table name to open the list of fields (see Figure 6 - 42).

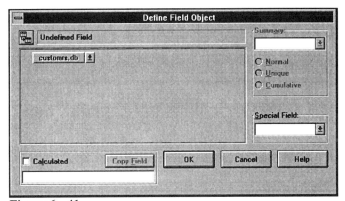

Figure 6 - 41

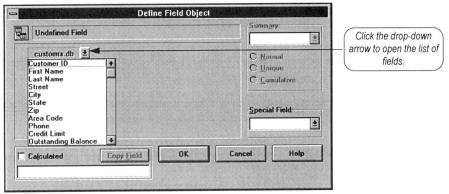

Figure 6 - 42

11. Click on **Outstanding Balance** at the bottom of the list.

    The list will remain open temporarily and the description in the top left panel should now say **CUSTOMRS.Outstanding Balance**.

12. In the **Summary:** section click on the drop-down arrow to open the list of summary calculations and click on **Sum** (see Figure 6 - 43).

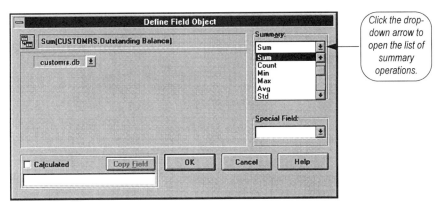

Figure 6 - 43

13. Click the **OK** button.

    The field is now defined so that it will calculate the subtotals, and the label is automatically changed to **Sum(Outstanding Balance):** *(see Figure 6 - 44).*

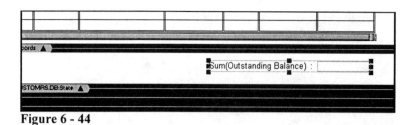

Figure 6 - 44

14. To change the subtotal's label to say **Total Balance for State,** click on the word
    Outstanding to get into the label portion of the field object (see Figure 6 - 45).

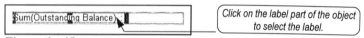

Click on the label part of the object
to select the label.

Figure 6 - 45

15. Click again on the word **Outstanding** to get the insertion bar, remove the old label with the
    BACKSPACE and/or **DELETE** keys, and type the new label **Total Balance for State.**
    Press the **ESC** key when finished typing.

16. Press the **ESC** key again to switch the selection to the overall field (see Figure 6 - 46).

Figure 6 - 46

17. Click the **View Data** button on the toolbar to see the grouped report with subtotals (see
    Figure 6 - 58).

18. Choose **VIEW/Zoom/Fit Width.**

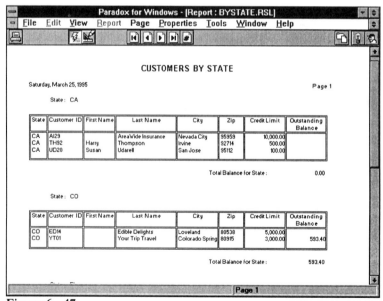

Figure 6 - 47

19. Click the **Next Page** button on the toolbar to jump to the second page.

20. Click the **Last Page** button on the toolbar to jump to the last page.

21. Click the **Design** button to return to the design.

22. Save the modified design with **FILE/Save**.

23. Print the report by clicking the **Print** button on the toolbar. Since you know the design fits on a single page width, you do not need to pick **Create Horizontal Overflow Pages As Needed**. Click the **OK** button.

24. Close all windows with **WINDOW/Close All**.

MULTI-TABLE REPORTS

Two or more tables can be included on the same report. The main table is called the *master table*; the secondary table is the *detail table*. The two tables must be related by a field that is common to both tables. That common field is the basis of the link or relationship between the pair of tables. Once there is such a link, *Paradox* will display the fields from the matching records from both tables simultaneously.

Remembering the discussion of relational tables in Lesson 3, we will create a report with data from both the **EMPLOYES.DB** and the **INVOICES.DB** tables. Both tables contain the linking field **Employee ID**. We will include the **First Name** and **Last Name** from the **EMPLOYES.DB** table and the **Invoice #**, **Date of Sale**, and **Customer ID** from **INVOICES.DB** (see Figure 6 - 48). The requirements for multi-table reports are the same as for multi-table forms:

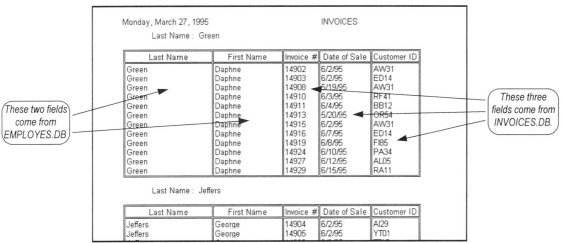

Figure 6 - 48

- The detail table must have either a primary index (key field) or a secondary index on the common field.

- The field types and sizes of the common fields must be identical in the two tables.

We will use the **Data Model/Layout Diagram** method for our multi-table report.

To create a multi-table report:

- Make certain the detail table has an index on the common field. If it does not, create a primary index (key field) or secondary index on that field.

- Pick **FILE/New/Report**. Alternatively, right-click the **Open Report** toolbar button or right-click the **Reports** icon in the Project Viewer and pick **New** from the self-contained menu.

- Click the **Data Model/Layout Diagram** button.

- Click on the master table name and click the arrow button to place it in the data model.

- Click on the detail table name.

- Drag from the master table to the detail table to begin the linking.

- In the **Define Link** dialog box pick the common field for the master table. Normally *Paradox* will match it by choosing the same field from the detail table, but, if not, pick the common field in the detail table.

- Click **OK**.

- Choose the design style, fields, and order of fields as in the previous report designs.

- Preview the report, make any desired modifications, and save the design.

Activity 6.7: A Multi-table Report

Management would like a report showing which invoices were sold by which employees. Since the invoice table only contains the Employee ID, but the report needs the names of the employees, we must link the **EMPLOYES.DB** table to **INVOICES.DB** to get the names. This link is possible because the **EMPLOYES.DB** (the detail table) table has the **Employee ID** field defined as a key field.

1. Click the **Open Project Viewer** button.

2. Click on the **Reports** category on the left side of the Project Viewer if it is not already selected.

3. Right-click (inspect) the **Reports** icon and pick **New** from the self-contained menu.

4. Click on the **Data Model/Layout Diagram** button in the **New Report** dialog box.

5. In the **Data Model** dialog box, click on **INVOICES.DB** in the **File Name:** list and click the rightward pointing arrow button.

   The rightward pointing arrow button does not appear to accomplish anything extra, but clicking it is required. Otherwise, the next table name you click will replace the current name, instead of being added to the data model.

6. Click on **EMPLOYES.DB** in the **File Name:** list to include that in the model (Figure 6 - 49).

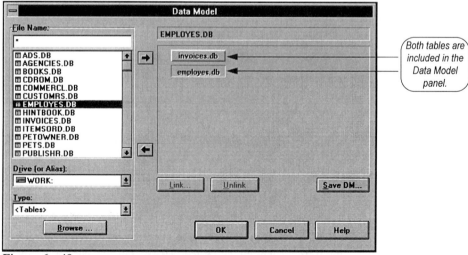

Figure 6 - 49

7. Move the mouse pointer on top of the embossed box for the **invoices.db** table. The mouse pointer will become an arrow with two tiny tables being connected by a bent arrow. Hold down the mouse button and drag down to the **employes.db** box immediately below it. When you release the mouse button, the **Define Link** dialog box will open (see Figure 6 - 50).

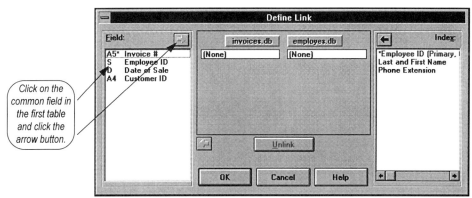

Figure 6 - 50

8. In the **Field:** list on the left side of the **Define Link** dialog box, click on **S Employee ID** and click the rightward-pointing arrow button.

   *Paradox will fill in both **Employee ID** field names and connect the two tables with an arrow (see Figure 6 - 51).*

   *The S in front of Employee ID signifies that it is a field of type **Short**.*

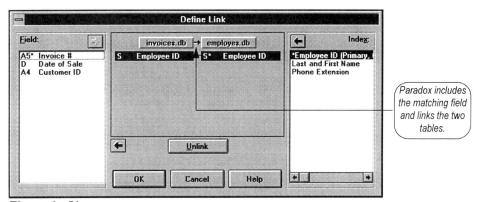

Figure 6 - 51

9. Click the **OK** button in the **Define Link** dialog box.

   *Paradox will connect the two tables with an arrow in the **Data Model** dialog box (see Figure 6 - 52).*

10. Click the **OK** button in the **Data Model** dialog box.

11. In the **Design Layout** dialog box make certain **Tabular** is the selection under **Style:**.

12. Click the **Show Fields** button at the top of the **Design Layout** dialog box.

    *Since two tables are involved, each field name is preceded by the table name in the **Selected Field:** list.*

13. As we do not want the **INVOICES.Employee ID** field, click on that field name in the **Selected Fields:** list and click the **Remove Field** button.

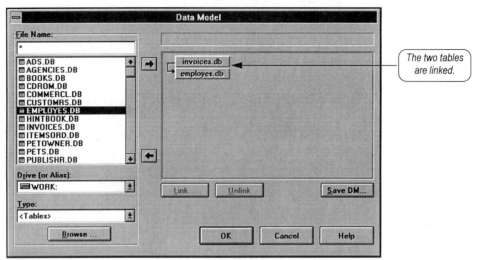

Figure 6 - 52

14. We also do not want the **EMPLOYES.Date Hired** field, so click on its name and click the **Remove Field** button.

15. Similarly, remove the **EMPLOYES.Salary**, **EMPLOYES.Commission**, **EMPLOYES.Extension**, and **EMPLOYES.Notes** fields. Do *not* click **OK** yet.

16. The **EMPLOYES.Last Name** field should be the first column, so click on that field name in the **Selected Fields:** list and click the **upward pointing arrow** button that is to the right of **Order:** four times to move **EMPLOYES.Last Name** to the top of the list of fields.

17. Similarly, use the arrow button to move **EMPLOYES.First Name** to the second position (see Figure 6 - 53).

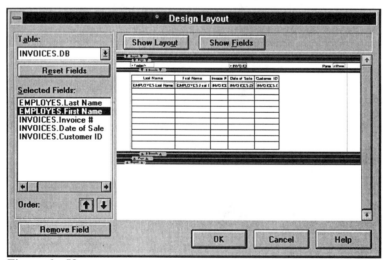

Figure 6 - 53

18. Click the **OK** button in the **Design Layout** dialog box.

19. To group by the **Last Name** field, pick **REPORT/Add Band**.

20. In the **Define Group** dialog box, make certain that **Group By Field Value** is the selected option, click on **EMPLOYES.DB** in the **Table:** list, click on **Last Name** in the **Field:** list (see Figure 6 - 54), and click **OK**.

21. Click the **View Data** button to see the report (see Figure 6 - 48).

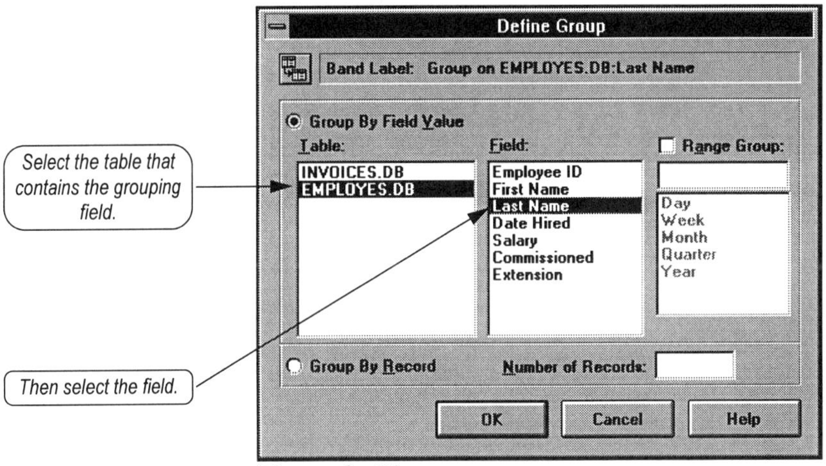

Select the table that contains the grouping field.

Then select the field.

Figure 6 - 54

22. Click the **Design** button to return to the design.

23. Save the multi-table design with **FILE/Save As**.

24. Enter the name **EMP-INV** and click the **OK** button.

25. Close all windows with **WINDOW/Close All**.

THE *LABEL EXPERT*

Another method for designing reports is to use the *Report Expert* or the *Label Expert*. Each asks a sequence of questions as to how you want the design to look, and then produces the report design for you, similar to the **Data Model/Layout Diagram** method. Once they have finished producing the report design, you may, of course, alter the design in any way desired in the **Report** window.

While the *Report Expert* is of questionable value for a tabular design because it does not do much more than the **Data Model/Layout Diagram** method and because of some of the curious decisions it makes about the sizes and positions of fields, the *Label Expert* makes the designing of sheets of labels vastly easier than the **Data Model/Layout Diagram** method.

To design labels with the *Label Expert*:

- Right-click (inspect) the **Reports** icon at the left side of the Project Viewer or the **Open Report** button on the toolbar and click on **New** in the self-contained menu. Alternatively, pick **FILE/New/Report** in the menu.

- Click the **Label Expert** button to have the *Expert* do most of the work for you.

- In Step 1 of 5, pick the category of the labels you are designing (address labels, diskette labels, name badges, etc.) and the specific type of labels you will be using.

- From the **Table Name:** list in Step 2 of 5 pick the table that is the basis for the labels.

- Choose the font, size, and any style options in Step 3 of 5.

- Pick whether the order of the labels should progress from left to right across the page or down the page like newspaper columns.

- Place the fields you need from the list the *Expert* presents in Step 5 of 5 into the label design panel by clicking on the appropriate label line, clicking the field name, and clicking the **Place Field on Label** button.

- Directly type any spaces, punctuation, or words that are needed into the label design panel.

- Click the **lightning bolt (Run)** button and the *Expert* will create the design.

Activity 6.8: Mailing Labels

A mailing will be sent to all customers, so we need a set of mailing labels. These will be regular mailing labels with First and Last Name on the top line, Street on the second line, and City-State-Zip on the third line. They should be sorted into zip code order, then by last name within each zip code.

1. Click the **Open Project Viewer** button.

2. Right-click (inspect) the **Reports** icon and pick **New** from the self-contained menu.

3. Click on the **Label Expert** button in the **New Report** dialog box.

4. Step 1 of the *Label Expert* asks for the type of label stock you will be using (Figure 6 - 55). Make certain the selection in the **Label Categories:** list is **Avery Address Labels**.

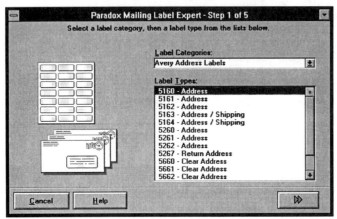

Figure 6 - 55

5. The most common pages of address labels for a laser printer are Avery 5160, the default choice. Click on **5160 - Address**, then click the double-arrowhead (>>) button.

6. In the **Table Name:** list, click on **CUSTOMRS.DB** (see Figure 6 - 56) and click the >> button.

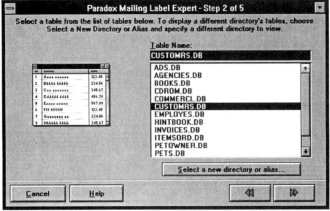

Figure 6 - 56

7. In the **Font:** list pick **Arial**, for **Size:** choose **10**, and do *not* check any of the options (see Figure 6 - 57). Click the >> button.

8. Pick **Left To Right** (row by row) as the print order for the labels (see Figure 6 - 58). Click the >> button.

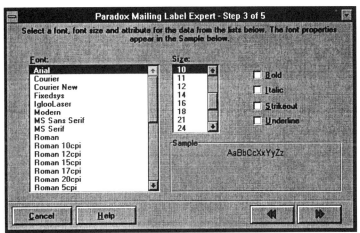

Figure 6 - 57

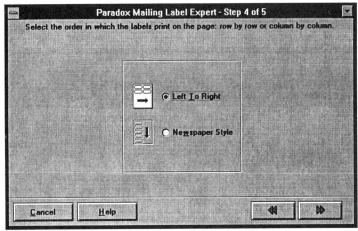

Figure 6 - 58

9. Click on line **1** in the **Example of Label Layout:** box to highlight that line.

10. In the **Fields:** list click on **First Name**. Then click the **Place Field on Label**>> button to copy the field name to the current line of the **Example of Label Layout:** box.

    The field name will be surrounded by curly braces. The highlight automatically moves to **Last Name** *(see Figure 6 - 59).*

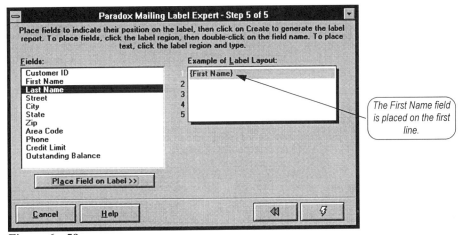

Figure 6 - 59

11. Press the **SPACEBAR** to put a space after the {**First Name**} field.

12. With the highlight on **Last Name** in the **Fields:** list, click the **Place Field on Label**>> button to copy it to the end of the first line of the **Example of Label Layout:** box.

13. The first line is finished. To move to line 2, either click the mouse on line **2** or press the **DOWN ARROW**. (If you press the **DOWN ARROW**, it may require two presses.)

14. The highlight is probably already on **Street**, but if it is not, click on **Street** in the **Fields:** list. When **Street** is highlighted, click the **Place Field on Label**>> button to copy it to the second line of the **Example of Label Layout:** box.

15. The second line is finished. To move to line 3, either click the mouse on line **3** or press the **DOWN ARROW**.

16. With the highlight on **City**, click the **Place Field on Label**>> button to copy it to the beginning of the third line of the **Example of Label Layout:** box.

17. Type a **comma** (,) and a **space** to follow the name of the city on the third line.

18. With the highlight on **State**, click the **Place Field on Label**>> button to copy it to the **Example of Label Layout:** box.

19. Type two **spaces** to follow the name of the state on the third line.

20. With the highlight on **Zip**, click the **Place Field on Label**>> button to copy it to the end of the third line of the **Example of Label Layout:** box (see Figure 6 - 60).

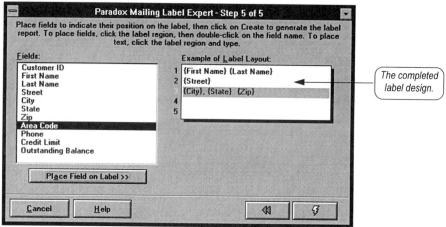

Figure 6 - 60

21. That completes the fields for the mailing labels, so click the **lightning bolt** button.

    The Expert puts the design together. You will see the message stating that it may take a few moments to complete the design and the multiple records will appear on the design screen in the background. Eventually, an alert box asking about running the report or remaining on the design screen will appear (see Figure 6 - 61).

Figure 6 - 61

22. Click the **Yes** button to run (preview) the labels (see Figure 6 - 62).

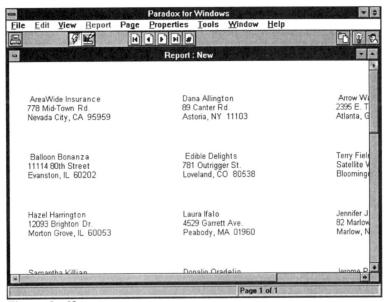

Figure 6 - 62

The labels are not yet in Zip code order, but are three across the page.

23. Pick **VIEW/Zoom/Best Fit** to see the overall page.

24. Switch to the design by clicking the **Design** button on the toolbar.

25. Pick **VIEW/Zoom/100%** to see the individual label design.

26. To sort the labels by the **Zip** field, right-click (inspect) the **All Records** band line or the margin just to the left of the label design (see Figure 6 - 63).

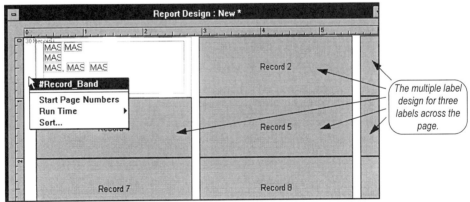

Figure 6 - 63

27. Click on **Sort** in the self-contained menu.

28. In the **Fields:** list of the **Sort Record Band** dialog box, click on **MASTER.Zip** and click the right-pointing arrow button to copy the field to the **Sort Order:** list.

29. Also click on **MASTER.Last Name** in the **Fields:** list. Click the **right pointing arrow** button to copy that field to the **Sort Order:** list as the second most important field by which to sort.

*Both fields should have plus signs in front of their name in the **Sort Order:** list for ascending order (see Figure 6 - 64).*

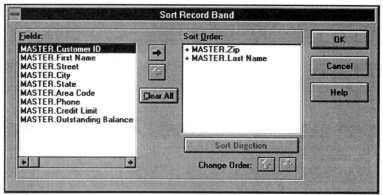

Figure 6 - 64

30. Click the **OK** button to apply the sort order.

31. Click the **View Data** button to see the resulting sort.

    The zip codes should be in order and if there were two of the same zip codes, the last names would be in order (see Figure 6 - 65).

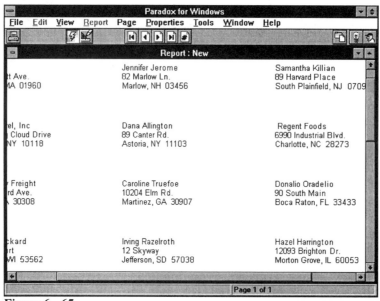

Figure 6 - 65

32. Switch to the design by clicking the **Design** button on the toolbar.

33. Save this design by picking **FILE/Save As**, entering the name **CUSTLABL** in the **New File Name:** text box, and clicking **OK**.

34. Print the labels by clicking the **Print** button on the toolbar. You do not need to select **Create Horizontal Overflow Page As Needed** since the labels were designed to fit a single page width. Click the **OK** button.

35. Close the design with **FILE/Close**.

SUMMARY

In this lesson we have produced three different reports based on the data in the **CUSTOMRS.DB** table and one from the combined data in **INVOICES.DB** and **EMPLOYES.DB**. The first tabular report contained the customer listings sorted in descending order of outstanding balances. The second design included grouping by state and subtotals. We changed the column widths to fit the design onto a single page width and removed the unwanted table name object. We also added a report title and changed its formatting (appearance). We then linked two related tables in a report design. The fourth and final design was for sheets of mailing labels, which were sorted by zip code and last name.

KEY TERMS

All Records section	*Label Expert*	Portrait orientation
Footer	Landscape orientation	*Report Expert*
Grouping	Mailing label report	Single-record report
Handle	Multi-record report	Tabular report
Header	Object	

INDEPENDENT PROJECTS

Independent Project 6.1: The School Newspaper

This Independent Project continues working with the Newspaper Ad database from Independent Project 5.1. The newspaper's business manager requires a report of the sales of ads grouped by the salesperson. The **Salesperson ID**, **Ad Number**, **Price**, **Purchased By**, and **Date Paid** fields are needed. Subtotals should be included for the **Price** field. The table name, **ADS.DB**, should be deleted from the page header and the report title **ADS SOLD PER PERSON** should be added to the report header.

The top portion of the finished report should resemble Figure 6 - 66.

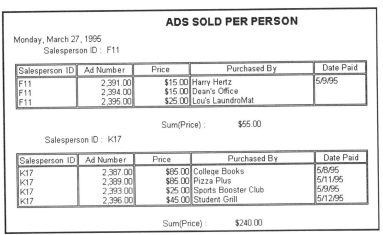

Figure 6 - 66

1. Run *Paradox*.

2. Click the **Paradox** button to close the Welcome to Paradox screen if it is open.

3. Maximize the *Paradox* window if it does not already cover the entire screen.

4. Click the **Open Project Viewer** button on the toolbar if it is not already open. Check that you are in the correct working directory.

5. Right-click on the **Reports** icon on the left side of the Project Viewer.

6. Click **New** in the self-contained menu to start a new report.

7. Click the **Data Model/Layout Diagram** button.

8. Click on the name **ADS.DB** in the list of tables and click the **OK** button.

9. As this will be a tabular report, make certain **Tabular** is the selection under **Style:**.

10. Click the **Show Fields** button.

11. In the **Selected Fields:** list, click on **Size** and click the **Remove Field** button.

12. Similarly, click on **Issue Date** and click the **Remove Field** button.

13. To move **Salesperson ID** to the top of the list so it will be in the first column in the report, click on **Salesperson ID** in the **Selected Fields:** list and click the **upward-pointing arrow** button four times.

14. To move **Purchased By** from the third position to the fourth position in the list, click on **Purchased By** and click the **downward-pointing arrow** button once.

15. Click **OK**.

16. To group by **Salesperson ID**, pick **REPORT/Add Band**. Make certain **Group By Field Value** is the chosen option and click on **Salesperson ID** in the **Field:** list. Click **OK**.

17. Click the **View Data** button on the toolbar to see the report.

18. Pick **VIEW/Zoom/Fit Width** to see the whole width of the report.

19. Return to the design with the **Design** button.

20. To add the subtotal for the **Price** field, click the **Field Tool** button on the toolbar and move the mouse pointer into the **Group on ADS.DB.Salesperson ID** footer. At about the 3-inch mark on the top ruler, hold down the mouse button and drag out the box to about the 5-inch mark. Release the mouse button to place the field.

21. Inspect the new field and choose **Define Field** in the self-contained menu.

22. Pick **...** in the submenu.

23. In the **Define Field Object** dialog box that opens, click on the drop-down arrow to the right of the table name (**ads.db**) to open the list of fields and click on **Price**.

24. In the **Summary:** section, click on the drop-down arrow to open the list of summary calculations and pick **Sum**.

25. Click **OK**.

26. Pick **VIEW/Zoom/100 %**.

27. Click on the table name (**<ADS>**) at the center of the **Page** header section. When it shows selection handles, press the **DELETE** key to remove it.

28. Click on the **Report** header band line to highlight (select) it.

29. With the **Report** header band line highlighted, move the mouse pointer onto the top half of the **Page** header band line and, when the double-headed arrow shows, drag it down about ½ inch on the side ruler.

30. Pick **VIEW/Zoom/Fit Width**.

31. Click on the **Text Tool** on the toolbar, move the mouse pointer to the dotted line at the left margin, hold down the mouse button, and drag a box all the way across to the right margin. The frame should be about ☐ inch tall.

32. Type **ADS SOLD PER PERSON** as the title. Press the **ESC** key to switch back to the entire field being selected.

33. Inspect the title and choose **Alignment/Center**.

34. Inspect the title again and choose **Font/Size/14**.

35. Inspect the title a third time and choose **Font/Style/Bold**.

36. Click the **View Data** button on the toolbar to see the report (see Figure 6 - 66).

37. Return to the design with the **Design** button.

38. Save the report by picking **FILE/Save As**, typing the name **AD-SALES**, and clicking the **OK** button.

39. Print the report by clicking the **Print** button on the toolbar. You do not need to select **Create Horizontal Overflow Page As Needed** since the report was designed to fit a single page width. Click the **OK** button.

40. Close the report with **FILE/Close**.

41. If you need to exit from *Paradox* and/or Windows, do so properly.

Independent Project 6.2: The Bookstore

This Independent Project continues working with the Bookstore database from Independent Project 5.2. The owner has requested a report that lists the publisher, fax number, book titles, and cost for every book. Since that data resides in two separate tables, you will need to link **BOOKS.DB** and **PUBLISHR.DB**. **PUBLISHR.DB** has **Publisher Code** defined as a key field so that the link can be made.

The top portion of the finished report should resemble Figure 6 - 67.

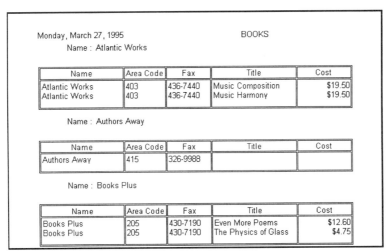

Figure 6 - 67

1. Run *Paradox*.

2. Click the **Paradox** button to close the Welcome to Paradox screen if it is open.

3. Maximize the *Paradox* window if it does not already cover the entire screen.

4. Click the **Open Project Viewer** button on the toolbar if it is not already open. Check that you are in the correct working directory.

5. Right-click on the **Reports** icon on the left side of the Project Viewer.

6. Click **New** in the self-contained menu to start a new report.

7. Click the **Data Model/Layout Diagram** button.

8. Click on the name **BOOKS.DB** in the list of tables and click the right pointing arrow button.

9. Click on **PUBLISHR.DB**.

10. Move the mouse pointer on top of the embossed box for the **BOOKS.DB** table. Drag down to the **PUBLISHR.DB** box immediately below it.

11. In the **Field:** list on the left side of the Define Link dialog box, click on **A4 Publisher Code** and click the rightward-pointing arrow button. *Paradox* will fill in both **Publisher Code** field names.

12. Click the **OK** button in the Define Link dialog box.

13. Click the **OK** button in the Data Model dialog box.

14. In the Design Layout dialog box make certain **Tabular** is the selection under **Style:**.

15. Click the **Show Fields** button at the top of the Design Layout dialog box.

16. As we do not want the **BOOKS.Book Code** field, click on that field name in the **Selected Fields:** list and click the **Remove Field** button.

17. Similarly, remove the **BOOKS.Author**, **BOOKS.Year of Publication**, **BOOKS.Publisher Code**, **BOOKS.Price**, **BOOKS.Quantity in Stock**, **PUBLISHR.Publisher Code**, **PUBLISHR.Address**, **PUBLISHR.City**, **PUBLISHR.State**, **PUBLISHR.Zip**, and **PUBLISHR.Phone** fields. Do *not* click **OK** yet.

18. The **BOOKS.Cost** field should be the last column, so click on that field name in the **Selected Fields:** list and click the downward-pointing arrow button that is to the right of **Order:** three times to move it to the bottom of the list of fields.

19. Similarly, use the arrow button to move **BOOKS.Title** to the second to last position, just above **BOOKS.Cost**.

20. Click the **OK** button.

21. Click the **View Data** button to see the current report.

22. After examining the current design, return to the design screen by clicking the **Design** button.

23. Click on the table object in the **All Records** section.

24. When the table object has selection handles around it, move the mouse pointer on top of the line at the right side of the column heading for **Name** and drag that line to the left to the 2-inch mark on the top ruler.

25. Scroll to the right so you can see the right edge of the design and drag the line at the right edge of the **Title** column heading to the 5-inch mark on the top ruler.

26. Click the **View Data** button to examine the current state of the design.

27. Return to the design screen by clicking the **Design** button.

28. To insert grouping, pick **REPORT/Add Band**.

29. Click on **PUBLISHR.DB** in the **Table:** list, **Name** in the **Field:** list, and the **OK** button.

30. Click the **View Data** button to see the report (see Figure 6 - 67).

31. Return to the design screen by clicking the **Design** button.

32. Save the report by picking **FILE/Save As**, typing the name **PUBBOOKS**, and clicking the **OK** button.

33. Print the report by clicking the **Print** button on the toolbar. You do not need to select **Create Horizontal Overflow Page As Needed** since the report was designed to fit a single page width. Click the **OK** button.

34. Close the report with **FILE/Close**.

35. If you need to exit from *Paradox* and/or Windows, do so properly.

Independent Project 6.3: The Real Estate Office

This Independent Project continues working with the Real Estate Office database from Independent Project 5.3. The owner has requested a report that lists the commercial properties grouped by agency. From the **AGENCIES.DB** table you should include the **Agency Name** and **Phone 1**. From the **COMMERCL.DB** table include the **Agent**, **Address**, **City**, and **Price**. Since that data resides in two separate tables, you will need to link the two tables. **AGENCIES.DB** has **Agency Code** defined as a key field, and so the linking will be possible.

The top portion of the finished report should resemble Figure 6 - 68.

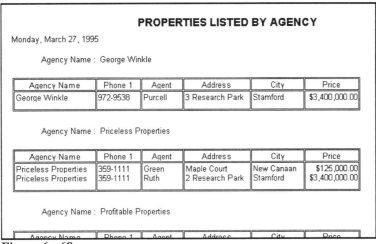

Figure 6 - 68

1. Run *Paradox*, close the Welcome to Paradox screen, and maximize the window.

2. Open the Project Viewer and confirm the working directory.

3. Right-click on the **Reports** icon and pick **New**.

4. Use the **Data Model/Layout Diagram** method.

5. Pick **COMMERCL.DB** as the master table.

6. Pick **AGENCIES.DB** as the detail table.

7. Drag the mouse pointer from **commercl.db** to **agencies.db** to begin linking the two tables.

8. Paradox will attempt to match **A4* Code** to **A4* Agency Code**. That is *not* the correct link. Click on **A4 Agency Code** in the **Field:** list and click the right-pointing arrow button to correct the link. The common field is **Agency Code** in both tables.

9. Click the **OK** button in the Define Link dialog box.

10. Click the **OK** button in the Data Model dialog box.

11. Use a **Tabular** design.

12. Click the **Show Fields** button at the top of the Design Layout dialog box.

13. Remove all fields except **COMMERCL.Address**, **COMMERCL.City**, **COMMERCL.Price**, **COMMERCL.Agent**, **AGENCIES.Agency Name**, and **AGENCIES.Phone 1**.

14. Arrange the order of the fields so they are **AGENCIES.Agency Name, AGENCIES.Phone 1, COMMERCL.Agent, COMMERCL.Address, COMMERCL.City,** and **COMMERCL.Price**.

15. Click the **OK** button.

16. View the report and use **VIEW/Zoom/Fit Width** to see what changes need to be made to column widths.

17. Return to the design.

18. Narrow the **Agency Name, Address,** and **City** columns so that the design will fit on a single page width.

19. Insert a grouping band based on the **Agency Name** field in the **AGENCIES.DB** table.

20. Remove the table name, **<COMMERCL>**, from the **Page** header band.

21. Open the **Report** header band for a report title.

22. Use the **Text Tool** button to place an object from margin to margin. Type the label **PROPERTIES LISTED BY AGENCY** into the text box.

23. Inspect the title and center it. Also make its characters 14 point in size and bold.

24. View the report (see Figure 6 - 68).

25. Return to the design.

26. Save the report as **BYAGENCY**.

27. Print the report.

28. Close the report design.

29. If you need to exit from *Paradox* and/or Windows, do so properly.

Independent Project 6.4: The Veterinarian

This Independent Project continues working with the veterinarian database from Independent Project 5.4. She has requested a report that lists the pets grouped by owner. She hands you a sample of what the report should look like (see Figure 6 - 69). Since that data resides in two separate tables, you will need to link the two. Create the report, save the report design, and print the report.

Owners and Their Pets

Monday, March 27, 1995

Name : Albert Smith

Name	Area Code	Phone	Name	Type	Date of Last Visit
Albert Smith	203	359-4181	Fifi	cat	2/20/95
Albert Smith	203	359-4181	Homer	dog	2/1/95
Albert Smith	203	359-4181	Runner	horse	2/1/95
Albert Smith	203	359-4181	Wild Thing	dog	4/20/95

Name : Dan Wilson

Name	Area Code	Phone	Name	Type	Date of Last Visit
Dan Wilson	203	972-3571	Spot	dog	2/1/95
Dan Wilson	203	972-3571	Wilhelm	horse	1/15/95

Name : Mureen Utley

Name	Area Code	Phone	Name	Type	Date of Last Visit
Mureen Utley	203	359-8152	Fluffy	cat	3/8/95
Mureen Utley	203	359-8152	George	dog	1/15/95
Mureen Utley	203	359-8152	Kuddles	cat	3/8/95

Figure 6 - 69

Appendix:
Features Reference

Features	Mouse Shortcut	Menu Bar Commands	Shortcut Keys	Lessons
Exit Paradox	Double-click Application Control Menu	FILE/Exit	ALT+F4	I
Run Paradox	Double-click Paradox icon		ENTER when name is highlighted	I
Open a table	Double-click table name in Project Viewer or click Open Table button on toolbar	FILE/Open/Table	ENTER when name is highlighted in Project Viewer	I
Close a table	Double-click Document Control Menu	FILE/Close	CTRL+F4	I
Print a table	Click the Print button on the toolbar	FILE/Print		I
Help		HELP/Contents or HELP/Search for Help On	F1	I
Set Working Directory	Click drop-down arrow at top of Project Viewer and pick from list	FILE/Working Directory		1
Create a new table	Right-click Tables icon in Project Viewer or Open Table button on toolbar and pick New	FILE/New/Table		1
Move to next column	Click in next column		ENTER or TAB or RIGHT ARROW	1
Close a design window	Double-click Document Control Menu	FILE/Close	CTRL+F4	1
Move to previous column	Click in previous column		LEFT ARROW or SHIFT+TAB	1
Switch into Edit Mode	Click Edit Data button	VIEW/Edit Data	F9	1
Switch into or out of Field View	Click Field View button	VIEW/Field View	F2	1
Leave Edit Mode	Click Edit Data button	VIEW/View Data	F9	1
Switch into or out of Memo View	Click Field View button	VIEW/Memo View	SHIFT+F2	1
Modify a table's structure	Click Restructure button on toolbar when table is open	TABLE/Restructure Table		1

Features	Mouse Shortcut	Menu Bar Commands	Shortcut Keys	Lessons
Delete a row		RECORD/Delete	CTRL+DELETE	1
Primary Key	Double-click Key column		any character key when in Key column	1
Move to next record	Click Next Record Navigation Button	RECORD/Next	DOWN ARROW or F12	2
Move to previous record	Click Previous Record Navigation Button	RECORD/Previous	UP ARROW or F11	2
Move to first record	Click First Record Navigation Button	RECORD/First	CTRL+F11	2
Move to last record	Click Last Record Navigation Button	RECORD/Last	CTRL+F12	2
Move to first field	Use scroll bar, then click in field		HOME	2
Move to last field	Use scroll bar, then click in field		END	2
Size a field	Drag right edge of Field Heading box			2
Move a field	Click on Field Name, then drag to new position			2
Search	Click Locate Field Value button on toolbar	RECORD/Locate/ Value	CTRL+Z	2
Locate Next	Click Locate Next button	RECORD/Locate Next	CTRL+A	2
Delete a record		RECORD/Delete	CTRL+DELETE	2
Open Project Viewer	Click Open Project Viewer button	TOOLS/Project Viewer		3
Switch windows	Click on other window	WINDOW menu and click on desired name at bottom	CTRL+F6	3
Pick multiple items in list	Click on first and CTRL+click on next			3
Index a table	Click Restructure button and pick Secondary Indexes in Table Properties list	TABLE/Restructure Table and pick Secondary Indexes in Table Properties list		3
Activate a secondary index	Click Filter button and pick index from Order By list	TABLE/Filter and pick index from Order By list		3
Create a form	Right-click Forms icon in Project Viewer or Open Form button and pick New	FILE/New/Form		3
Open a form	Double-click name in Project Viewer when Forms category is chosen or click Open Form button and pick name	FILE/Open/Form		3

Features	Mouse Shortcut	Menu Bar Commands	Shortcut Keys	Lessons
Save a form design		FILE/Save As		3
Create a query	Right-click Queries icon in Project Viewer or Open Query button and pick New	FILE/New/Query		4
Include a field in a query	Click check box in field		F6 in field	4
Include all fields in QBE Grid	Click check box under table name		F6 in table name column	4
View ANSWER	Click the Run Query button on toolbar	VIEW/Run Query	F8	4
Sort ANSWER	Use Check or Check Descending or click Sort Answer Table button	PROPERTIES/Answer Sort		4
Save a query design		FILE/Save As		4
Add a table to query	Click Add Table button on toolbar	QUERY/Add Table		5
Join multiple tables in query	Click Join Tables button and click in each of the two common fields in the two tables		F5 followed by example element in each of the two common fields in the two tables	5
Create a report	Right-click Reports icon in Project Viewer or Open Report button and pick New	FILE/New/Report		6
Select an object on a report design	Click on the object		TAB repeatedly until object is selected	6
Select multiple objects on report design	Click on first object and SHIFT+click on next			
Scale view of design		VIEW/Zoom/100 % or VIEW/Zoom/Fit Width		6
Sort a report	Inspect (right-click) the All Records band and pick Sort in the self-contained menu	PROPERTIES/Current Object/Sort when All Records band is selected	F6 and pick Sort when All Records band is selected	6
Preview a report design	Click View Data button	VIEW/Run Report	F8	6
Return to the design	Click the Design button	VIEW/Design Report	F8	6
Open a report design	Right-click on report name in Project Viewer and pick Design	FILE/Open/Report and check Design in Open Mode section of dialog box		6
Add grouping to a report	Click Add Band button	REPORT/Add Band		6
Add an object to report design	Click the appropriate tool on toolbar			6

Index